FRAMINGHAM STATE COLLEGE
3 3014 00304 0583

D1287900

METAPHYSICS AND COMMON SENSE

By the same author

LANGUAGE, TRUTH AND LOGIC

THE FOUNDATIONS OF EMPIRICAL KNOWLEDGE

BRITISH EMPIRICAL PHILOSOPHERS
(*ed. with Raymond Winch*)

PHILOSOPHICAL ESSAYS

THE PROBLEM OF KNOWLEDGE

THE REVOLUTION IN PHILOSOPHY (*with others*)

LOGICAL POSITIVISM (*ed.*)

THE CONCEPT OF A PERSON AND OTHER ESSAYS

THE ORIGINS OF PRAGMATISM

METAPHYSICS AND COMMON SENSE

A. J. AYER

WYKEHAM PROFESSOR OF LOGIC IN THE UNIVERSITY OF OXFORD AND FELLOW OF NEW COLLEGE, OXFORD

FELLOW OF THE BRITISH ACADEMY

MACMILLAN

First published 1969 by
MACMILLAN AND CO LTD
Little Essex Street London W C 2
and also at Bombay Calcutta and Madras
Macmillan South Africa (Publishers) Pty Ltd Johannesburg
The Macmillan Company of Australia Pty Ltd Melbourne
The Macmillan Company of Canada Ltd Toronto
Gill and Macmillan Ltd Dublin

Printed in Great Britain at the
PITMAN PRESS
Bath

TO

GULLY AND NICHOLAS

CONTENTS

PREFACE

THE essays which I have collected into this book fall into several overlapping classes. Four of them, including the essay from which the book takes its title, are concerned with the purpose and method of philosophy and the way in which philosophical questions are related to questions of empirical or formal fact. The essay 'On Making Philosophy Intelligible', which belongs to this group, is also one of the seven essays in the book which were written with a wider audience in view than that of professional philosophers. The other essays which fall into this class are those entitled 'What is Communication?', 'Chance', 'An Appraisal of Bertrand Russell's Philosophy', 'Reflections on Existentialism', 'Man as a Subject for Science' and 'Philosophy and Politics', in which I make an amateur excursion into modern history. Of the more strictly professional essays, three deal with the work of other philosophers in a mainly critical spirit. My reason for including these polemical pieces is that the views which are criticized in them are well-known and still influential. This is also my excuse for reproducing my mainly unfavourable impressions of existentialist philosophy.

All the essays have already been published, or accepted for publication, elsewhere. In most cases, I have reprinted them as they stood, except for minor grammatical or stylistic emendations. I have, however, rewritten the last section of the essay on 'Chance' and I have cut out passages from the original versions of 'What Must There Be?' and 'Metaphysics and Common Sense', in order to avoid repetition. Insofar as I have still not succeeded in avoiding it entirely, I can only apologize.

Taking the essays in the order in which they appear in this book, their provenance is as follows:

1. 'On Making Philosophy Intelligible'. Delivered in 1963 as one of the Guildhall Lectures, organized annually by the British Association for the Advancement of Science and sponsored by Granada Television. First published by Granada Television in a pamphlet

entitled *Communication in the Modern World—Guildhall Lectures 1963*.

2. 'What is Communication?' Delivered as a lecture at University College London, as one of a series organized by the University College Communication Research Centre. First published by Secker & Warburg in 1955 in a book entitled *Studies in Communication.*

3. 'Meaning and Intentionality'. First published in vol. I of the Proceedings of the 12th International Congress of Philosophy held in Venice in 1958. The publishers are G. S. Sansoni of Florence.

4. 'What Must There Be?' Delivered as a lecture, under the title 'On What There Is', before the Israel Academy of Sciences and Humanities in the spring of 1968 and to be published in their proceedings. I have changed the title to avoid confusion with a substantially different essay 'On What There Is' which I published in the *Supplementary Proceedings of the Aristotelian Society* for 1951 and reprinted in my *Philosophical Essays* (Macmillan, 1954).

5. 'Metaphysics and Common Sense'. First published in 1966 in an anthology entitled *Metaphysics*, edited by Professors W. E. Kennick and Morris Lazerowitz, and published by Prentice-Hall.

6. 'Philosophy and Science'. First published in a Russian translation in *Voprosy Filosofii* (1962) and reprinted in the original English version in *Ratio V*.2, 1963.

7. 'Chance'. First published in the *Scientific American*, vol. 213, no. 4, 1965, and reprinted by permission of the agents for *Scientific American*, W. H. Freeman & Co., San Francisco, U.S.A.

8. 'Knowledge, Belief and Evidence'. First published as the *Danish Yearbook of Philosophy*, vol. I, 1964, in a number dedicated to Professor Jørgen Jørgensen. The *Danish Yearbook of Philosophy* is published by Munksgaard, Copenhagen.

9. 'Has Austin Refuted the Sense-Datum Theory?' First published in *Synthese*, 17, 1967, by the D. Reidel Publishing Company of Dordrecht, Holland.

10. 'Professor Malcolm on Dreams'. First published in 1960 in the *Journal of Philosophy*, vol. LVII, no. 16.

11. 'An Appraisal of Bertrand Russell's Philosophy'. First published in *Bertrand Russell, Philosopher of the Century* (George Allen & Unwin, 1967).

12. 'G. E. Moore on Propositions and Facts'. Written for a forthcoming volume to be entitled *G. E. Moore—Essays in Retrospect*, edited by Professors Morris Lazerowitz and Alice Ambrose, and published by George Allen & Unwin.

13. 'Reflections on Existentialism'. Delivered in December 1966 as the Presidential Address to the Modern Language Association. First published in *Modern Languages*, March 1967.

14. 'Man as a Subject for Science'. The August Comte Memorial Lecture for 1964. Delivered at the London School of Economics under the auspices of the August Comte Memorial Lectureship Trust and published by the Athlone Press.

15. 'Philosophy and Politics'. The Eleanor Rathbone Memorial Lecture for 1965. Delivered at Bristol University under the auspices of the Trustees of the Eleanor Rathbone Memorial Fund and published in 1967 by the Liverpool University Press.

My thanks are due to the editors, publishers, and authorities concerned for permission to reprint these essays, and to Mrs Guida Crowley for her help in preparing this book for the press.

A. J. AYER

10 Regent's Park Terrace
London, N.W.1

I

ON MAKING PHILOSOPHY INTELLIGIBLE

'WHAT do you do?'; people sometimes ask me. 'I am a philosopher.' If I am lucky, the conversation ends there, but often it continues: 'Well, I suppose we are all of us philosophers in our different ways; I mean we all have our own ideas about the purpose of life. Now what I think. . .' Or else: 'A philosopher: I envy you in these difficult times. To be able to take things calmly, to rise above the petty vexations that trouble us ordinary men.' Or again: 'That must be fascinating: really to understand people, to be able to reach their souls. I am sure that you could give me some good advice.' Or, worst of all: 'What *is* philosophy?'

All these approaches are mildly annoying, but they all have some historical justification. From Socrates and Plato onwards, philosophers have frequently concerned themselves with the question of man's place in the universe, as well as with the rather more tractable question how men ought to live. The man who insists on giving you his own views on these subjects, whereas he would not, for example, think of lecturing a physicist on the theory of relativity, has perhaps caught on to the modern idea that these are not questions which demand professional expertise. That the philosopher is indifferent to everyday concerns, because his gaze is fixed on higher things, and that he therefore is able to bear misfortunes calmly, is a doctrine which was made popular by the Stoics. It is, indeed, one of the curiosities of history that although the Stoics contributed nothing of interest to philosophical theory, their image of a philosopher is still the predominant one. It is enshrined in our language, 'To take things philosophically' means to react like a Stoic. I need hardly say that this image nowadays bears little relation to the facts. No doubt academic persons still tend to lead cloistered lives, but philosophers are not more cloistered than the rest, rather the reverse: neither, as a class, do they seem to be any less nervous and irritable than the general run of scholars. There is indeed no good reason why they should be.

It is equally false to credit present-day philosophers with any special insight into practical psychology. Psychology is now a science and psychologists are extremely resentful if it is thought that their subject falls within the province of philosophy. Their emancipation is, indeed, of fairly short standing and is, perhaps, not yet so complete as they would like to think it; in the domain of mental science there is still a kind of no man's land where the lines between philosophy and psychology are not clearly delimited. But even if it is not always sharp or continuous, the boundary does exist.

The only mistake that could be attributed to the man who simply asks 'What is philosophy?' might be that of presupposing that it is one single thing. Not only has the conception of the subject changed in the course of its history, but even at the present time it covers such disparate activities that it seems only a historical accident that they are brought under a single heading. This would, indeed, not greatly matter if these several activities were sharply defined. It might be thought undesirable that the word 'philosophy' should be used ambiguously, but any misunderstanding to which this gave rise could easily be cleared up. In fact, however, the confusion is more than verbal. It is not so much that there is a difference of opinion about the range of problems which are to be regarded as philosophical. It is rather that there is disagreement and uncertainty about the character of these problems, the methods by which they are to be tackled, and the status and even the possibility of the solutions to them. Thus one of the reasons why it is hard to explain to laymen what philosophers are trying to do is that they are often not wholly clear about it themselves. In saying this, I do not mean to make a confession of incompetence, still less to pass strictures on my colleagues, but rather to make the point that it is characteristic of philosophy that its problems are elusive. To assign this or that status to them, to fasten on to this or that method of approaching them, is already to adopt a philosophical position.

One of the main questions in dispute is that of the relation between philosophy and the natural sciences. This was not a question which troubled the Greeks, from whom western philosophy takes its starting point and from whose language the word 'philosophy' is itself derived. Etymologically it meant no more than 'love of wisdom' and it was used by the Greeks to cover any attempt to understand the world as a whole or any feature of it. Thus the pre-Socratic philosophers were primarily cosmogonists; they wished to know what the world was made of. Plato, among much else, was a mathematician; Aristotle, the father of logic, was also an aesthetician, a political theorist, a constitutional historian, and a very eminent biologist. The intertwining of philosophy with science persisted until well after the Renaissance. Descartes and Leibniz were physicists and mathematicians, and, like Spinoza, they aimed at building philosophical systems in which all the scientific knowledge of their day would find its proper place. The empiricist philosophers, Locke, Berkeley and Hume, were not so closely concerned with the physical sciences, though Berkeley was confident enough to join issue with Newton, but Locke at least aspired to found a science of the mind which would be a counterpart to Newton's philosophy of nature, and to a lesser extent this is also true of Hume. Again, Kant was a physicist in his own right, and his *Critique of Pure Reason* was primarily an attempt to provide a foundation for Newtonian physics. Even Hegel, however unscientific in his methods, believed that he could incorporate the natural sciences in his all-embracing system.

It is, in fact, only in the nineteenth century that the paths of philosophy and science begin to diverge: indeed the very word 'scientist' is a nineteenth-century coinage. There are various reasons for this. One practical reason is the multiplication of scientific knowledge, and the consequent increase of specialization, not only as between the different sciences, but also within the various departments of what is loosely classified as a single science. This has made it exceedingly difficult, if not practically impossible, for any one person to take a synoptic view. But a deeper and more serious reason is that it has come to seem doubtful whether the ideal of giving a unified picture of reality is capable of being realized in any interesting or fruitful way. No doubt, if one had the resources of UNESCO one could compile a scientific encyclopaedia. It would be such a vast undertaking that there would be a danger of its being out of date before it was completed, but if it were well done it would serve a useful pedagogic purpose. But it would be a compilation, not a synthesis. It would not meet the demands of those who wish to transcend the partial views of the sciences and arrive at a unified picture of reality.

But now the question is whether such a demand is even significant. What could a unified picture of reality be like? I can imagine something of the following sort. It might turn out that mental phenomena could be accounted for in terms of physiology, that the laws of physiology could be derived from those of biochemistry, that biochemistry could in its turn be reduced to physics and that within physics something like Einstein's ideal of a unified theory came to be realized. We should then have a scientific theory of very great generality, which would serve as the ultimate explanation for every sort of thing that went on in the world, so far as this was known to us. As a picture of reality it would be exceedingly schematic, but this is unavoidable. Only a highly abstract picture could be sufficiently comprehensive.

It is, however, an open question whether such a programme could be fulfilled, and moreover it is a question which could only be decided, one way or the other, by experimental work within the special sciences. Only experience can show, for example, whether the bridge which biochemistry attempts to build between the organic and the inorganic can sustain the weight which it would need to bear. There is no room here for philosophy to intervene.

Nevertheless, the idea persists that it is open to philosophy, in some *a priori* fashion, to disclose the most general features of reality. This is a view which is tenaciously held by Marxists; it comes to them as a legacy of Hegel. But since any general hypothesis which is empirically testable is to be classified as scientific, a set of laws of even greater generality would have to be one that was consistent with anything whatsoever; a theory so all-embracing that no observations could possibly refute it. But then the price which the theory pays for this security is that it is devoid of any factual content. From this point of view, the hypothesis that everything happens in accordance with the laws of the dialectic is as vacuous as the hypothesis that everything happens in accordance with the dictates of providence. A hypothesis which explains everything, in the sense that nothing is counted as refuting it, explains nothing.[1]

In fact, if we look at the practice of the most intelligent Marxists, rather than their professions, we find that they do not treat the laws of the dialectic as laws of nature at all, but rather as constituting a conceptual framework into which scientific laws and theories are required to fit. And this is a perfectly legitimate procedure so long as the belief in the adequacy of the framework is not made into a dogma. For the value of any conceptual system depends upon the success with which it operates. As the recent history of physics has shown, a situation may arise in which the most firmly entrenched of concepts may need to be refurbished, modified or even discarded.

So far, my account of the relation of philosophy to science has been rather inimical to philosophy, but I by no means wish to imply that there is no longer any place for a philosophy of science. On the contrary I think that there is a very great need for what I believe that it should

[1] This point is developed in my 'Philosophy and Science'. See below, pp. 84–6.

furnish, a critical interpretation of scientific ideas and theories. One of the main problems of communication in our time is that while our civilization depends upon the application of science, the content and purport of scientific theories have become increasingly esoteric. The greater part of the educated public has simply to take them on trust. The reason for this is not just that there is a systematic division in our culture, but rather that scientific concepts tend to grow more abstract, with the result that there is a widening gulf between the scientific account of the world and the outlook which is fostered by the assumptions, and indeed by the vocabulary, of common sense. This creates a problem for which there is no easy remedy.

The attempt to popularize science by supplying abstract theories with pictorial models is praiseworthy in its intention; but it runs the risks which are inherent in any method of analogy, besides being limited by the fact that not every abstract theory lends itself to a treatment of this kind. What is more greatly needed is a painstaking analysis of the ways in which such theories are related to their evidence; an account of what the pragmatists call their cash-values in operational terms. It would seem, however, that to undertake this successfully one would need to have some personal experience of scientific practice; and I am afraid that the same condition would apply, though in a lesser degree, even to its being properly understood.

The illusion that it is possible to transcend science, in the sense of providing an explanation of the world which would not be subject to empirical tests, is one which philosophy has at times shared with theology. To trace the relations between the two disciplines at different historical periods would be laborious and perhaps not very profitable. It is sufficient to say here that since the time of Kant it has been a matter of fairly general agreement among philosophers that the existence of a deity is not logically demonstrable. This is not to say that respectable philosophers are bound to be atheists or at least agnostics. Many are not, but most of these would admit that their faith was not supported by philosophical argument.

The greater circumspection of philosophy in this domain is well illustrated by a story which is told of the great American philosopher and psychologist, William James. He was being teased by a theological colleague who said to him: 'A philosopher is like a blind man in a dark cellar looking for a black cat that isn't there.' 'Yes,' said William James, 'and the difference between philosophy and theology is that theology finds the cat.'

With the decline of metaphysics, at least in this country—they still order these matters differently in France—the relations between philosophy and theology have grown more distant. The philosophers have gone into a different line of business. There is, however, one important field in which it might be suspected that they would still compete, and that is the field of morals. For is not the philosopher concerned with values? Is it not his function, no less than the theologian's, to prescribe to us how we ought to live?

That this is at least one of his primary functions is a belief that is still widely held. I suppose that when young people take up philosophy, it is chiefly in the expectation that it will answer questions of this kind. Perhaps they have become critical of the morality in which they have been brought up and are looking for some proof or disproof of its validity. They are indeed right in thinking that this is a problem to put to a philosopher, but the result may disappoint their expectations. For what they will most probably come to learn is just that there is no foundation for morality. I do not mean by this that all moral judgements are arbitrary or even that they are all subjective, in the sense that 'there is nothing either good or bad but thinking makes it so'. It is rather that there is nothing external to morality on which it could logically be founded. It cannot be founded on authority, since the appeal to authority itself rests on the moral premiss that what the authority commands is right, and it cannot be founded on nature since there is no logical transition from a statement of fact about the way things are to a judgement of value about the way they ought to be. Of course, natural facts are relevant to morals. In making moral assessments, whether it be a matter of judging the conduct of others or of deciding what to do ourselves, we try to take account of motives and intentions and to estimate the possibility of different courses of action and their probable consequences. But while we may appeal to such motives or consequences as justifying an action, we shall thereby always be relying on some unproved moral assumption; if the consequences justify the action it is because they are good. In the last resort, then, it is a matter of finding a set of principles that we are prepared to stand by; and the question whether they are the right principles comes down to the question whether we really are prepared to stand by them. It can have no other meaning.

This is not to say that moral philosophers are debarred from giving moral guidance. If they have original ideas about morals, there is no reason why they should not try to organize them into a system and persuade other people to adopt them. Whether they would thereby be acting as philosophers is a question of nomenclature which is not in this instance of any great importance. But the fact is that there seems at present to be no call for any fundamental revision of our moral outlook. Not that our age is destitute of moral problems; far from it. But they relate to the application and extension of moral standards which are at least nominally accepted, rather than to the security of the standards themselves. By and large we find ourselves still at home in the moral climate of liberal humanism which was fostered by the Enlightenment and developed, anyhow theoretically, by the nineteenth-century Utilitarians. The main difference is that we are more concerned with social welfare and less with the virtues of individual self-reliance; being no longer quite so sure that God is on the side of the big battalions, we are less content, even in practice, to let the Devil take the hindmost. But this is a welcome shift in emphasis, rather than a fundamental change of principle.

The recognition of the autonomy of morals on the one hand, and on the other the continued adherence to a well-established set of moral values, have led to a certain narrowing of the scope of moral philosophy. It concerns itself less with the question what our duties are and more with the question what our talk about our duties means. The promulgation of moral judgements has given way to their analysis. This is primarily a matter of establishing the character of moral concepts and determining their relation to one another and to concepts of other kinds. In itself, this field is fairly restricted, but it does broaden out into the philosophy of mind. We have to try to find out exactly what is comprised in the idea of human action, to analyse the concepts of motive and intention, to bring out the psychological and other factual assumptions which underlie our ascriptions or disclaimers of moral responsibility. These questions are by no means easy, neither are they lacking in theoretical interest; but if someone has come to moral philosophy in the hope of being shown a way of life they may perhaps strike him as a trifle abstract. However, even in this sphere, abstract problems can have practical importance. The most obvious example, about which I hope to say something later, is the problem, or set of problems, relating to the freedom of the will.

This preoccupation with the analysis of concepts, though it perpetuates a philosophical tradition which at least goes back to Socrates, is sometimes held against contemporary philosophers. They are reproached with fighting shy of the grand questions, the nature of reality, the meaning of life. But if I am right in what I have been saying, these reproaches are unjustified. For there can be no meaning to life except the meaning that we give it; but this is a function of our values and I suggest that our present need is not for new principles but rather for the diffusion and wider application of those that we already profess. And as for the nature of reality there is after all no other way of discovering what the world is like than by exploring it. But here science holds the field: as we have seen, there is a call for a philosophical interpretation of scientific theories, but an attempt to usurp the function of science, to proceed by some other method than that of formulating hypotheses and testing them by observation, can yield nothing of factual significance.

That philosophers look askance at these larger questions is therefore to their credit. But while it is no doubt a mark of grace to abstain from meddling in other people's concerns, it hardly constitutes a profession in itself. Either philosophy is merely masquerading as an academic discipline, or there must be some range of questions which it is especially equipped to answer. Being a professional philosopher, I make no doubt that there are such questions, but I have to acknowledge that we have not been very successful in making clear what their nature is and why they are important. It is this problem of communication that I have in mind when I speak of the need for making philosophy intelligible.

At this point, I can think of no better way to proceed than by giving examples, and the first example which I shall choose is that of the philosophical approach to the question of reality. I have just said that it is vain for philosophy to compete with science in trying to depict and explain the world as we find it, but this does not mean that the question of reality raises no problems for it at all. These problems are, however, of a special character. They are concerned not straightforwardly with what there is, but rather with what we say there is and the reasons why we say it. In other words, they bear on our criteria of reality.

Let me illustrate this at the most fundamental level. All our knowledge of the world in which we find ourselves is ultimately based on sense-perception. We tend to take it for granted that through sense-perception we become aware of physical objects which exist independently of our perceiving them. We think that for reasons of perspective, or some peculiarity in the physical medium, or some disorder of our perceptual organs, these objects may appear different in some respects from what they really are, but that normally they are what they appear to be; we conceive of them as persisting unperceived in very much the same form as that in which we perceive them. These real, objective physical things are contrasted with our no less real, but subjective, mental states and with the unreal objects or events of our dreams, delusions and imaginings.

But now it may occur to us to inquire a little more deeply into these assumptions. What exactly are the marks by which we distinguish the mental from the physical? What grounds can we have for supposing that the things which we perceive continue to exist when we are not perceiving them? And even if this can be established, what grounds have we for supposing that they persist in anything like the same form? In what sense, if any, can it be maintained, for example, that things preserve their colours when no one is seeing them? And, in general, what are the criteria by which we distinguish the properties which things really have from those which they only appear to have? By what means can we distinguish real things at all from the figments of our imagination?

The attempt to deal with these questions gives rise to different philosophical theories of perception. Thus it has been maintained by many eminent philosophers that perception primarily consists in our having sense-impressions, more commonly nowadays called 'sense-data', which do not exist otherwise than as the momentary contents of private sensations. The question then arises how on the basis of these private, fleeting sense-data we can arrive at any knowledge of a public, enduring physical world; and one answer which has been given to it is that physical objects are constituted by sense-data. As John Stuart Mill put it, the theory is that things are nothing more than permanent possibilities of sensation. The criterion of reality would then be one of coherence. We regard perceptions as delusive when they present us with sense-data which do not fit in with the general system.

This theory has the merit of economy, but it plainly encounters very serious difficulties. In particular, it threatens to imprison each of us within a circle of his own ideas. For other people are known to me only through my perception of their bodies; but if, so far as I am concerned, their bodies are nothing but constructions out of my sense-data, it is not clear how I can consistently regard them as subjects possessing sense-data of their own; neither is it clear how these wholly independent sets of sense-data can constitute a common physical world. On any view, there is a problem about one's knowledge of other people's experiences, but for a theory of this kind it is especially acute.

An alternative theory, which tends to find favour with amateurs of science, is that we do not perceive physical objects as they really are, but only the effects of their action upon us. On this view, our ground for believing in the physical world is purely inferential: physical objects are postulated as the causes of our sense-data, and they are credited with whatever properties contemporary physics attributes to them. This theory draws some support from scientific accounts of perception, in so far as they establish that the way in which physical objects appear to us depends not only on their own constitution but also on the perceptual medium and on the physiological and psychological condition of the observer. But it too faces the difficulty which besets any theory which takes sense-data for its starting point; it has to explain how we can ever get beyond them. The trouble with the causal answer is that it is not at all clear how we can be justified in believing in a causal relation one party to which, the physical object, is never itself observed.

In face of this difficulty, the modern tendency has been to give up the concept of the sense-datum, which was never very adequately defined, and return to the naïve realism of common sense. There is then no problem of accounting for our knowledge of the physical world, since it is assumed that physical objects are directly given to us in perception, and that one and the same physical object is presented in this way to different observers. Even so, our right to make these convenient assumptions has to be vindicated and a way has to be found of reconciling the naïve realist view that we commonly see things as they really are with the scientific facts which, at least on the face of it, appear to show that what we see is transmuted by the process of seeing it. The introduction of sense-data may have been a mistake, but it was not a wanton mistake. The considerations which led to it have still somehow to be met.

I shall not attempt here to decide between these rival theories or to develop an alternative to them. The point to which I want to draw attention is that they are not theories in the scientific sense. They are not testable by observation. No experiment could be devised which would decide between a follower of Berkeley who thought that all that people ever perceived was ideas in their own minds and a naïve realist who thought that he directly perceived material things. For the experiment would itself have to produce a perceptual state of affairs; and then this would simply be interpreted by either party in accordance with his own view. So Doctor Johnson's kicking a stone with mighty force and saying 'I refute it thus' was nothing to the purpose; Berkeley would never have thought of denying his power to acquire a painful idea of solidity.

This brings out the important point that philosophical disputes of this kind are not disputes about matters of fact, or at least not in any straightforward sense. They are disputes rather about the way in which facts are to be categorized, and so, one may say, about the nature of what is to constitute a fact. For though I do not dispute that the world exists independently of our thinking and talking about it, nevertheless the world as we conceive it—and it is only as we conceive it that it enters significantly into discourse—is partly a function of our system of description. So, if a theory like Berkeley's is to be refuted, it has to be on logical or semantic grounds. Perhaps it can be shown that the notion of a sensible idea is incoherent or that in introducing persons as percipients Berkeley is tacitly bringing in material bodies in a sense which he repudiates. One step towards achieving this would be to show that the only viable criterion of personal identity was that of the physical identity of the person's body. If this could be demonstrated, it would have the interesting consequence of eliminating at least one popular version of the hypothesis that we survive our deaths.

If a theory like Berkeley's cannot be refuted logically, it would seem that the only remaining grounds on which to judge it are pragmatic. I do in fact think it possible to give a neutral description of the data of perception, that is, a description which is non-committal with regard to the status of what is perceived. Such a description would, as it were, supply the raw material which can then be made to bear the imprint of such distinctions as that between the objective and the subjective or the real and the hallucinatory. It is a fact about the material that such distinctions can be applied to it, but it is for us to decide whether it is useful to apply them. A system which made no provision for things existing unperceived might not be logically defective or even false to our experience, since it could furnish a means of recording any actual data. It would, however, be extremely inconvenient, since the only natural laws which it would enable us to formulate would be of limited scope and of intolerable complexity. By synthesizing our data in such a way as to make room for the concept of persisting physical objects, we achieve an enormous gain in simplicity and predictive power.

But surely, it will be said, this is not simply a question of convenience. Either there really is a table here, which exists independently of anyone's perceiving it, or there is not; and if it really does exist, then either it really is the solid, coloured object which it appears to us to be, or it really is a set of colourless electrons with empty space between them, or whatever. This is a natural objection to make, but a misguided one. It trades too naïvely on the use of the word 'really'. We must distinguish the case in which the word is used *within* a given conceptual system from that in which an attempt is made to use it outside any system from a conceptually neutral standpoint.[1] In the former case it can have a clear descriptive meaning. If we presuppose a system in which the concept of a physical object, like a table, is given its ordinary application, then the answer to the question whether there really is a table here, which exists independently of our perceiving it, is that there really is. For all that is here at issue is the question whether the conventional criteria which we use for determining the independent existence of such objects, criteria such as the object's accessibility to different senses and to different observers at different moments of time, are satisfied in this instance, and we can easily assure ourselves that they are. But this gets us no further with our philosophical problem. For the question which we were trying to ask was not whether these criteria can be satisfied but whether the objects which really exist in terms of these criteria really do exist. But now it is not clear even what this question means. In this second use of the word 'really' we have cut it loose from the system in which it was provided with definite criteria and have failed to supply any other criteria to take their place. No doubt we could supply criteria from a different system, but this would not serve our purpose; we should still be begging the question in another form. But it is only within a conceptual system of some sort or other that the word 'really' can acquire a descriptive meaning. So, if we are using it from a neutral standpoint, its function can only be evaluative. It simply marks our preference for one type of system over any other.

Much the same considerations apply to the question whether the table really is the solid, coloured object that it appears to be or whether it really is as the physicists represent it. If we are talking at the level of common sense, then we need have no hesitation in saying that the table really is solid and that it really is coloured; for there is no doubt that it satisfies the criteria by which, at this level, the ascription of these properties is determined. This does not mean, however, that the

[1] I give an account of this distinction in my essay 'What Must There Be?' See below, pp. 49–52.

physicists' description of it is mistaken. For here the question is whether the physical theories in which such concepts as that of the electron figure are empirically verified; and the answer is of course that they are. But once more, one is inclined to protest that we cannot simply leave it at that. Either what is really there independently of our perceiving it is a continuous coloured surface, or it is a group of discrete colourless particles. It surely cannot be both. But again this argument is too naïve, and again the trouble lies in the uncritical use of the word 'really'. From what standpoint is this question of the 'real' nature of the table being raised and what are the criteria for deciding it? So far as I can see, it comes down at this stage not to a question of fact at all, in the way that the common-sense question about the table's colour was a question of fact, but rather to a choice between two rival pictures.[1] We can imagine things persisting unperceived in very much the same form as that which they display when we do perceive them, or we can imagine them, with rather greater difficulty, as transmuted into the guise in which they are represented in the theories of contemporary physics. Which picture we prefer will depend upon our interests and purposes. We can indeed make the decision that only one of them portrays things as they really are, but all that this will come to is that we have found reason to attach primary importance to one of the competing points of view. This can be construed as a preference for a particular way of speaking or as a preference for a particular way of looking at the world. At this level, the two come to the same.

As I said before, I am not attempting to put forward an authoritative solution of these philosophical problems. My aim has only been to try to make as clear to you as possible what kind of problems they are and in what sort of way one might set about them, to give you, as it were, a glimpse of a philosopher in action. If you have followed me, you will, I hope, have a clearer idea of what a philosopher's activity consists in, but it may still occur to you to wonder why it is thought to be important. If no experiment can decide between the various theories of perception and if in the end we come to the conclusion that the common-sense view of the world is perfectly acceptable on its own terms, and indeed for many purposes the most convenient, then what do we gain in practice from going through these elaborate ratiocinations? Are we not like the Red Queen in *Through the Looking-Glass*, running very hard in order to stay in the same place?

[1] This question is discussed in my essay 'What Must There Be?' See below, pp. 58–63.

Well, one answer is that the exercise is good for us, but there is more to it than that. It is true that it makes no practical difference whether one agrees with Berkeley or not. But even the aim of science is not wholly practical. We want to control our environment, so far as possible to make nature serve our purposes, but we also want to understand it. And philosophy in its way does contribute to our understanding. It does not tell us directly how nature works, but it does tell us about the conceptual tools on which our investigation of the workings of nature depends. We can use these tools without thinking about them, but it will always occur to persons of a certain intellectual temperament to raise the question whether and how they are adapted to their work. And once these questions are raised, it is not at all easy to suppress them. They create a puzzlement which demands to be resolved.

In any case, it is not always true that a philosophical inquiry will, for all practical purposes, leave things just as they were. A conspicuous counter-example is one which I mentioned earlier in passing, the problem of the freedom of the will. As often happens in philosophy, this problem takes the form of a dilemma. On the one hand, we are inclined to believe that all spatio-temporal processes, and therefore also human actions, are governed by natural laws; and from this we are inclined to infer that given the initial circumstances whatever actually happens could not have happened otherwise. On the other hand, all our moral assessments of our own and other people's conduct and all our legal practice depend on the assumption that people are responsible for their acts; but this seems to imply that, even given the existing circumstances, they *could* have acted otherwise. But these conclusions are mutually contradictory. It has to be shown, then, either that there is some flaw in this reasoning, or that at least one of the premisses of one or other of these arguments is false.

Again, I do not propose to offer you a solution of this problem. To do so would mean going very carefully into a set of notions of which the correct analysis is by no means obvious; the notion of causality and of natural law on the one hand, and on the other the whole group of concepts; which figure in the teleological explanation of human action, as well as our idea of moral responsibility. The concept of a person would itself come under review. One would have to consider exactly what was involved in the shift from causal to statistical laws in microphysics, and whether this was relevant to the present issue; whether there were any logical reasons for denying that every human action could be predicted; whether there was anything at all about a human being that could not be explained in physiological terms. My own view, which I give you without argument, is that we have as yet no very strong reason to believe in the emergence of a physiological theory which will account for every facet of our behaviour, but that the possibility of it cannot be excluded *a priori*.[1]

The point which I now wish to make is that it may very well turn out, in the course of such an inquiry, that the picture of ourselves which underlies much of our moral thinking, the idea of our actions as proceeding from the unfettered choices of self-propelling agents, did not stand up to critical scrutiny. If this did prove to be the case, it would not follow that the idea of freedom would have to go by the board. We could still draw a distinction between the actions which a person chose to do, never mind how the choice came to be made, and those which were forced upon him, in the sense that he was subject to unusual pressures, or even deprived of any power to choose; and there might be utilitarian grounds for our responding to actions of these different sorts in different judicial ways. But certainly a great strain would be placed on the conventional ideas of merit and of guilt; and if these ideas were given up or greatly modified, it is hardly to be expected that our moral and our legal outlook would remain unchanged.

This again illustrates the general point that even our most central concepts are constantly on trial. The clearest proof of this in recent times is to be seen in the development of classical into modern physics. But here the boundary between science and philosophy is not sharp. Einstein's Theory of Relativity, for example, is as much a philosophical as a scientific achievement.

It has recently become the fashion to speak of philosophy as an inquiry into language. We are told that what philosophers are, or anyhow should be, doing is investigating how words are used. This is true in a way, but it is also misleading. It is true in so far as any analysis of concepts can be viewed as an inquiry into the use of the words in which the concepts are deployed; there is, indeed, on way of getting at concepts except through the symbols which deploy them. So, in the examples which I have given you, instead of saying that I was raising a philosophical question about the nature of reality or about the possibility of free will, I could have said that the question at issue was how the word 'really' was used in certain contexts, or whether an expression

[1] I try to deal with some of these questions in my essay 'Man as a Subject for Science'. See below, pp. 218–39.

like 'doing something of one's own free will' had any application. But then I should have had to explain that this was not an inquiry into the niceties of English idiom or into the canons of grammatical propriety. The knowledge which one might hope that it would yield is not the sort of knowledge that could be obtained from a dictionary or a phrase-book. In a sense which I have tried to bring out, such inquiries are indeed concerned with the way we speak about the world, rather than with the way the world operates. But since we are bound to look at the world through the prism of language, this is not a hard and fast distinction. To understand the demands which our language makes upon the facts is also a way of understanding the nature of the facts themselves.

Why then is there so much prejudice against what is called linguistic philosophy? Partly through sheer misunderstanding. We sometimes talk of a question's being purely verbal in a way which implies that it is trivial; and it is mistakenly thought that philosophical questions are represented as being verbal in this sense. But the philosophers themselves are partly to blame for being excessively modest in their estimation of the influence of their inquiries. They have tended not sufficiently to appreciate the extent to which their approach to language is critical as well as descriptive. They are not at all interested in the morphology of words, and not very greatly interested in detecting ambiguities or bringing out fine shades of meaning, except where the ambiguity has lent support to some fallacious argument, or the distinction illuminates some central feature of our thought. Their interest is in the architecture of language, rather than its decoration, and this includes the uncovering of hidden flaws in the structure, repairing it, extending it, and even rebuilding parts of it in a slightly different style. Since these activities have to be carried out *in* language, they often throw new light upon a certain set of facts by exhibiting them, as it were in a different projection. The world is not changed, but we are made to see it differently.

One of the great merits of the linguistic movement in philosophy is that it has focused attention upon the problem of language itself. Much work has been done in recent years with regard to the mechanism of communication; we have learned a great deal about the transmission of signals, the way in which information is stored in the brain, the way it is coded and decoded, the methods of translation from one language to another, the art of teaching, the technique of persuasion both in its sinister and beneficent forms. But underlying all this is the question what communication itself consists in. What is it exactly to use and understand a sign? How are signs related to the things which they signify? How diverse are their functions? What is the range of purposes which they serve?

I do not think that we yet have a satisfactory theory of language, but we are making progress towards it. Thanks largely to the later work of Wittgenstein, and to that of the pragmatists before him, we have substituted a dynamic for a static model of the relation of words to things. We no longer think of words as pictures, but rather as tools, and tools which are adapted to a wide variety of ends. The rather crude but still very valuable distinction between the descriptive and the emotive uses of language, which was drawn forty years ago by Ogden and Richards in their pioneering work *The Meaning of Meaning*, has been refined, and the heterogeneous set of linguistic acts which were lumped together as emotive have been largely differentiated and independently analysed. Here we owe much to the work of Professor Austin who, among other things, drew attention to what he called the performative use of language, the cases where we use a linguistic expression not to describe an action, but as an essential part of its performance. The classic example is the expression 'I promise' which is used not to state that one is making a promise but actually to make one. As we quite often find in philosophy, the point seems obvious once somebody has drawn attention to it; but it had in fact been largely overlooked and the extent of its application is surprisingly wide. It has, for example, a very important bearing on the theory of law.

The shift from a static to a dynamic conception of the operation of signs is well illustrated by the theory of truth. The classical model is the metaphor of reflection; it was thought that the truth of a statement consisted in its faithfully mirroring some fact. But apart from other difficulties, this metaphor could simply not be cashed. Most languages are not ideographic, and anyhow there is no particular virtue in a pictorial symbolism. It is merely one method of representation among others, and for most purposes not the most effective. Then it came to be seen that the only correct way of answering the question what makes a given statement true was to assert the statement, or some equivalent to it. What makes it true that I am trying to make philosophy intelligible is just that I am trying to make philosophy intelligible. But what does this consist in? All that can follow is some redescription of what I am doing. But this made it look as though we were imprisoned in a circle of words, since the only way of explaining what makes a statement true is to make another statement. However, the circle is easily broken. The key is the fact that understanding a declarative sentence consists in one's being disposed to accept or reject it in certain concrete situations. If you understand the meaning of the words 'I am trying to make philosophy intelligible', and if you are so placed that you can tell from the context who it is that the word 'I' refers to in this usage, then you can decide whether these words are being used to make a true or false statement just by listening to me. The relation of signs to what they signify is to be elucidated not in terms of any direct link between them but in terms of the behaviour of the people by whom the signs are used and interpreted.

It is fortunate that practice does not always wait upon theory. We can rely upon our senses, even though we lack a satisfactory theory of perception. We can communicate successfully without having an altogether clear idea what communication is. It can even be argued that at a certain stage of research it is inhibiting to a science if its concepts are too closely scrutinized. Nevertheless in the long run it is better to understand what we are doing, if we can. With his reluctance to take things at their face value, the philosopher is an intellectual trouble-maker. He sets out to disturb complacency. But ignorance is not altogether bliss; and in the field of learning, as in politics, it is only because some people are prepared to make trouble that anything of importance ever gets done.

2

WHAT IS COMMUNICATION?

I

IT may seem strange that one should begin a discussion of communication by asking what communication is. Surely, it may be said, you must already know what communication is before you can profitably start discussing it. And of course there is a sense in which we do know what it is. We know how to use the word 'communication'; we can understand English sentences in which the noun, or the corresponding verb, occurs. But it is one thing to be able to use a word correctly, and quite another to be able to give an account of its use. We know, for example, how to use the word 'time' correctly. At the level of common sense, we have no difficulty in understanding what people say about time: we are able to handle tenses and to make an informative use of words like 'earlier' and 'later', or 'past', 'present' and 'future'. But that does not mean that we are able to answer the question 'What is time?' Most of us, when confronted with this question, would be at a loss for an answer. We should be inclined to say, like St Augustine, 'I know so long as you don't ask me'. Much the same applies to such questions as 'What is freedom?' 'What is sovereignty?' 'What is life?' 'What is consciousness?' Sometimes what is wanted is a definition, but more often in cases of this sort a definition would not be of much help, even if it were obtainable. We need an explanation rather than a definition, a detailed account of the work that the concept has to do, a critical investigation of the territory that it is supposed to cover.

In the case of communication, this territory is very wide. We communicate information, but also knowledge, error, opinions, thoughts, ideas, experiences, wishes, orders, emotions, feelings, moods. Heat and motion can be communicated. So can strength and weakness and disease. We speak of communication cords and communicating rooms. A system of communications covers not only postal services, signals, telephones and telegraphs but roads and railways and vehicles of transport. 'Evil communications corrupt good manners' in more senses than one.

When a word is applied to such a variety of things, it is natural for us to assume that they have something in common, something in virtue of which the same word is applicable to them all. In this instance the connecting thread appears to be the idea of something's being transferred from one thing, or person, to another. We use the word 'communication' sometimes to refer to what is so transferred, sometimes to the means by which it is transferred, sometimes to the whole process. In many cases, what is transferred in this way continues to be shared; if I convey information to another person, it does not leave my own possession through coming into his. Accordingly, the word 'communication' acquires also the sense of participation. It is in this sense, for example, that religious worshippers are said to communicate.

But if there is a thread which ties the various uses of the word, it is to be noted that it does not bind them very firmly. The differences between them are in many ways more interesting than the resemblances. Thus, the very fact that my own stock of information, or of knowledge, is not, or need not be, diminished through my communicating part of it to others, at once weakens the analogy between this sort of communication and the communication of energy and heat. It suggests, indeed, that the idea of information as a commodity which can change or multiply its ownership is itself somewhat misleading. A further proof of this is that I can communicate information which I do not have, as when my behaviour enables others to know me better than I know myself. In such a case my communication is not intentional. When it is intentional, the intention may or may not be fulfilled. When it is not fulfilled, I may still communicate something, though not what I intended: and here too, I may communicate information which I do not have. Again, we sometimes speak of communicating feelings, where what is transferred is the feeling itself, as when rage or panic spreads throughout a crowd. But more often when a feeling is said to be communicated, what the recipient of the communication is supposed to be acquiring is not the feeling itself but, a very different thing, the knowledge that the other person has it. In most cases this knowledge will then be shared, but it need not be. I can, in either of these senses, communicate feelings which I do not know that I possess.

Such examples indicate that, while there are connecting links between the different things that are brought under the heading of communication, there is no single feature, or set of features, which is common and peculiar to them all. What they have, to borrow a fashionable expression from Wittgenstein, is a family resemblance to each other. The proper method of approach, therefore, is not to try to fit them all into a rigid scheme, but to set about describing them as accurately as possible. The comparison between them may prove to be instructive: it may be found that one, more simple, type of instance can serve as a useful model which helps us to understand the more complex character of another, just as, for example, the study of electronic machines is expected to throw light upon the workings of the human brain. But the existence of such a resemblance has to be exhibited rather than assumed. If a systematic classification is needed here at all, it will have to come at the end, and as the result, of our inquiries rather than at the beginning.

II

The type of communication that I particularly wish to discuss is the transference of information, in a very broad sense of this term, which may be taken to include not merely the imparting of news, in a factual sense, but also the expression of feelings, wishes, commands, desires, or whatever it may be. It covers all deliberate uses of language by human beings as well as voluntary or involuntary exclamations, movements, gestures, singing, crying, laughing, dancing, in so far as they are informative. Thus I can communicate my unhappiness to you by telling you that I am unhappy but also by sighing, or groaning, or simply by looking sad. You acquire the same information in either case, the knowledge that I am unhappy; we are not now concerned with the case where my communicating my unhappiness to you is my infecting you with it, my causing you to share it. In short, there are other ways of conveying information than by the use of language, though the use of language is the most important and, from my point of view at least, the most interesting to investigate. And they too must be reckoned as methods of communication.

It is clear that this admission should be made, but it is not clear how far it is to carry us. We shall want to say, for example, that a patient communicates to his psycho-analyst not only, or even primarily, the facts which he is ostensibly reporting, but also his unconscious memories or desires, which his actual statements vainly attempt to screen. But how does this differ from any other case in which the patient's manifestation of certain symptoms enables the doctor to diagnose his complaint? Yet we should not, in these other cases, speak so readily of communication. We should, I think, hesitate to say that one communicated one's measles to the doctor, in the sense of informing rather than infecting him, by coming out in spots. It seems, however, to be a fairly arbitrary question where we are to draw the line. Perhaps the cases which we are most ready to consider as examples of communication are those where the data from which an inference is made are regarded as signs of something that would otherwise remain hidden, rather than those in which the data merely fit into an observable pattern. Communication tends to be conceived as the making public through the appropriate intermediaries, the verbal or non-verbal signs, of things which cannot themselves come out into the open. But this conception is misleading, if not actually mistaken, as I shall presently try to show.

The fact is that in every case in which different events are associated by a natural law, or by convention, or by a combination of the two, it is open to us to regard one of them as the sign of another. How far it is profitable for us to extend the concept of language, how seriously we are to take the metaphor of the book of nature, will depend upon the fruitfulness, in particular cases, of the analogies it enables us to bring out. As always, there is the danger that we may press them too far. Thus many, perhaps most, people are prepared to regard the production of works of art, not merely in the field of literature but also in that of music and the visual arts, as a species of communication. And I do not wish to say that they are wrong. But let us note that if we are to say that a piece of music conveys a message, it will be a strange sort of message; one that, unlike the normal message, is not expressible in other terms. Not all pictures tell stories; or if they do it is in a markedly Pickwickian sense.

How difficult it is to isolate what we want to call communication is shown by the case of non-human animals and machines. 'I shall not ask Jean-Jacques Rousseau if birds confabulate or no.' Professor Haldane can satisfy me that they do. And bees, he will inform you, are in their fashion particularly loquacious.[1] But whether there is any justification for making a sharp distinction between such phenomena and other cases in which the behaviour of one animal is causally dependent upon that of another is a question which I am content to leave to him. I should not be surprised if he held that there was not. Again, our interest in warfare has led to the construction of machines which carry out

[1] J. B. S. Haldane gave the second lecture 'Communication in Biology' in the series of lectures of which this was the first.

such operations as make it quite natural to say that they communicate with one another. But if we look at the facts we find that nothing more is involved than a set of rather complicated causal connections, resembling those displayed by a great many physical phenomena, with regard to which we should not ordinarily say that there was any question of communication. If we choose to speak of communication in the case of the machines, it is, I think, because we wish to stress the analogy between their operations and the use of language by human beings. And we are perfectly entitled to do so, if the comparison is any way illuminating.

Reverting to the use of language by human beings, which I take to be the central point of our inquiry, we find that it presents us with a very wide range of material for study. The standard situation in which one person converses with another appears, on a superficial analysis, to contain many different factors. There is the person who makes the communication and the person who receives it, the thought or feeling which is communicated, the encoding of that thought or feeling in some set of symbols, and the meaning or reference which these symbols have. This may be identical with the thoughts or feelings which they are supposed to encode, but it usually is not. I may in some sense be expressing my thoughts when I talk to you about the weather or whatever it may be, but I am certainly not talking about them; few people are such egotists that all their conversation is about themselves. Then there are the physiological processes attendant on the publication of the message, which may be regarded as part of the means by which it is transmitted. The question of transmission brings in such extensions of the human voice as pens, ink and paper, printing presses, telephones, telegraphs, wireless sets and so forth. Further, we have the physiological processes attendant on the reception of the message, its decoding by the recipient, and the meaning or reference of the symbols in which his interpretation of it is expressed. Since the processes of transmission are not infallible, the message which he finally receives may be different from the message that its originator actually sent: and different again from the message that he meant to send.

It will be seen that there is something here for almost everyone. There are philosophical, psychological, aesthetic and biological problems about the relationship between the experiences, the thoughts and feelings, of the subject and the symbols in which they are expressed. Consideration of the symbols themselves brings in phonetics, sociology and all the departments of philology. The question of the relation of the symbols to their meaning goes closely together with the consideration of the symbols themselves, but it independently raises a number of philosophical problems. Finally the questions connected with the transmission of the message bring in psychology again and sociology, physiology, physics and engineering, and, given the inter-dependence of the physical sciences, almost everything else besides.

III

I shall confine myself to philosophy. The questions with which I shall now try to deal are those concerning the relationship of symbols, verbal or other but primarily verbal, first to the experiences which they are supposed to encode and secondly to what they signify. These questions to some extent overlap, but it will be convenient to consider them in turn.

The first of them is particularly difficult, because it at once involves us in the mind–body problem, the inner–outer dichotomy which bedevils modern philosophy. The physical world, we think, is public. Allowing for difficulties due to defective sense organs, or lack of the appropriate scientific instruments, or limitations of the power to travel, we are all equally able to observe it and report upon it. We are in a position to understand one another's reports because the things to which they refer are things to which we all have access. The table which I see is the same as the table which my neighbour sees. In describing it to him I am telling him something which he could, in principle, find out directly for himself. But he does not, in this direct way, have access to my thoughts and feelings. Our experiences are private. We try to communicate them but we can never, so it is suggested, be sure that we succeed. We can never compare our respective sensations, so that we can never know that we mean the same by the words which we use to describe them. All that we can know is that we systematically apply these words on the same occasions. What my neighbour sees as green may be very different from what I see as green; I cannot get into his mind to tell nor he into mine; but at least his usage corresponds with mine. We cannot communicate the content of our experiences, but we can at least determine that they have the same structure.

Philosophers have accepted this line of argument without always seeing how far it can be made to take them. For once it is laid down that content cannot be communicated, the public world, with which we so securely started, dissolves in its turn. We say that we see the same table, but how, if you can never gain access to my experiences, nor I to yours, can we ever know that it really is the same? Communication then becomes like a game of postal chess. Each of us plays on his own board, sending out signals to report the position of his pieces and moving them in accordance with the signals which he in turn receives. He does not know that the boards and pieces of the other players are in any way like his own; he does not know even that they have any boards and pieces; he does not, if it comes to that, know even that there are any other players. He does not know and he need not care. It is enough for him that the signals which he records, no matter where they come from or what they mean to the person, if any, who sent them, can be correlated with the disposition of the pieces on his board. So long as this is so, he can get on with his game; and so long as he can get on with his game, these philosophical questions about the source and character of the signals need not worry him.

All the same, few of us would be content to leave the matter there. Although solipsism is a bogy that no one seriously believes in, it has the power to haunt us. But I cannot here do more than indicate the way in which it might be exorcised.

To begin with, the conception of public and private worlds is seriously misleading, above all when we try to remove the dualism, either by dissolving the public world, in the sort of way I have outlined, or else, in an attempt to make everything public, by interpreting all references to inner experiences as descriptions of physical events. The first is a course which perhaps only a philosopher would think himself obliged to follow: the second has an attraction for some scientists, especially when they have become a little infected with philosophy. The physical events which are selected for this work may be events in the subject's brain, which, unlike his mind, is taken to be publicly accessible. There are still certain practical difficulties in the way of our inspecting one another's brains, but it is enough for the argument that it be theoretically possible.

Both courses, it seems to me, are wrong. It is wrong to say that there are no such things as private experiences; in a very obvious sense, there are. It is wrong to say that we cannot describe them to one another; we can and do. It is wrong to say that when we describe them we are really describing something else, the condition of our bodies, whether inside or outside the skin. But equally it is incorrect to say that when we talk about physical events, we are really describing our private experiences. So far the dualism is to be upheld. But we shall get into a muddle if we conceive it as a dualism of worlds, as a distinction between different sorts of property, on the legal analogy of public and private ownership. The distinction between what is public and what is private is, in the sense with which we are now concerned, a logical distinction. It is the distinction between the cases in which it does, and those in which it does not, make sense to say of two different people that they are observing the same object, and so in a manner having the same experience. It is not that my own experiences, my private thoughts and feelings, are so firmly anchored in me that I cannot convey them to you, but have to give you tokens instead, the tokens being my words, which I issue like bank notes in a currency system where the gold is pledged but never actually delivered, 'the eternal repetition of the promise to pay being made to pass for its eternal performance'. Words are not tokens in this sense, for all that John Locke said they were. I cannot convey my experiences to you, for the sufficient reason that experiences are not the sort of thing that it is significant to speak of conveying, if conveying is understood in the sense of transferring an object, of the physical conveyance of property. And I do not, in this sense, convey substitutes for them either. But I can and do inform you about them. I make statements about them which you are capable of understanding.

What has to be admitted is that we are often less well placed for testing some statements than we are for testing others. In general, we are not so well placed for testing statements about the past and future as those who were, or will be, living at the relevant times, and we are not so well placed for testing statements about another person's inner life as he is himself. This is not true of all such statements: a psychologist may come to know more about my motives than I do myself or, for psychological reasons, ever shall: but there are certain facts of immediate experience to which the subject is the best possible witness. I think, however, that these are differences of degree and not of kind. I suggest that even such difficulties as that of knowing whether another person sees the same colours as one sees oneself may not be difficulties of principle. It may, in this example, turn on the merely practical impossibility of acquiring his nervous system, of putting oneself sufficiently in his place. Of course, if putting oneself sufficiently in his place is to be construed as becoming completely identical with him, then the impossibility is logical. But for reasons into which I shall not now enter, I do not think we are bound to construe it so pessimistically.

Even if I am mistaken about this, we are still not reduced to saying that anything is incommunicable. For unless it is at least significant to say of something that it is communicated, it cannot significantly be said of it, and consequently cannot be true, that it is not communicated. And anything of which it makes sense to say that it is communicated is, at least in principle, communicable. This is, indeed, a tautology, though perhaps not so obvious as some. There is no doubt, on the other hand, that certain things are harder to communicate than others, whether it be that we have not devised, or mastered, a suitable set of symbols, or that the persons to whom we wish to convey the information have not had the experiences, or the appropriate training, which would enable them to understand it. But, in theory, all such deficiencies are capable of being remedied, although in some cases it may be practically unlikely that they ever will be.

Just as nothing is, in principle, incommunicable, so, I wish to argue, all language is public. There can of course be private languages, in the sense of private codes, which only a few people, or only two people, or perhaps even only one person, in fact understand. It is always open to any diarist, like Pepys, to invent a personal shorthand for recording what he wishes to keep secret, or even, if it be objected that a personal shorthand is merely an unconventional way of transcribing the phrases of some current language, to go further and invent a personal language. But it must remain logically possible for some other person to break the code, however difficult this may be. And here it makes no difference whether the statements, which are expressed in this language, refer to their author's private experiences or to things which are publicly observable. In either case it is possible for others to test them, at least to some degree, and consequently to understand them.

There is, however, an important distinction which remains even if we reject that between private and public languages. It is the distinction between indexical and non-indexical signs. Indexical signs are those that cannot be understood apart from the context in which they are produced. When they are verbal their presence in a sentence makes it necessary to know the occasion of its utterance before it can be interpreted. Pronouns, tenses, words like 'here' and 'now', proper names in some of their uses, are examples. It is characteristic of most of these signs that by locating the speaker they show how well he is placed for verifying the statements which he is using them to make. If I say, for example, that Napoleon died at St Helena in 1821, my use of the tensed word 'died' indicates that my own position in time is later than the event which I am describing, and consequently that my statement is one that I myself am not in the best possible position to verify. On the other hand, such a sentence as that the freezing point of water is 32° Fahrenheit is entirely non-indexical. It contains no indication of the personality of the speaker, or of his spatio-temporal position; it tells us nothing about his opportunity for verifying the statement which it is used to express. But even in the case of indexical sentences, the information about the speaker which is conveyed by the indexical words is not part of what is stated. The truth of what is expressed by 'Napoleon died at St Helena in 1821' is not dependent upon my subsequently existing, or indeed upon the subsequent existence of anything else. Consequently, so far as the factual content of the statement is concerned, it would make no difference what tense the verb had, or whether it had any at all. This would not be so if the date of the event in question were not mentioned. For then the tense would do the work of locating the event with reference to the temporal position of the speaker, which is not itself stated but taken to be known. But this work of dating which tenses do rather vaguely can always be more fully done by non-indexical expressions. From this point of view tenses are superfluous, though in a language like English there may be no idiomatic way of eliminating them.

The same applies to the other indexical signs. If I say, for example, 'I am now discussing a philosophical problem', the truth of my statement, like the statement that I made about Napoleon, does depend upon my now existing; but it does not depend upon the fact that it is I who make it nor upon the fact that I am in a strong position for testing it. These things are shown to be so by the use of the words 'I' and 'now' but they are not stated. Accordingly both words can be replaced, 'now' by some reference to a date, and 'I' by some descriptive phrase which in fact applies to me. We thus obtain a non-indexical sentence to the effect that a person of such and such a kind discusses a philosophical problem at such and such a time. This will not, indeed, be logically equivalent to the original, since it is not logically necessary that I should satisfy any particular description or that now should be any particular time; but, if the descriptions are suitably chosen, the same information will be conveyed.

In this way we can make all our sentences non-indexical. I am arguing only that this is possible, not that it should actually be done. The use of indexical expressions has obvious practical advantages; they serve as pointers which save one the trouble of formulating descriptions, or, in the case of an audience, of searching for the object to which a description refers. If in your presence I describe a man of a certain sort, you may not know who is meant, though it is in fact myself. If I say 'I' you do. But the fact that indexical words *could* be dispensed with reinforces the claim that language is public. In this context, Professor Haldane has reminded me that scientists are apt to write the reports of their experiments in the third person, saying not 'I observe' but 'it was observed that'. This practice should not, I think, be ascribed to a modesty which some might consider false. It is, at a certain sacrifice of elegance, a tribute paid by these scientists to their ideal of objectivity.

IV

I have maintained that words are not tokens in the Lockean sense. They are not reflections of thoughts nor are they emissaries which thought sends out, being itself unable to travel. They are expressions of thoughts in a way that does not allow of any clear-cut distinction between the two. It is, in my view, not unduly misleading to conceive of thinking as a form of operating with signs. Of course there is a difference between talking intelligently, thoughtfully if you will, and merely babbling, just as there is a difference between writing intelligently and merely scribbling. But the difference is to be found in the arrangement of the signs themselves, the manner in which they are produced, the general attitude of the speaker, rather than in the presence of any factor 'behind' the signs for which the word 'thought' might be a name. I do not want to deny to psychologists the right to investigate, and so the possibility of discovering, what they describe as imageless thought. But I want to insist that if the thought is to be a thought *of* something or a thought *that* such and such is so, it must be expressed in symbols of some sort. This is, indeed, analytic: unless it were so expressed I should not allow that it was a thought of anything or a thought that anything was so. And this applies equally whether the signs in question are publicly produced, that is, spoken or written or danced or gesticulated or whatever it may be, or whether they are used by the thinker in silent soliloquy. Words, just as much as thoughts, can be kept to oneself.

One reason why many people are reluctant to accept this line of argument is that they feel that they are capable of having, perhaps often do have, thoughts which they cannot put into words. Does not our thesis set altogether too high a value on being articulate? I do not think that it does. Of course, the people who talk of having difficulty in putting their thoughts into words are describing something that actually occurs; I am not trying to deny this empirical fact. But I think that we shall be misunderstanding the character of this fact if we conceive it as being analogous to a man's going to his tailor and trying to get a suit to fit him; as if the thought were already there, fully-fledged, and it were just a matter of finding words to clothe it. The thought which we are unable to put into words is vague and inchoate; the symbols in which it is embodied are fragmentary; they do not fit together, or not in any way that satisfies us. As we find more appropriate expression for it the thought itself becomes more definite. In the end one may say 'Yes, this is what I meant all along', but the fact is not that one had a meaning all along, which the different sets of words more or less faithfully reflected, as an artist may make several attempts at a portrait, with his model in front of him, before he gets the likeness that he wants. In this case there is no such model. The words say 'what we meant all along' because it is they that finally give its sense to the whole previous process of groping; we are satisfied with them in a way that we were not satisfied before. A part of this process may consist in fitting words to images; but then the images themselves are symbols. In identifying thinking with the use of signs, to the extent that I do, I do not wish to imply that these signs must necessarily be verbal.

The case of feelings is somewhat, but not very, different. It is clear that they are not simply to be identified with their manifestations, but neither are they wholly separable from them. A man's yawning is not the effect of his boredom in the way that the flaming of a match is the effect of its being struck upon the box. It is the expression of his boredom, though not its complete expression. It is an element in a pattern which includes other features of his behaviour together, perhaps, with certain 'inner feelings' which he alone directly detects: and it is the whole of the pattern which constitutes his boredom. In saying this, I am merely calling attention to the linguistic fact that words which we ordinarily construe as referring to feelings are most often used in such a way that they include the expression of these feelings in their references.

V

We are now in a position to simplify things a little. Ignoring questions relating to the transmission of messages, which fall outside our province, we find that the analysis of communication, in the sense that primarily concerns us, reduces to the analysis of the expressions '*A* issues *x* as a sign of *y*' and '*B* receives *x* as a sign of *y*': *A* and *B* are normally persons, but they may also be non-human animals or even machines. In most cases they will be different from each other, but they need not be; there is no reason why we should not allow it to be possible for a person to communicate with himself. If the sign that *A* issues is isomorphic with the sign that *B* receives and *y* has the same value for them both, the communication is successful. For our present purposes we need not dwell on the distinction between 'issues' and 'receives'. We can therefore simplify still further, and consider only the expression '*A* uses *x* as a sign of *y*'.

The problem consists in the analysis, or explanation, of 'being a sign of'. It is an old philosophical problem, a part of which sometimes takes the more specific form of the question 'What is the meaning of a word?' or 'What do sentences mean?' But the trouble with questions of this kind is just that they are couched in general terms. We can give the meaning of particular signs by definition, by explanation, by translation into another language, or in the cases where the sign denotes something that can be pointed to, by ostentation. But the proper answer to such a question as what do sentences mean in general would seem to be that some mean one thing and some another. It might be thought that a recourse to semantics would produce a more illuminating answer: but this is not so. Semantics will enable us to set out, and in certain cases to formalize, the rules of designation or, what comes to the same thing, the truth-conditions for the sentences of some particular language, and so to give their meaning. But then the notion of designation, or some other such semantic concept, is taken as primitive. In this way we can learn what certain expressions mean, but not, it may be objected, what meaning is.

But if we are not permitted to say what meaning is by defining one semantic concept in terms of another, it is clear that no answer of the form that meaning is such and such can be forthcoming. Our only resource will be to turn the question by giving an account of the way in which people must behave, or be disposed to behave, if it is to be true that they are using signs meaningfully. Various attempts have been made to work out analyses of this sort; but none of them appears to me to be at all satisfactory. Most of them follow the line that if *x* is to be a sign of *y*, *x* must be either a substitute, or a preparatory, stimulus for *y*. That is, it is suggested that *A* uses *x* as a sign of *y* if and only if he is disposed to react to *x* as he reacts to *y*, or if his reaction to *x* tends to initiate a reaction to *y*. But it is easy to show that neither theory fits the facts in more than a special set of cases. I doubt, indeed, whether any such theory will be successful, so long as it remains at this level of generality. What I think can be done, on the other hand, is to analyse a series of particular cases and show what it is in each of them for someone to be using signs meaningfully. Thus for a particular *x* and *y*, it might be shown that *A*'s being disposed to utter the words *x* in a certain way was an ingredient in the pattern of behaviour which constituted his believing that *y*; this could then be represented as at least a sufficient condition of his using *x* as a sign of *y*.[1] A procedure of this sort may not lead to any useful definitions, or indeed to any definitions at all, but it is not necessarily the worse for that. Our aim is to get to understand the various ways in which signs can be endowed with meaning, and this can be achieved by an illustrative method as well as any other.

One merit of a behavioural analysis, whether general or piecemeal, is that it helps to rid us of the conception of meaning as a simple two-termed relation between a sign and the thing that it signifies. To see how inadequate this conception is we have only to consider the cases where a descriptive expression fails to denote anything, or a sentence is used to state what is false. For then this other term of the supposed relation does not exist. Philosophers have sometimes tried to meet this difficulty by bringing in such entities as propositions to fill the gap, saying in effect, that what a sign corresponds to is its meaning: and this in turn has led them into sterile debates as to whether or not these meanings are real. But such questions should not be permitted to arise. The proper answer to any discussion of this sort is that the notion of correspondence, or portrayal, does not provide us with an adequate model for the relationship of meaning. If we represent it in this way, we may expect to be philosophically misled.[2] Since many people do make this mistake, it is important to show that a different form of analysis is possible.

In view of their concern with truth and falsehood, it is natural that philosophers, in giving their accounts of meaning, should have concentrated mainly on the fact-stating use of language. The danger of this is

[1] I say a little more about this in my essay 'Meaning and Intentionality'. See below, pp. 44–6 and footnote to p. 46.

[2] I develop this point in my essay 'G. E. Moore on Propositions and Facts'. See below, pp. 191–3.

that one may try to make it cover too much, and so force certain types of utterance into a mould where they do not fit. An example is to be found in ethics, where the analysis of statements to the effect that something is good or that something ought to be done has foundered on two opposing errors, one being to treat these normative statements as descriptions of natural facts, facts about human happiness or the progress of evolution or whatever it may be, and the other being to treat them as descriptions of something mysterious and other-worldly, an objective realm of values. Whereas the truth is that, in their ethical aspect, they are not descriptive of anything at all. They are prescriptive; they lay down standards; they are, what they are said to be, normative: and the fact that normative statements are not deducible from, or reducible to, descriptive statements is central to any adequate treatment of moral philosophy or aesthetics. In the same way, one will make no advance in the philosophy of law unless one does justice to the prescriptive element in legal utterances. A judge who passes sentence is not making a prediction, he is delivering a verdict; and we falsify the character of his performance if we treat it, in a positivistic way, as consisting in his making a statement of fact. Ogden and Richards have indeed made us familiar, in their *Meaning of Meaning*, with the distinction between the descriptive and the emotive use of language, but the word 'emotive', though useful in its time, is apt in this context to be misleading. It is not just a matter of our having to distinguish between the assertion of facts, or would-be facts, and the expression of feelings. There are very many uses of language, prescriptive, ritualistic, playful, or performative, which are not fact-stating and cannot just be lumped together as forms of emotional expression. They have functions to fulfil, which have to be carefully distinguished and analysed for what they are, not fitted into a single preconceived scheme.

The undertaking of such analyses is an important philosophical activity, but its importance can be over-emphasized. Many problems are linguistic, a matter of our having to be clear about the way in which words are used, or to prescribe the ways in which they should be used, but many, even in philosophy, are not, or at least not in any straightforward sense; and outside philosophy most are not. There is a great deal to be achieved by the study of semantics; but the successes which it has recently obtained must not deceive us into thinking that all our troubles would be over if only we could become clearer about the use of words, perhaps even that all that we need is to find suitable definitions. For instance it has been suggested that many political difficulties would vanish if only we could all agree upon a definition of democracy. But this is to put things in the wrong order; it is only when the difficulties have already been removed that any such agreement is at all likely to be secured. As it is, when one party says that a certain procedure is democratic and another says that it is not, they are not simply, or even primarily, disputing about the meaning of a word. What is at issue between them is a different conception of the way in which society ought to be organized, no doubt involving different practical interests; and this is not a verbal problem. Similarly, a definition of a fair wage will not solve labour disputes. Or rather, getting people to admit that a wage is fair is not just a matter of getting them to agree about the use of a word: it is a matter of inducing them to be satisfied with the amount of goods that a certain sum of money will buy, and with its relation to what others are earning. It sometimes happens that what appear to be practical disputes are really verbal; but very often it is the other way about.

This is not to say, however, that even in these cases linguistic analysis is trivial or useless. By itself, it does not solve the problems; but it can fulfil the extremely important function of enabling us to see more clearly what the problems are.

3

MEANING AND INTENTIONALITY

IF a word means something, it is tempting to infer that there is something which it means. In the case of a proper name, or a pronoun, or a singular noun, one's first inclination may be to identify the meaning of the word with the object which it denotes. But the attempt to generalize this procedure leads to obvious difficulties. We may say that verbs denote states or activities, but what about adjectives? Do they denote properties or the things which have them? Do common nouns denote classes or their members? Must we say that abstract nouns denote abstract entities? But in what sense, if any, do abstract entities exist? Then there are prepositions to be considered, and conjunctions and other parts of speech. And words are used to form sentences which themselves have meaning. What are we to say that they denote?

Under the influence of Wittgenstein[1] and others, we have mostly ceased to be troubled by such questions. We dismiss them as illegitimate. They arise, it is said, out of the mistaken assumption that all words function as names. What is not so generally recognized is that even in the model case of proper names it is incorrect to identify the meaning of the name with the object which it denotes. The proof of this is that the meaning of the sentences in which the name occurs is not affected by the question whether any such object exists. For example, I do not know whether there ever was such a person as King Arthur of the Round Table. I am inclined to believe that there was, but I may very well be wrong. But whether he existed or not, the meaning of the sentence 'King Arthur fought the Saxons' remains the same. If he did not exist, the sentence misses its intended reference, but it does not thereby become meaningless. Yet it would become meaningless if the proper name meant what it denoted: for then the failure of the denotation would wholly deprive the name of meaning. It may, indeed, be objected that my example is not typical. Normally, when we use proper names, we are quite sure that their intended reference is successful. Even so, the argument still holds. For, however little doubt there

[1] See especially his *Philosophical Investigations*, 2nd ed. (1967).

may be that the objects in question do exist, it remains conceivable that they should not; and even if they did not, it would make no difference to the meaning of the sentences in which the proper names occurred.

The only cases in which it is plausible to identify the meaning of an expression with its denotation are those in which the success of its reference is a condition of the expression's being meaningfully used. Thus it might be held that all demonstrative words, or expressions, fell into this category; that talk of *this* or *that* object would be meaningless unless there really were things to which the demonstratives referred. But I am not at all sure that this must be so. Certainly, when such demonstratives are used, as they may be, to refer to absent objects, it is not necessary that the objects should exist: and even when it is implied that the objects are present, I do not think that their failure to exist need deprive the demonstratives of their meaning. The sort of cases that I have in mind are those in which the use of a demonstrative expression serves only to pretend that some object exists, or those in which the subject is suffering from a hallucination. In the case of hallucinations, we may bring in a special class of objects, sense-data, which will provide the demonstratives with something to denote, but while we may choose to do this it is by no means clear that we are bound to. There are, however, certain demonstratives, such as 'here' or 'now' or 'I', the meaning of which does logically depend, in their standard usage, upon their succeeding in their reference. But even in these cases it is questionable whether the meaning and the reference are to be identified. For the places and times and persons, which are referred to by the demonstratives, may have a great many properties which it would appear strange also to ascribe to the meanings of words.

Having remarked that expressions which are taken to be referential are not deprived of meaning when the objects which they seem to denote do not exist, some philosophers have concluded, not that the meaning even of names is different from their denotation, but simply that these referential expressions are not genuine names. They have assumed that if we were able wholly to unravel the meaning of the sentences that we ordinarily use, we should find that it was to be expressed by sentences which had an ultimate logical simplicity; and these sentences would contain, or perhaps even consist of, logically proper names; the mark of a logically proper name being that its significant use entailed the existence of the object which it was supposed to denote. This is the doctrine of logical atomism, to which both

Russell[1] and Wittgenstein[2] at one time subscribed. But while it may be possible to endow a language with logically proper names, it surely is not necessary; I can see no good reason to hold that every descriptive language implicitly contains them. The assumption made by the logical atomists is that logically proper names are required, as it were, to furnish the language with an anchorage in nature; but, so far as I can see, this assumption is just false. If the language is to be descriptive, it is indeed necessary that some of its expressions should be capable of having a denotation; it must afford the means of referring to objects that could exist. But, even if we make the further stipulation that some of these objects do in fact exist, it still does not follow that there need be any expressions in the language which have to refer to existent objects in order to be meaningful. Even if some demonstratives in our language do function in this way, I see no reason to take them as a paradigm. They do not even perform an essential service; it would be no sacrifice to replace them by names, or definite descriptive phrases, for which this special condition did not hold.

To refute the logical atomist theory, in its extreme form, it need only be remarked that a sentence which consisted entirely of logically proper names could not be used to say anything false. Either it would express a truth, or it would be meaningless. But surely to credit a sentence with descriptive meaning is to imply that what it is used to state can be either true or false. It is for this reason, indeed, that the desire of some philosophers to identify the meaning of indicative sentences with facts cannot be satisfied. For, setting aside the question what facts are, and in what sense, if any, they can be said to exist, in the case where a sentence is used to state what is false there is no fact for it to mean. And from this it follows that the sentence does not mean a fact, even though what it states is true. For whether what it is used to state is true or false, its meaning remains the same.

Having failed to locate the meanings of words in the external part of nature, philosophers may then be tempted to house them in the mind. Words, it is said, are the signs of ideas: and ideas are here identified with thoughts or images. But this view has nothing to commend it. If it is taken literally, it implies that we never do, or indeed can, talk about anything except our own mental processes; and, mercifully, this is not the case. If, on the other hand, the theory is that words refer in the

[1] See 'The Philosophy of Logical Atomism', lectures published in the *Monist* in 1918, and reprinted in *Logic and Knowledge*, ed. R. C. Marsh (1956).

[2] See *Tractatus Logico-Philosophicus*, tr. Pears and McGuiness (1961).

first instance to ideas, that is, that they signify things by way of ideas, then it runs against the objection that people very often use words significantly without having any accompanying images and without engaging in any processes of thinking other than those which are embodied in their intelligent use of words. But what is still more serious is that this introduction of ideas meets none of the difficulties relating to the significance of words. We are told that words signify by way of ideas: but then how do ideas signify? There are exactly the same objections to identifying the meaning of ideas with their denotations as there are to identifying the meaning of words with theirs. The appeal to ideas, so far from serving to explain how words have meaning, merely brings in a second set of symbols, which have in many cases a dubious title to existence and in no case fulfil any function that is not already fulfilled by the corresponding words. We can say, if we like, that words are used to express ideas, though even this will be incorrect if it implies that having an idea necessarily precedes or accompanies the significant use of words as a separate mental process; but we must not say that they mean them.

There would seem, then, to be nothing in nature with which the meanings of words can be identified. And so philosophers, who think that there must somehow be such things as meanings, are forced, as it were, to go outside nature to find them. The view taken is that singular nouns mean individual concepts; common nouns mean class concepts; adjectives mean universals; indicative sentences mean propositions. And these concepts and universals and propositions are not mental entities, nor yet physical; they do not exist in space or time. Nevertheless they are held to be real, just as it may be held that numbers are real, though they do not exist in space and time. Moreover, they are easily accessible to us, just as numbers are. We can discover their properties and their relations to one another. For, on this view, whenever we understand a word, we apprehend its meaning, in the form of a concept or a universal; whenever we understand an indicative sentence, we apprehend a proposition; when we reason validly we are aware how propositions are related. And these relations are not in any way dependent upon us. They depend upon the nature of the propositions in question: and the propositions, as has been said, are objectively real. They would be what they are, even though no one ever thought of them; even though no one had ever devised a language in which they were capable of being expressed.

I suppose that the fundamental objection to this Platonic theory is that it puts too heavy a strain on one's credulity. It does not require a very robust sense of reality to make one hesitate to charge the Universe with a host of incorporeal entities, corresponding not only to every actual but to every possible set of meaningful words. The class of propositions alone will contain an infinite number of objective falsehoods, and even of objective contradictions, if it be allowed, as I think it should, that a contradictory sentence is not meaningless. Can we seriously admit that such things are real? A further argument is that the introduction of these entities fulfils no purpose: there is nothing that it serves to explain. To be told that adjectives mean universals, or that sentences mean propositions, is really to be told no more than that they mean what they mean. As so often in philosophy, this recourse to a 'realistic' theory is in effect a way of putting an end to the discussion. It does not provide us with an analysis of meaning so much as deny that any analysis is possible. To settle for meanings as objective entities is an explanation of meaning only in the sense that it implies that no more 'natural' explanation can be given.

At this point, many philosophers would say that the source of our difficulties is that we are trying to answer an illegitimate question. There can be no general answer to the question what do words, or sentences, mean, for the very good reason that they do not all mean the same. Except in the rare cases where they are synonymous, different words have different meanings. Thus, if one is presented with the question What do words mean? the proper course is to ask What words? And then if one is told the words, one will, if one understands them, be able to give their meanings. Furthermore, in giving their meanings, one will not be specifying any objects. It is just a mistake to suppose that because a word is meaningful, there must be some entity which it means.

I think that this resolution of the problem is correct so far as it goes, but also that it does not go quite far enough. It forbids us to treat meaning as a relation between a sign and what it signifies, but the only reason that it gives for this prohibition is that we get into trouble if we disregard it. And thus it fails to attack the problem at its root. Why is it that it seems so natural to assume that there must be some object which is the meaning of a word?

The answer, or an important part of the answer, is that this assumption is strongly suggested by the way in which we talk about meaning. The transitive employment of verbs like 'mean', 'signify', 'designate', 'state', 'record', 'describe', 'express', requires that they be supplied with accusatives; and the status of these accusatives is uncertain. It is not evident that they are independently existing entities, and it is not evident that they are not. But, if we go by grammar, we shall be tempted to assume that they are.

The technical way of describing verbs of this kind, which was introduced, I believe, by Brentano, is to say that they are intentional. There are some transitive verbs, like the verbs 'to eat' or 'to kill', which logically imply the reality of their accusatives; there can be no eating or killing unless there really are things that are eaten or killed. Other transitive verbs, like the verb 'to seek', are logically non-committal in this respect. Many things that are sought do exist, but one can also seek things that never have existed, and never will; it may be necessary that we should believe in their existence, but the belief need not be true. Now, it is verbs of this second class that are said to be intentional; and verbs like 'signify' are commonly included among them. But if we are to follow this procedure, we must make a distinction which is often overlooked. The things that one seeks may or may not exist; but the question which is here left open is normally a question of fact. In certain rare cases, such as the search for a method of squaring the circle, the object sought may be one that logically could not exist, but in general the object sought is one that might have existed, even though it in fact does not. When it comes to verbs like 'signify', on the other hand, the question about the reality of the accusative is normally not a question of fact but a question of logic. To ask whether there really are such things as universals or propositions is to raise a question of an entirely different order from the question whether there is uranium in the British Isles or even whether there is such a thing as a golden mountain. If there can be universals, there is no difficulty about finding them: what has to be decided is not whether they do in fact exist, but whether they could.

It is to be noted that the same problem arises with 'cognitive' verbs, like 'believe', 'opine', 'imagine', 'doubt', 'suppose'. They also are intentional in the sense that they can be said to have accusatives of which the logical status is not clear. Thus, if various people believe the same thing, and others doubt it, it is tempting to assume that there is some single entity, a proposition, towards which these attitudes are directed. We refer to beliefs as being true or false, but it can be argued that this is an elliptical way of speaking: what is true or false is the proposition which is believed; and its truth or falsehood is independent of the attitude which anyone may have towards it. So, these propositions fulfil a triple role. They are the vehicles of truth and falsehood, the objects of the various cognitive attitudes, and the meanings of the sentences in which these cognitive attitudes may be expressed.

Now it is not disputed that it is convenient to talk of propositions, or even of universals. Since there is plainly some good sense in which different words, or sentences, may have the same meaning, and different cognitive attitudes may have the same object, we need to be able to refer concisely to what they have in common; and it is more correct, and less cumbersome, to attribute truth and falsehood to propositions than to sentences. As we have seen, this does not in itself commit us to the view that propositions, or other such entities, are real. Our use of intentional language may suggest their reality, but it does not logically imply it. It is still open to us to hold that the mention, or apparent mention, of these objective meanings is only a verbal convenience. But if it is only a verbal convenience, it should be dispensable. And if it is dispensable, we should be able to find a non-intentional way of stating the facts about meaning which seem to require an intentional form of expression. Our problem, then, is to discover how this can be done.

The most simple method, if it were successful, would be to have recourse to what Carnap used to call 'the formal mode of speech'. The theory then would be that talk about meaning can always be replaced by talk about the formal relations of words. Thus, to use Carnap's own examples,[1] it is suggested that to say that 'the word "daystar" designates (or : means: or: is a name for) the sun' is just a way of saying that 'the word "daystar" is synonymous with "sun"'; to say that 'the Latin word "luna" designates the moon' is to say that there is a valid translation 'of the Latin into the English language in which the word "moon" is the correlate of the word "luna"'; to say that 'the sentence S_1 means that the moon is spherical' is to say that 'S_1 is equipollent to the sentence "the moon is spherical"'. But the answer to this is that the suggested translations are all demonstrably incorrect. The statement that the word 'daystar' means the sun neither entails nor is entailed by the statement that the words 'sun' and 'daystar' are synonymous: for to be told that these words have the same meaning is not to be told what meaning they have; their being synonymous is logically consistent with their each meaning not the sun, but the moon, or anything else you please. In the same way, the information that a sentence means the same as the sentence 'the moon is spherical' is not sufficient, or even

[1] See R. Carnap, *The Logical Syntax of Language* (1937), part v, section 75.

necessary, for us to infer that it means that the moon is spherical; not sufficient, for we have not been told what 'the moon is spherical' means; and not necessary, for the sentence in question might mean that the moon is spherical, even though the English words 'the moon is spherical' meant something else, or had no meaning at all. And there is the further objection, which comes out most clearly in the Latin example, that in saying that a word means what it does, one may be using English words but, unless the word in question happens to be English, one is not talking about them. The Latin word 'luna' would have the meaning that it has, even though the English language had never existed. Thus, not only does the proposed translation fail to give the information which is contained in the original sentence, but it adds a piece of gratuitous information about the existence of an English word, which the original sentence did not contain.

It may be thought that these objections are captious. Surely, if someone asks what the word 'daystar' means, it is proper to tell him that it is, or can be, used as a synonym for 'sun'; we are taking for granted that he knows what the word 'sun' means, but why should we not? If he were unfamiliar with English, we should try to substitute the corresponding word in some language which he did know. There would be no point in telling anyone that two words were synonymous unless it could be assumed that the meaning of one of them was known to him. But while this may be true, it is not to the purpose. The idea of talking about synonymity was to recast a typical set of statements about meaning in non-intentional language. It turns out, however, that this language does not do the work required of it unless statements of the kind that it was intended to eliminate are presupposed. Consequently, our object is not attained: nor can it be attained by this method. We may seem only to be talking about the relations that words bear to one another, but we shall always find that this has to be supplemented by some explicit or tacit reference to their meaning. In short, syntax cannot be made to do the work of semantics, and the language of semantics is irreducibly intentional.

If we are to find a solution to our problem, therefore, we must go further afield. The possibilities that remain are to elaborate either a causal theory of meaning, or some version of a behavioural theory, and of these I think the second is much the more promising. To my mind, the fatal defect of the causal theory, either as developed by Russell in his *Inquiry into Meaning and Truth* and elsewhere, or as developed by Ogden and Richards in their famous *Meaning of Meaning*, or indeed in any other version, is that the identification of 'using *x* as a sign of *y*' with 'being caused to produce *x* by *y*' breaks down entirely in the case where *x* is a substantival expression which fails in its denotation or a sentence which expresses what is false: for then there will be no *y* to act as a cause. Yet the meaning of *x* must remain the same, whether *y* exists or not; so that even where *y* does exist and has some causal relation to *x*, the causal and the symbolic relations cannot be identified. To this it may be replied that even if *y* does not exist, the production of *x* must be causally related to something like *y*, or, in the case where *x* is a sentence, to factors resembling those that enter into *y*. If I now say that there is a cat asleep on the floor beside me, I state what is false; there is, then, no such present fact to be the cause of my uttering these words. But, it is argued, I should not attach to these words the meaning that I do, unless I had some previous experience of cats and floors and being asleep and finding things beside me: and it is reasonable to assume that these experiences have left traces which are causal factors in my present utterance. But while this may be true, it does nothing to rescue the theory. At the best, it accounts for my being able to use such a sentence correctly, but to say how certain words have come to acquire the meaning that someone gives them is not the same as saying what he uses them to mean. The false statement which my sentence serves to express does not itself refer to my past experiences, even though they may be a condition of my being able to make it; if it did refer to them it would not be false. It is about a cat and a floor, not about the words 'cat' and 'floor' or the way in which I have come to learn them. A simple proof of this is that the statement could equally well have been made in French: and surely no one would then wish to maintain that what I was really talking about was the genesis of my acquaintance with the English language.

This leaves us with what I have called the behavioural theory. In the versions of it which have so far been developed,[1] the guiding principle is that a sign tends to evoke the same behaviour as that which it signifies. The model used is that of the conditioned reflex in animals, or one's normal reaction to a fire alarm. Sometimes the sign is supposed to function as a preparatory stimulus, sometimes as a substitute stimulus; the distinction is in any case not sharp. On either interpretation, the theory fits certain simple cases but it falls a long way short of supplying the necessary conditions for a sign to be meaningful. The difficulties of

[1] See especially the work of Charles Morris, in particular his *Signs, Language and Behaviour* (1946).

dealing with signs that refer to the past, for example, or to fictitious events, are obvious. The proponents of this type of theory are, indeed, aware of this; they do not claim more at present than that they are laying down 'a set of conditions sufficient for something to be a sign'.[1] But I do not think that even this claim can be sustained. One counter example arises in the case where someone is mistaken about the effect which a certain situation will have upon him. Then, his response to a given sign *S*, which he takes to be a sign of the situation *A*, may mimic the responses that he thinks he would make to *A*; but though he does not know it, these responses, which he is mimicking, are not those that he would in fact make to *A*, but those that he would make to a quite different situation *B*. It would then seem very paradoxical to say that he was really taking *S* to be a sign of *B*. Yet this is what the theory requires.

One reason why it is difficult to make a behavioural theory work is that one's reaction to a sign will be different according as one does or does not believe in the existence of that to which it refers: if the sign is a sentence, one will react to it differently according as one does, or does not, believe in the truth of what it is used to express. Yet it may be equally well understood in either case, and understood in the same sense. It would seem, therefore, that the most promising course is to try to analyse meaning in terms of belief.[2] If this approach is successful it will, in the first instance, account for no more than the meaning of sentences. But, if the meaning of sentences can be analysed, then I think it is only a syntactical problem, though not necessarily an easy one, to deal with the meaning of individual words.

I can here give only the outline of the theory which I wish to develop. I say that a person A *assents* to an indicative sentence *S* when he is disposed to utter *S* seriously and confidently and without mental reservations and to be acquiescent when it is uttered to him. And I say that assenting to a sentence *S* is *constitutive* of a belief that *p*, when there is a *prima facie* logical incompatibility between assenting to *S* and disbelieving that *p*, and between dissenting from *S* and believing that *p*. Thus, for an English-speaking person there is a *prima facie* logical incompatibility between assenting to the sentence 'lions are carnivorous' and disbelieving that lions are carnivorous, and between

[1] Ibid. p. 10.

[2] I owe this suggestion to Dr R. W. Ashby, who has developed it in an unpublished thesis on 'Criteria of Descriptive Meaning', University of London (1954).

dissenting from the sentence 'lions are carnivorous' and believing that lions are carnivorous. It is necessary to put in both conditions, because with the first alone, if assenting to *S* were constitutive of a belief that *p*, assenting to *S* and *S′* would also be constitutive of a belief that *p*, however *S′* were chosen, and with the second alone, if assenting to *S* were constitutive of a belief that *p*, assenting to *S* or *S′* would also be constitutive of a belief that *p*, however *S′* were chosen. By combining them we, as it were, tailor *S* to *p*. And it is necessary to qualify the logical incompatibility as *prima facie* because in the case of some beliefs there may be a conflict of criteria. One might judge that a man believed something if one went only by his words, but when one considered his actions, one might come to think that he did not believe it after all.

I suggest, then, that the meaning of indicative sentences can be analysed as follows: given that *S* is a sentence, *p* a proposition, and *A* a person, *S* means *p* to *A* if and only if *A*'s assenting to *S* is constitutive of his believing that *p*. It is not of course implied that *A* does actually believe that *p*; all that is required is that if he did believe it his assent to *S* would be constitutive of the belief.

Even if this is satisfactory, so far as it goes, our task is not yet done. For our formula does not eliminate propositions; they still appear as the objects of beliefs. What is needed, therefore, is a non-intentional analysis of believing. This has fairly often been attempted but never yet with complete success.[1] The most obvious course is to set up some such pragmatic formula as '*A* believes that *p* if and only if *A* is disposed to behave in a way that is appropriate if and only if *p*'. But, apart from other difficulties, this is exposed to the fatal objection that *A*'s behaviour may in fact be quite inappropriate because of his holding other false beliefs. Thus a doctor who believes that his patient has a certain disease, and wishes to cure him, may act in a way that is unlikely to achieve his end owing to his lack of medical knowledge. I think, however, that this difficulty might be met by specifying that *A*'s behaviour must be appropriate *for him*, where the qualification 'for him' covers not only *A*'s special circumstances and desires but also the general body of his beliefs. Clearly this brings in an element of circularity, but I think it may not be vicious; for in any particular case the behaviour which is appropriate for a given person could be specified, without our having explicitly to mention the beliefs that made it so.

[1] Cf. R. M. Chisholm, 'Sentences About Believing', *Proceedings of the Aristotelian Society* (1955–6).

I think then that this behavioural theory can be made to work.[1] If it cannot, I see no way of avoiding the admission that our talk about meaning is basically intentional. As we have seen, this need not in itself commit us to a belief in the existence of objective meanings. We could still argue that this was not a genuine theory; but it might well be regarded as a weakness in our position that we had had no better theory to put in its place.

[1] I have made a further effort to develop a theory of this type in my book *The Origins of Pragmatism*. See especially pp. 40–9 and 175–9 (Macmillan, 1968) or pp. 29–38 and 164–8 (Freeman, Cooper, 1968).

4

WHAT MUST THERE BE?

It has often been assumed that one of the main problems of philosophy is to determine what there is. This goes with the view that the way in which philosophy principally differs from the natural sciences is through the greater generality of its approach. Thus, G. E. Moore once gave it as his opinion that 'the most important and interesting thing which philosophers have tried to do is no less than this; namely: To give a general description of the *whole* of the Universe, mentioning all the most important kinds of things which we *know* to be in it, considering how far it is likely that there are in it important kinds of things which we do not absolutely *know* to be in it, and also considering the most important ways in which these various kinds of things are related to one another'.[1]

This sounds a very large undertaking. Exactly how large it is will depend upon what is counted as an important kind of thing. At first sight it might appear as if the philosopher were expected to compile a vast Encyclopaedia, in which every known type of object, of scientific or historical interest, was listed and cross-classified. This would indeed turn him into an under-labourer, though hardly in the sense that Locke intended. Neither is it what Moore intended. Though he does not lay down any criteria of importance, it soon becomes clear that he is concerned only with very broad classifications. Thus, he looks to philosophy to pronounce on the truth of what he calls the common-sense view of the world, and takes this to consist in the belief that the world contains two substantial sorts of things, physical objects and acts of consciousness. As an afterthought, he also ascribes to common sense a belief in the existence of space and time, but does not regard these as substantial entities, in the sense in which he takes physical objects and acts of consciousness to be substantial. Another class of entities, the possible existence of which is treated by Moore as a philosophical question, though not one that forms part of the assessment of the common-sense view of the world, is that of propositions. At one

[1] G. E. Moore, *Some Main Problems of Philosophy* (1953), ch. i, p. 1.

point he declares it to be certain that there are propositions, but later in the same series of lectures he comes to the conclusion that there are not.

How are such questions to be answered and why should they be thought to be philosophical? In the case of physical objects, especially, it seems strange that one should look to philosophy to settle the question of their existence. If science, or indeed ordinary common sense, cannot come up with an answer to this question, what is the philosopher expected to do? What sources of knowledge are at his disposal, that are not available to anybody else? Moore did in fact offer a proof of the external world which, following Kant, he equated with the existence of things in space, but the proof simply consisted in his appealing to his knowledge that there were such things. To be precise, it took the form of his holding up his two hands, saying to his audience, 'this is a human hand' and 'that is a human hand' and deducing from this that at least two physical, and therefore by definition two external, objects existed. He insisted that the proof was valid on the ground that its conclusion followed from its premiss and that he knew the premiss to be true.

But even if it be concluded that this proof is valid, what is the point of it? What purpose does it serve? The answer is that it is directed against other philosophers. Metaphysicians have at various times denied the reality of matter, or of mind, or of space or time. Moore points out that if what these metaphysicians say is taken literally, it is at variance with obvious facts. If Moore really does know the propositions which he claims to know, and these are propositions of a sort which we should all claim to know, at least in our unphilosophical moments, then the metaphysicians who have contradicted these propositions, which are known to be true, must be wrong. We know that they are wrong, even if we cannot see through their arguments.

But now it begins to look as if something has gone awry. Not all metaphysicians are fools or charlatans. Whatever it is that they are trying to say when they deny the existence of matter, or mind, or whatever it may be, it is rash to assume that it is anything so simple as to be capable of being refuted merely by appealing to what everybody knows. But then how are we to interpret it? I shall offer some suggestions later on.

Moore's technique is to prove the existence of entities of a given type simply by adducing examples. So the presence of this lectern or this chair proves that there are physical objects; the fact that I can see them and that I remember coming here this morning proves that there are acts of consciousness, and so on. But then how is it proved that these examples exist? By their being found to satisfy whatever are the appropriate criteria. There are accredited procedures for deciding whether this is a real physical lectern, and not a dummy or a phantom. They are not infallible—perhaps there is no situation in which the possibility of error is logically excluded—but if there is no ground for suspecting any error, then I am fully justified in accepting their verdict. There is anyhow nothing more that I can do than carry out the relevant tests. The case of acts of consciousness is rather more complicated, because of difficulties about publicity. Nevertheless, it would generally be held that introspection, in one's own case, or certain forms of behaviour, in the case of other people, provide sufficient evidence of their existence.

But then how far will these procedures take us? We can provide examples, in this sense, of all sorts of abstract entities—numbers, classes, propositions, universals; we can provide examples of mythological entities, or characters in fiction. Do we want to say that they exist? Presumably not, or not in all cases. Yet why should an example of one kind be better, why should it count for more, than an example of another?

Carnap has an interesting way of dealing with this problem. In an article entitled 'Empiricism, Semantics and Ontology', which originally appeared in the *Revue International de Philosophie* in 1950, and has since been reprinted in various anthologies, he drew a distinction between what he called internal and external questions of existence. Internal questions, as the name suggests, are questions that arise within the framework of a conceptual system and are settled by the application of the criteria which the system supplies. Thus, if we are speaking at the level of common sense, the question whether there are chairs in this room, or elephants, is a question to be settled by observation, the answer being yes in the one case and no in the other. If we are speaking in terms of physics, then the question whether there are mesons (yes) or whether there is a *perpetuum mobile* (no) are questions which are decided in the last resort by observation, but also in terms of the acceptability of certain theories. If we are operating inside mathematics, then there are formal procedures for deciding such questions as whether there is a rational square root of 2 (no) or a prime number between 11 and 15 (yes). If we are talking about mythology or literature then such questions as whether there is a Greek god of the Underworld (yes) or a woman married to Mr Pickwick (no) are settled by looking up the relevant texts. Of course the answers are not always so easy. Even in mathematics there may be questions like that of the validity of Goldbach's conjecture, which no one has yet been able to decide. There may also be disputes concerning the criteria themselves; a mathematical example would be the disagreement about the status of *reductio ad absurdum* proofs. The point remains that once the criteria have been settled the question whether they are satisfied is internal to the relevant discipline.

Now if we raise very general questions like 'Are there physical objects?', 'Are there numbers?',' Are there fictitious characters?', and treat them as internal questions, the answers to them are always obvious, either obviously yes or obviously no, according as the conceptual system does or does not make provision for them. Yes there are physical objects; this chair is a physical object. Yes there are numbers; 2 is a number. Yes there are fictitious characters; Mr Pickwick is a fictitious character. Or, if one is speaking within a universe of discourse where the criterion of existence is location in space and time, then of course there are no fictitious characters, and for that matter no numbers either.

But now, Carnap goes on, these very general questions can also be interpreted externally. That is to say, they can be interpreted not as questions arising within a given conceptual or linguistic framework, but as questions which bear upon the framework itself. But when they are interpreted in this way, how are they to be construed? Carnap's answer is that they are to be construed as questions of policy. Are we going to employ a language which contains the means of referring to entities of this kind? So extreme nominalists, who renounce abstract entities, will, if they are consistent, think themselves bound to restrict their discourse so that they refer only to individuals, not classes, to numerals, not numbers, to sentences conceived as strings of words or noises, and not to propositions. But why should one restrict oneself in this way? Only, Carnap thinks, for metaphysical motives, which leave him cold. Of course not everything is admissible. Statements which are not analytically true have to be empirically testable. But so long as this requirement is satisfied, Carnap is in favour of a principle of tolerance. We are free to employ any form of language that we find useful, no matter what sort of entities it refers to.

Though Carnap's handling of external questions may be thought to be carrying pragmatism rather far, I think that the distinction which he draws between them and internal questions is extremely important, indeed crucial. It has, however, been challenged by Professor Quine, in an essay 'On Carnap's View on Ontology' which was first published in 1951 in volume 2 of *Philosophical Studies*, and is reprinted in Quine's *The Ways of Paradox*. He characterizes Carnap's dichotomy between external and internal questions as one between category questions and sub-class questions. Thus the question 'Are there numbers?' is a category question, whereas the question whether there are irrational numbers is a sub-class question. 'Are there so and so's?' is a category question when the so and so's purport to exhaust the range of a particular style of bound variables; it is a sub-class question when they do not. Quine remarks of Carnap's external questions that they are category questions conceived or propounded before the adoption of a given language, and he agrees with Carnap that, as so conceived, they are properly to be construed as questions of the desirability of a given language form.

But now, Quine goes on to argue, this distinction between category questions and sub-class questions turns out to be a fairly arbitrary one. For instance, the question whether there are numbers would be a category question only with respect to languages which have a special style of variables for the purpose of referring to numbers. In a language, like the language normally used in set theory, in which the variables which take numbers for their values, can also take as values classes which are not numbers, the question whether there are numbers becomes a sub-class question. And the same would hold good, Quine implies, for any of the other categories. Even if we adopt Russell's theory of types, which favours compartmentalization of variables, we can still use a single style of variables for all types by adopting what Quine has called the device of stratification, which comes down to imposing certain grammatical restrictions on the sort of repetition patterns which variables can display in formulae. And if we do use a single style of variables, then the basis for Carnap's distinction between category and sub-class questions has gone. In fact, Quine thinks, this would be no great loss to Carnap. He can get all he wants out of the analytic-synthetic distinction. Ontological statements which are the answers to internal questions are those which are analytic or contradictory given the language. Thus the statement that there are physical objects is analytic, relatively to the language of common sense. We don't have to find out that there are physical objects; the assumption that there are is part of the framework in which our observations have to be fitted. On the other hand, the statement that there are chairs is synthetic or empirical. Our language makes provision for there being chairs, just as it makes provision for there being unicorns, but it leaves it open whether the necessary conditions are satisfied in either case. Admittedly, we can't now make a similar distinction within mathematics, where the statement that there are numbers and the statement that there are prime numbers above a hundred are equally analytic, but Quine doesn't see why this should worry Carnap. He himself, of course, has the much more radical objection that he does not accept the analytic-synthetic distinction.

I think that what Quine says here about the arbitrariness of the distinction between category and sub-class questions is correct, but I also think that his criticism of Carnap misses the point. The point is that the distinction between external and internal questions is not just a distinction with respect to levels of generality. It is rather a distinction between questions which can be answered affirmatively by giving an example of the sort of entity whose existence is being queried, and questions which cannot be answered in this way. So, 'Are there prime numbers greater than a hundred?' is an internal question which is answered by giving examples—101 is such a number, 103, 107, and so forth; but 'Are there numbers?', when treated as an external question, is not to be answered in this way. It is possible for a philosopher to admit that '2 is a number' is a true statement and yet deny that there are numbers, to admit that France is a nation-state and yet deny that there are states, as opposed to the individuals who are members of them, to characterize 'Queen Anne is dead' as a proposition about the past, and yet deny that there are propositions, as opposed to sentences.

But how are these denials possible? Here I part company with Carnap, though not very radically. I don't think it is just a matter of declaring a preference for a certain sort of linguistic framework. I think the position is rather that one may find it convenient to talk about all sorts of things—propositions, numbers, states, mythological entities, and yet not want to regard oneself as committed to a belief in their existence.

But is this just a matter of choice? How is it decided what one is committed to and what one isn't? And anyway, how can one be sure that one makes the right commitments? On the face of it, it would seem that one could commit oneself to a belief in what does not exist, and fail to commit oneself to a belief in what does exist. And how is this to be decided?

It would seem, then, that we have first to find some means of determining what ontological commitments are, and then to find some means of assessing them. Let us begin with the first problem. The most systematic attempt to lay down a criterion of ontological commitment has been made by Quine. His suggestion is that an entity is assumed by a theory, in a sense of 'theory' in which any set of statements that one accepts constitutes a theory, if and only if it must be counted among the values of the variables in order that the statements of the theory be true.[1] Hence his famous slogan 'To be is to be the value of a variable'. A minor defect of this way of putting it is that it ties the criterion to a particular notation, namely to that of quantification, but the point can be generalized. The idea is that we incur ontological commitments through our employment not of names but of predicates. We are committed to believing in the existence of whatever satisfies the predicates in question. We can reduce our commitments within a given language only by showing that certain of the predicates which it contains are dispensable; and here the criterion of the dispensability of a predicate is the strong one of the possibility of translating out the sentences in which it occurs. So someone, using ordinary language, who wishes, say, to deny the existence of mental states, will be required to show that the statements which he accepts about people's thoughts and feelings can be translated into statements about people's physical condition or behaviour; someone who wishes to dispense with numbers as entities will have to show that mathematical statements can be treated formalistically as statements about numerals and so on.

This looks promising, except that the requirement of translatability may turn out to be too strong for comfort, but there are snags. The main difficulty, as Scheffler and Chomsky pointed out in an article on 'What is said to be', which appeared in the *Proceedings of the Aristotelian Society* for 1958, is that if we follow Quine's procedure it will be very hard, if not impossible, for us to speak about the ontological commitments of a theory which we do not accept, without incurring them ourselves. So, to use their example, if the theory is that $(\exists x)$ x is phlogiston, then in speaking about the theory's commitments we have to say '$(\exists x)$ x is phlogiston and assumed by T', which involves us in the assumption of phlogiston ourselves. We might try to get round this by saying that we are committed to the existence of objects of a certain sort only if there is at least one member of the class which actually satisfies the relevant predicate, but while this absolves us from

[1] W. V. Quine, 'On What There Is', *From a Logical Point of View* (1953).

committal to phlogiston, it has the undesirable consequence, from our present point of view, that the believers in phlogiston are not committed to it either, since nothing actually does satisfy the predicate of being phlogiston. And there are other difficulties. For instance, a theory which admits the existence of the Young Pretender but denies the existence of Charles Edward Stuart is not self-contradictory. It is an empirical fact that Charles Edward Stuart was identical with the Young Pretender. Yet since the function '*x* is the Young Pretender' is in fact satisfied by the Charles Edward Stuart, we have to say that the theory is implicitly committed to the existence of something the existence of which it explicitly denies.

These difficulties arise out of referential opacity. They raise the whole question of intentional objects into which I shall not enter here, partly because I do not know what ought to be said about them. I believe them to be eliminable, but have not yet found any wholly satisfactory way of eliminating them. Failing this, I think the best course, with regard to our present problem, will be to have special rules about existential generalization. That is to say, we make a list of verbs which take intentional objects, verbs like 'desired', 'feared', 'loved', 'assumed by', 'believed in' and so on, and then lay it down that the statement that an object satisfies these predicates is not to count as an ontological commitment. This does, however, mar the purity of Quine's programme. We no longer have a general criterion.

I don't very much mind this, because I want to look at it the other way; that is, to study the denials of ontological commitment. It is normally what a philosopher tells you when he argues that there are not things of such and such a sort that gives you the clue to what ontology is about. These denials fall into several not very clearly demarcated groups.

(i) The least interesting and least problematic cases are those where you can operate a straightforward reduction. If you can define *x*s in terms of *y*s or translate out references to *x*s in favour of references to *y*s you will not want to maintain the existence of *x*s independently of *y*s. Thus, if you accept the view that irrational numbers can be defined in terms of rationals by Dedekindian section, you will not think of them as having an independent title to existence. To take a more obvious example, no one wants to think of the average Englishman as an entity existing independently of Jones, Smith and Robinson, because it can so easily be shown that talking about the average so and so is just a way of summarizing statistics about so and so's.

(ii) A related case is one in which we do not, or at least do not obviously, have a method of translating out, and yet it would be generally agreed that something's being true of *x*s comes down to something's being true of *y*s. The best example here is that of nations. I doubt if it is possible to find a rule for translating statements about England and France into statements about Englishmen and Frenchmen and yet it seems obvious that what makes it true to say that England is undergoing an economic crisis is a set of facts about the behaviour of individual men and women, the scarcity or abundance of certain types of goods and so forth, and nothing over and above facts of this kind. In this case the negative ontological thesis seems obvious, but there are other cases, not evidently different from this, where it does not seem obvious at all. Do we say that talk about unconscious states of mind is a summary of talk about overt behaviour, that someone's being, say, unconsciously jealous of his brother is nothing over and above his being disposed to do and say certain things, to reply in such and such ways to the psycho-analyst or whatever? Probably most of us would want to say this. But then again, do we say that talking about atoms and electrons comes down in the same way to talking about the actual and possible results of carrying out certain operations, that the wire's being electrically charged just consists in a set of hypothetical facts to the effect that under such and such conditions bells will be rung, shocks received and so forth? Here the general tendency is to go the other way, the reason being that we have theories which explain these facts in terms of the structure, the constitution of the wire. But don't we also in the psycho-analytic case? Is it just that we are more sceptical about allegedly mental structures? And anyway how are these physical theories themselves interpreted? How are their ontological commitments assessed? The trouble is that once the requirement of translatability is relaxed, it ceases to be clear under what conditions we are to say that the truth of one type of statement *comes down* to the truth of another. I shall argue later on that this is in the end a matter of our taking a more or less arbitrary decision.

A good example of this sort of uncertainty is the case of numbers. Someone who says that there are not numbers may be committing himself to the kind of programme that Quine and Goodman outlined in their 'Steps towards a Constructive Nominalism', actually rewriting references to classes, so that we only quantify over individuals; and then it is a precise technical question whether this programme can be carried out, whether we can preserve all the mathematics we want in this restricted notation, a question which probably has to be answered in the negative. But one may be claiming something weaker and vaguer. Like Wittgenstein in his posthumous work on the *Foundations of Mathematics* one may try to show in an unsystematic way that doing mathematics comes down to carrying out certain operations, including pencil and paper operations. And then just because the procedure is unsystematic, it is not clear whether it succeeds or not: it is not clear what we are to count as its succeeding.

(iii) The motives for renouncing abstract entities are various, but one of them is that they fail to do the work that they have been called upon to do. Thus someone who asks 'Are there propositions?' is not, or anyhow ought not to be, asking for an inventory of the contents of some Platonic heaven. How would this inventory be taken? He is asking whether we need to bring in propositions to get a satisfactory theory of meaning and truth. Do we learn anything by being told that sentences acquire meaning by standing for propositions, or that truth consists in the correspondence of propositions to facts? The answer is that so far from learning anything useful, we are if anything misled. This way of speaking suggests the false idea that understanding a sentence (or a general term, for what I am saying about propositions applies *mutatis mutandis* to universals) is a matter of contemplating an abstract entity. It suggests, again falsely, that finding out that such and such a series of signs has been used to say what is true is a matter of looking upon this picture and upon that, propositions being made to intervene between signs and concrete states of affairs as unnecessary reduplications of one or the other or both. So to deny that there are abstract entities like propositions or universals is to say that the postulation of such entities plays no useful part in linguistics. To bring them in as the designata of signs is only to pretend to have a linguistic theory. It is to treat the relation of signifying as unanalysable, and cover up by supplying it with dummy accusatives.[1]

It is the same with values. Someone who says that there are no objective values may be conducting a campaign of moral nihilism, but more likely, if he is a philosopher, he will either be sponsoring a naturalistic or attitudinal theory of ethics, or, at the very least, making the valid point that to say that moral predicates stand for moral properties, that moral statements, if true, record objective moral facts, is totally unilluminating. It does not tell us how moral discourse

[1] These points are restated in my essay 'G. E. Moore on Propositions and Facts'. See below, pp. 191–3.

functions, but only that it functions in whatever way it does. And again this emptiness, this lack of enterprise, is covered up by bringing in dummy entities.

It is interesting to note in this class of cases that thesis and antithesis are reversed. It is the philosopher who says that there are not so and so's who is making the positive claim. He is implying that he can give an adequate account of meaning on morals or whatever it may be, without having to fall back on such *dei ex machina*. The philosopher who says that there are such things is taking the negative position. He is saying that these naturalistic explanations do not work.

(iv) Next I come to a set of cases which perhaps fit most closely into the pattern of Carnap's treatment of what he calls external questions. These relate to the choice of conceptual systems. I am not thinking here of predominantly technical questions such as whether it is possible to eliminate singular terms. I am thinking rather of one's general idea of the way the world works, of what one regards as a possible form of explanation, of what one counts as evidence in favour of a theory. Consider, for example, the passage from a medieval to a modern scientific view of the world, and in particular the abandonment of the belief in good and evil spirits. One could say that a theory like the theory of witchcraft had been empirically refuted, but that would be an over-simplification. The truth is that it comes out badly when tested by scientific procedures which belong to a different way of thinking. I do not wish to be completely relativistic here. There is a sense in which what we call scientific theories do correspond better to the facts, though it must be remembered that we make use of scientific theories, for example the theory of rigid bodies, in determining what are the facts. What may save us from complete relativism, each party being judge and victor in its own cause, is that we are working on recalcitrant material. I do not want to talk of brute facts, because I do not want to deny that even the most rudimentary perceptual judgements depend on some process of interpretation, but there is an element of bruteness in perceptual situations which sets limits to what can be believed. So one system can be better than another in the sense that it is better in accord with the perceptual judgements which are, so to speak, forced upon us: but this still leaves room for very great variety.

(v) Finally, one of the strongest motives for reducing ontological commitments has been the belief that we have to restrict ourselves to what we are capable of knowing. Curiously enough, this motive has led, in different hands of course, both to the subordination of matter to mind and to the subordination of mind to matter. Physicalist theories of the mind have resulted not from a dispassionate examination of the way in which psychological statements function, but rather from the assumption that it is only if they are interpreted physicalistically that these statements become epistemologically respectable: and conversely the view that statements about physical objects have to be analysed phenomenalistically has resulted not from a dispassionate examination of the way these statements function but from the assumption that only sense-data are immediate objects of knowledge.

I shall not attempt to discuss the merits of these positions here. I still adhere to what might be described as a very weak form of phenomenalism, in the sense that I think that the physical system of common sense can be represented as a theory with respect to a primary system of qualia, but I do not want to argue for this now. I do, however, want to conclude by saying something about the question of the reality of the external world. I am able to do this, without going deeply into epistemology, because I believe that the question what there is, in this sense, is very largely independent of what is known in terms of what. To put it succinctly, I see no reason to assume that epistemological and ontological priority necessarily go together.

There seem to me to be various possibilities, of which perhaps the best would be to take no ontological decision at all. Questions about the reality of different categories of objects would be construed only internally as questions whether or not the statements which figure in different types of theory are true.

This does not mean that we do not allow ourselves to talk of all manner of things existing. It is just that the criteria for existence will all be internal. The question whether such or such a thing exists will always be construed as a question whether such and such a function is satisfied, whether it is true for at least one value, or, if we have a wholly predicative language, whether the predicate is satisfied. What we shall not do is go on to raise ontological questions about what satisfies the functions. When we have shown how statements referring to numbers are related to statements referring to numerals, or how experiential statements are related to physical statements, we shall have done all that is required in these domains. We are not obliged to find a sense for such metaphysical questions as whether numbers or physical objects form part of the ultimate furniture of the world. They will simply not be admissible.

If we do find it necessary to have an ontology and if we decide, for fairly obvious reasons,[1] that sense-qualia are not suited to fulfil this role, the choice would appear to lie between naïve realism and what I propose to call physical realism. Let us first consider naïve realism. I shall be concerned with it only as a form of ontology not as a theory of perception.

The naïve realist position, as I interpret it, is that the things with which the world is mainly furnished are the physical objects of common-sense belief. There are thought to be other things as well; fluids, vapours, shadows, images, perhaps minds and their contents, considered as distinct if not separable from bodies: but for the most part the world is taken to consist of solid three-dimensional objects like trees, mountains, stars, tables, chairs, books, motor cars, dogs, cats, birds, stones and so forth. These objects are thought to be literally coloured, in the sense that their colour enters essentially into their description, no less than their size, shape, position and solidity. There is, indeed, a sense in which their colour is a fundamental feature of our conception of them, since it is only in so far as they are coloured that we can distinguish them at all by sight, and so assign other visual properties to them.

Now the fact that these objects appear to us as they do is open to a causal explanation; and into this explanation come scientific entities like protons and electrons. The question then arises how these scientific particles are related to the physical objects of common sense. One possible answer is that they are literally parts of them. There is, however, the difficulty that the particles are not themselves endowed with colour nor are they thought to be continuously spread over the area which a common-sense physical object occupies; and even if we admit the possibility that a number of colourless particles can combine to form a coloured object, it is difficult to see how a continuous surface could be composed of discontinuous parts. It might be argued that the physical objects which we perceive do not really have the continuous surface that they appear to have, that there are gaps which we are unable to detect; but this would be contrary to the naïve realist's principle that things really are as they normally appear to us. I think, therefore, that the naïve realist will have to say that things like protons and electrons, as opposed to things like chairs and motor cars, are theoretical constructs which exist only in the sense that the theories into which they enter can be verified. This need not commit him to a

[1] Cf. my *The Origins of Pragmatism*, pp. 334–5 (Macmillan, 1968), or pp. 322–3 (Freeman, Cooper, 1968).

thoroughgoing operationalism—he does not have to maintain that statements about scientific particles can be translated into statements about their observable effects—though he might have to adopt some weaker thesis of a reductive sort.

On this interpretation, the adoption of a naïve realist ontology just consists in the decision to think only of the objects in which common sense believes as constituting what there really is, and to treat the entities which figure in scientific theories as explanatory fictions. This decision can be criticized along the well-known lines that have tended to discredit naïve realism as a theory of perception, but so long as it is a matter not of the truth of any particular theory but of the picture which we choose to form of the world, I assume that these criticisms can be withstood.

What I call physical realism is not the only conceivable alternative to naïve realism—we could, for example, take space-time points or regions as the only existent individuals and there are other possibilities—but it is the only alternative that most people would consider seriously. It consists in awarding the ontological palm to the entities, the atomic particles or whatever, which figure in physical theories. How experiences are accommodated in it will not, indeed, be merely a matter for decision: it will depend on the resolution of the mind–body problem, and in particular on the question whether states of consciousness can be logically or factually identified with states of the nervous system. If this turns out not to be feasible, the physical realist will have the choice of adding minds to his ontology, treating experiences as entities alongside the entities of physics and causally dependent on them, or, what he is likely to prefer, of regarding consciousness as an emergent property of certain groups of physical particles. The physical objects of common sense are squeezed out, or to employ a more accurate metaphor, flayed. The flesh, the colours and shapes which one perceives, is taken off the bones and housed in consciousness, the bones are transmuted into the physical particles which take over their spatial positions.

Well then, if we are going to have an ontology, and if we are not going to bother with the more fanciful candidates, which are we to choose, naïve realism or physical realism? And here let me say at once that I am taking them to be competitive, as I do not see how it is possible to combine them. I lay stress on this point because many philosophers who are respectful of science but attached to common sense have held that one can combine them. Professor Ryle, for example, in his *Dilemmas* compares the situation of the physicist to that of the clerk who records all the activities of the members of a college in the college audits; there is nothing that the accounts do not deal with and yet it would be a great mistake to identify the whole life of the college with these accounts. Another analogy which he uses is that of the distinction between a landscape as seen by a painter and the same landscape as seen by a geologist. In both cases the suggestion seems to be that the physicist's and the plain man's conceptions of the external world are not in competition: they are looking at the same world from different aspects. 'A bit of the theory of ultimate particles', says Ryle, 'has no place in it for a description or misdescription of chairs and tables, and a description of chairs and tables has no place in it for a description or misdescription of ultimate particles. A statement that is true or false of the one is *neither* true *nor* false of the other. It cannot therefore be a rival of the other. The very fact that some statement in physical theory is true requires that some statement or other (it cannot be stated which) about such things as chairs and tables are true.'[1]

I have no quarrel with this if it just means that statements about chairs and tables and statements about electrons and protons are independently verifiable, and, what I take to be the purport of the last sentence of the passage I quoted, which as it stands is rather obscure, that the truth of some statements about chairs and tables can be explained by adducing true statements about protons and electrons. Nevertheless I do not think that this justifies Ryle's contention that naïve realism and physical realism are not ontological rivals, because he is adopting a position where no ontological questions are raised, the position in which all that one asks is whether certain sorts of statements are true. But if ontological questions are being raised, then I think that these two forms of realism must be rivals, if only for the reason, which Ryle appears to have overlooked, that they compete for the same regions of space. We can reconcile saying that there is a table here with saying that there is a group of electrons here, because there are independent ways of testing both statements, and these sets of tests can both be satisfied. But if we are constructing a picture of the world, I do not see how we can consistently think of this area both as being exclusively occupied by a solid, continuous, coloured object and as being exclusively occupied by a group of discontinuous, volatile, colourless, shapeless particles. We have to choose.

How then are we to choose? The weakness of the naïve realist

[1] *Dilemmas* (1954), p. 79.

position is that science psychologically undermines it. Once we have learned even a little physiology, it is hard to think of colour as anything but a causal property of physical objects, and the removal of colour brings down the edifice. In favour of naïve realism is the fact that we are habituated to it and that it does supply us with a picture.

Conversely, what is in favour of physical realism is that it is scientific. Against it is the fact that it does not supply us with a picture; to make a picture out of it we have to falsify it a little by visualizing the particles as little silvery specks, which they are not. It also encounters another psychological difficulty, which is perhaps more serious. It is not too hard for me to think of this table as being really a group of electrons, because I am more interested in its function than its appearance, but even in the case of an inanimate object, this attitude becomes quite difficult to sustain if the object is one to which I attach aesthetic value. And in the case of persons, especially those for whom one has affection, it is very difficult indeed. When I think of my small son in absence, I cannot bring myself to picture him as a group of electrons; if I get so far as the way he would look in an X-ray photograph I am doing very well. Of course, with this ontology, it is not so much a question of our forming images as of our being prepared to say that this is all that there really is. But how seriously do we mean it?

In conclusion, there are two points that I wish to make. The first is to repeat that what we have here is a question for decision. One may be tempted to protest: 'Never mind what *we* want to say. What is the truth? What is *really* there, the table as common sense conceives it, or the physical particles? What does God see?' But then one would be forgetting that the word 'really' is here being used externally; we are no longer speaking within a conceptual system which provides us with criteria for determining what there really is. It is not like asking whether there really was a man in the iron mask, where we have established criteria for settling the question. In fact we do not know whether the man to whom this description refers existed or not, and are not now very likely to find out, but at least we know what sort of evidence would satisfy us one way or the other. Neither is it like asking whether there really are positrons, when their existence has been postulated on theoretical grounds, and the question is whether the theoretical assumption is going to be confirmed by experiment. When it comes to such philosophical questions as 'Do things exist unperceived?' and 'In what form do they exist: as we perceive them or as physicists depict them?', the point is that they cannot be settled by experiment. They ask for an assessment of the framework in terms of which experiments are to be interpreted. As I said before, we do not have to admit these questions: we are probably better advised not to admit them. But if we do admit them, then in answering them we are not straightforwardly reporting what there is, but deciding what there is to be. We are, if you like, expressing a normative judgement. To say: this is what God sees, is to say: this is how we ought to look at the world. As we have seen, it is not an arbitrary judgement. One can give reasons for going one way or the other. But they are not compelling reasons. Whether we opt for naïve realism, or physical realism, or phenomenalism, or whatever, there are going to be some consequences which make us feel intellectually uncomfortable. If most of us feel least uncomfortable with naïve realism, it is mainly, I suppose, because it is the picture of the world with which we are most familiar, having lived with it since our childhood, and also because it occupies a safe, or comparatively safe, middle position, the phenomenalist picture being too fragmentary and the physical realist one too abstract.

My second point is that the question whether or how this decision is taken does not seem to me to be of any great importance. The important question for the plain man is whether the statements that are made within his conceptual framework are true: the same applies to the scientist at his level of discourse. The important questions for the philosopher are how these different sorts of statement are related, and what are the criteria by which their truth or falsehood is determined. Once these questions are satisfactorily answered, it does not very greatly matter how the ontological medals are bestowed.

5

METAPHYSICS AND COMMON SENSE

If we go by appearances, it can hardly be disputed that metaphysics is nearly always in conflict with common sense. This is most obvious in the case of the metaphysician who professes to find a logical flaw, a contradiction or a vicious infinite regress, in one or other of the ways in which we commonly describe the world, and so comes to such startling conclusions as that time and space are unreal, or that nothing really moves, or that there are not many things in the Universe but only one, or that nothing which we perceive through our senses is real or wholly real, or that there is no such thing as matter, or no such things as minds. It is, however, also true of those who maintain not that the features which common sense ascribes to the external world are unreal, but that they are dependent upon our consciousness of them, that space and time are merely forms of human intuition, or that none of the things which we classify as physical objects exist except when they are being perceived, or that the world is my idea. Even philosophers who wish to dissociate themselves from metaphysics often advance theories which are shocking to common sense, as that there are no private experiences, or that everything that exists is constructed out of sense-data, or that no one ever does anything of his own free will, or that the past is determined by the future as much as the future by the past.

In the eyes of many contemporary philosophers, the fact that such assertions do conflict with common sense is sufficient to condemn them. This is something of a new departure in the history of philosophy, where common sense has not on the whole been treated with very much respect. It is mainly due to the work of G. E. Moore who looked at metaphysics with the devastating simplicity and candour of the child in the Hans Andersen story of the Emperor's Clothes. His technique was to take metaphysical assertions at their face value and show how extraordinary their implications were. Thus he pointed out that if time is unreal, it follows that nothing ever changes or decays or grows, that a man's birth does not precede his death, and indeed that almost every would-be empirical proposition is false, since they nearly all imply that something happens before or after or simultaneously with something else. If matter is unreal, then the stars and the sun and the earth and everything in it, including human beings themselves, are as mythical as unicorns or gorgons. It follows also that if such theories are true, nobody holds them. For if matter is unreal, there are no metaphysicians: and if time is unreal, then nobody ever makes a statement or acquires a belief.

So again, if the world is my idea, it follows that it came into existence with my birth and will disappear at my death; if things exist only when they are perceived, then unless we rely on the perpetual vigilance of a problematic deity, we have to conclude that they are constantly popping in and out of existence, as well as holding that there never has been and never will be a time at which the Universe fails to contain sentient beings; if space and time are merely forms of human sensibility, it follows that the Universe is co-terminous with the existence of the human race. This result may not be quite so ludicrous as that of holding that space and time are unreal. But can any sane man seriously believe it?

Now it might be expected that the defenders of such metaphysical positions would have made some attempt to protect themselves against this sort of treatment, and in some cases they have done so. In the case of those whom Moore was especially attacking, the English neo-Hegelians like Bradley and MacTaggart who maintained the unreality of matter and of space and time, the line taken was to mitigate the charge of unreality; things which were not ultimately real might nevertheless be real as appearances. In this way an attempt was made to give common sense its due: it was able and entitled to distinguish between reality and illusion at its own level, the level of appearances, and the same would apply to science which was, indeed, only a sophistication of common sense. But the metaphysician was bound to go deeper, to probe for the more genuine reality which lay beneath the appearances, and this was discovered to be very different; so different that the most central concepts which served for the description of appearances were wholly inapplicable to it.

The trouble with this defence is that it is hardly more than a sham. To begin with, it is not at all clear what can be meant by saying that something is real as an appearance. If it is interpreted as meaning that the thing only appears to be real, then we have to conclude without qualification that it is not real. If what is meant is that the thing really appears, then we have to conclude without qualification that it is real, though here we may allow for the possibility of its appearing under some disguise. In neither case is any proviso made for any half-way stage. But these are the only natural interpretations of the curious expression 'real as an appearance' and we are not given any other.

Moreover the ground which philosophers like Bradley advance for saying that space and time and matter are not ultimately real is that the ordinary notions of a material object or of things standing in spatial or temporal relations to each other are self-contradictory. But if a concept is self-contradictory, it is hard to see how anything could even appear to fall under it, let alone really fall under it as an appearance. A man who is older than another may look younger, but how could he be said to look both older and younger? What should we understand by this? Perhaps, that he looked older in some respects and younger in others; but then we are interpreting the description so that it ceases to be contradictory. So long as a description is contradictory it necessarily applies to nothing and nothing can even seem to satisfy it, for the sufficient reason that there is nothing in such a case which the delusive appearance can be taken to fall short of. If it really were self-contradictory to speak of things as being temporally related then there would be no possible state of affairs which talk of this kind would represent, and therefore nothing that events which merely appeared to be in temporal relation would be counterfeiting. The most that could be claimed would be that real things had properties which caused us to categorize them in self-contradictory ways; but it would be highly misleading to translate this into the assertion that their appearances were self-contradictory: and even if this translation were allowed to pass, it would entail the conclusion not that such appearances were real at their own level, but rather that they were not real in any sense at all.

This thesis is so obviously untenable that it is tempting to assume that its proponents were using words like 'real' and 'self-contradictory' in peculiar senses of their own. But the trouble with this suggestion is that the arguments which they bring against the world of appearances purport to be logical; they are designed to show that the categories under which we try to order it are self-contradictory in the normal sense. And while they do tend to use the word 'real' in a rather elastic fashion, so that sometimes a thing is said by them to be unreal when all that seems to be meant is that it is limited or relatively unimportant, nevertheless they do pass from the premiss that appearances are not ultimately real to the conclusion that the descriptions which are given of them are not true, or at any rate not wholly true: and this would indicate that in this context at least they also intended the word 'real' to be understood in something like a normal sense. The notion of degrees of truth is again an escape clause to which no evident meaning is attached.

It would seem, then, that the attempts of metaphysicians of this kind to make the best of both worlds, to return with one hand at least part of what they have taken away with the other, have only led them into trouble. They would have done better to accept the conclusion that their views were quite irreconcilable with common sense, and not put themselves to dubious shifts in a vain attempt to save the appearances. They would indeed still be under some obligation to explain how we all can come to be so grievously mistaken; but if the appearances really are contradictory they are not worth saving.

Let us then suppose that we have to deal with a metaphysician who takes this more resolute attitude. His position, which has in fact been held at least by some oriental thinkers, is that the concepts of space and time and matter do not apply to anything at all. With or without argument, he maintains that reality falls under concepts of a totally different kind from these. How could he be refuted?

Well again he is exposed to the objection that if his view were true, he could not hold it, since he himself would not exist. But while this is enough to make the man appear ridiculous, it does not strictly demolish his opinion. For logically the opinion might be true, even though it entailed that nobody could exist to hold it. In practice the proponents of these views invariably fall into contradiction by advancing them as views of their own or implying that other people are in error. For example they speak of the common sense view of the world as a popular delusion, which it cannot possibly be if there are no people to be deluded by it. But with sufficient care these contradictions can be avoided.

At this point many people would be content to say that any view of this kind is palpably false, and this in effect was the position which Moore took, though he reached it indirectly. His contention was that he knew for certain the truth of such propositions as that he had a body and that this body was frequently in contact with the surface of the earth and that the earth had existed for many years past, and since such propositions all implied the reality of space and time and matter it followed that if he really knew them to be true, any propositions which denied the reality of space and time and matter must be false.

This argument is perfectly rigorous. If its premisses are true, its conclusion must also be true. And no doubt the premisses are true. No doubt Moore did know many propositions of the type which I have just mentioned and no doubt each one of us knows many similar propositions about himself and his environment. Nevertheless it looks like a weakness in Moore's position, as he himself acknowledged, that he does not explain how we know these things; he does not show us how we are to vindicate these claims to knowledge. The answer to this may be that while there are many propositions which we could not reasonably claim to know unless we knew others which supported them, there must be some that are known immediately, if we are not to be saddled with an infinite regress; and a case might be made out for saying that Moore's examples belong to this primitive class. Even so, the metaphysician against whom this argument is directed might not think it difficult to counter. To what would seem to him an entirely dogmatic objection he might make an equally dogmatic rejoinder. He might say that since his own theory is true it follows that these common sense propositions are false and *a fortiori* that nobody knows them.

There is, however, a further argument on which it seems to me that Moore tacitly relies though I do not know that he ever made it explicit. What makes us so sure that there are physical objects which stand to one another in spatio-temporal relations is that it seems to us that we perceive them. We have sense-experiences which we take as establishing the truth of such propositions as that there is a chair over here and a book-case over there and a table in between them, or that the sun came out just after the rain had stopped. Now the question is raised whether our experiences can ever establish propositions of these kinds. But, so the argument runs, it just is in the nature of these propositions, it is characteristic of the meaning of the sentences which serve to express them, that they *are* established by those sorts of experiences. The rules which govern the use of sentences of this type are such as to correlate them with observable states of affairs; we understand the sentences when we know what observations would verify or falsify the propositions which they express. On certain occasions, indeed, we may have reasons for distrusting what appear to be such observations; we may have grounds for thinking that the appearances are deceptive in one way or another. But in default of any such special reasons for mistrust, to have what appear to be the appropriate experiences and to refuse to accept the proposition which is expressed by the sentence with which they are conventionally correlated is simply to violate the canons of the language which one purports to be using. In short, there are accepted criteria for deciding in particular cases whether these common sense propositions are true or false, and the question whether these criteria are satisfied in any given instance is a question not for philosophical argument but simply for empirical observation.

It is easy to see that this argument can be generalized, and also that when it is generalized it naturally leads to the conclusion that the only positive contribution that philosophy can make to knowledge is in the field of analysis. This position was not formally held by Moore himself, but it is implied in his practice and was explicitly adopted by most of his followers. For it is true not only of the propositions of common sense that there are recognized criteria for deciding when they are true or false. This applies equally to the technical theories and hypotheses of science and, though in their case the criteria are not empirical, to the *a priori* propositions of logic and pure mathematics. In these domains also there are recognized standards of proof and recognized procedures for determining whether these standards have been met. If someone refuses to regard a favourable experiment as confirming a scientific theory, then unless he has some special reason for mistrusting the experiment, unless he has grounds for suspecting that there has been an error of observation, or that there is some other special reason why the apparent result of this experiment is not to be taken at its face value, he simply has not understood what the theory is. If someone refuses to accept the result of a logical or mathematical demonstration, without having any special reason for thinking that the procedure which was employed in this instance was faulty or incorrectly carried out, he simply does not understand how logic and mathematics work.

The upshot of this is that the truth or falsehood of these propositions is not even a matter for philosophical discussion. It depends only on the satisfaction of the appropriate criteria; and whether the criteria are satisfied is a matter of empirical or formal fact. There is no place here for philosophy to intervene. But what then is there left for it to do? The official answer is, as I have indicated, that while it is not equipped to estimate the truth or falsehood of these propositions, it can and should attempt to elucidate their meaning; it should devote itself exclusively to the task of analysis. Exactly what is analysed, whether words or concepts, sentences or propositions or facts, how the analysis proceeds, what purpose it serves, and how its results are to be assessed are all matters of dispute. No very general agreement has been reached on any of them. There is just the feeling that philosophy must after all be good for something, and that the avenue of analysis, whatever that may be, is the only one left open to it.

But now let us look a little more closely at the argument which leads to this result. At first sight it is very persuasive. How could a philosophical discussion contrive to show that, in these perfectly normal circumstances, I am mistaken in believing in the existence of the physical objects which I can see around me? Of course I may fail to identify all of them correctly; it is conceivable even that I am the victim of some more serious illusion. But then there are ways of finding out whether this is so; and if they show that nothing is amiss, the question is settled. It would be merely neurotic to embark on an endless series of further tests, when one had no reason at all to expect that they would yield any different result. Theoretically, we may have to admit the possibility of our being deceived by our senses in any given instance, but to suppose that they invariably deceived us would be nonsensical. We can only attach meaning to the statement that our perceptions are sometimes delusive because we contrast them with the normal case in which they are veridical.

So far, so good. But now let us suppose that someone has been convinced by Berkeley that the things which he perceives are not material objects, as we understand the term, but only collections of ideas in his own mind. How would this argument serve to disabuse him? The answer is that it would not serve at all. There will never be an occasion on which we can show him that because of his fidelity to Berkeley his judgements of perception run counter to the evidence. In the relevant circumstances, he will be as ready as we are to admit the truth of such propositions as that this is a piece of paper or that the clock has just struck four. Of course he interprets them differently; he does not think that they commit him to holding that these objects exist when he is not perceiving them, except perhaps as permanent possibilities of sensation, or as ideas in the mind of another person, or in the mind of God; but this does not mean that we can expect his judgement to dissent from ours in any concrete situation. We may say that he misunderstands these propositions, but if this is his mistake, it is not one that has any practical consequences.

But is it even obvious that he does misunderstand them? It might indeed be argued that this example exhibits not the weakness but the strength of Moore's position, on the ground that what is in dispute between the follower of Berkeley and ourselves is not the truth of any common sense propositions, but merely their analysis. His contention is that what I really mean when I say that this is a piece of paper is that I am having an idea, that is, a sense impression of a certain sort, which is linked in certain ways with other ideas: and the way to refute him would be to show that this is not what one ordinarily means when one makes a statement of this kind. He misunderstands these propositions, not in the sense that he does not know when to accept or reject them, but rather in the sense that he gives a false account of what they mean.

There is a good deal of support for this interpretation in Berkeley's own writings, but surely it does him an injustice. For if he really were contending that what is ordinarily meant by a physical object is a collection of ideas, it would be all too obvious that he was wrong. When the ordinary man speaks of a chair or a clock or a piece of paper, he plainly does so with the implication that these things exist unperceived. Perhaps he ought not to, but that is another question. There is no doubt that he does. This is the common sense view and Berkeley is not analysing but attacking it. He is not elucidating the way in which we systematize our experiences: he is putting up a rival system.

But how is this possible? How can the common sense view of the world be open to attack? In trying to answer this, we shall again find it helpful to draw upon Carnap's distinction between what he calls internal and external questions.[1] The salient feature of Moore's technique is that it treats metaphysical questions internally, as though they arose within the framework of common sense. It is in this way that he refutes the metaphysician who makes the outrageous claim that time is unreal, by giving impeccable examples of events which occur in time. It is in this way that he proved the existence of external objects, simply by holding up his own two hands.[2] On these terms, his victory is complete; there is nothing more to be said. Even so the metaphysician feels that his position, so far from being overthrown, has not even been considered: and fundamentally he is right; the victory has been won on the wrong terrain. To say this is not to detract from Moore's achievement. He did more than anyone to dispel the

[1] See above, pp. 49–51.

[2] See 'Proof of an External World', British Academy lecture 1939. Reprinted in G. E. Moore, *Philosophical Papers* (1959).

cobwebs which prevented all of us, and not least the metaphysicians themselves, from seeing what they were about. Even so he misinterpreted them: for if anything is now clear, it is that metaphysical questions are external.

But this only gets us a little further forward. We still have to explain, much more precisely, what external questions are and also why anyone should wish to raise them. Why, to continue with our example, was Berkeley dissatisfied with the conception of the physical world which, whether he admitted it or not, is in fact the outlook of common sense? Why did he want to disallow the criteria in terms of which we are able to say with confidence and truth that things exist unperceived? Was it simply a matter of caprice? Did he have a psychological need to look at the world, or to speak about the world, in a different way? Was he trying to elaborate a conceptual system which would prove more useful to us than the system of common sense?

None of these is quite the correct answer. I do not deny that a philosopher may have psychological reasons, most probably unknown to himself, for mounting an attack against certain concepts, or that it would be of interest to discover what these reasons were. But this still would not explain to us what the philosopher was doing. For this we need to look at his actual procedure, to study the way in which he comes by his conclusions. And here the clue to the problem is that he reaches them by argument. The typical metaphysician does not simply say: I do not like the idea of matter, or motion, or time, or numbers, or individuals, or universals, or propositions, or negative facts, or whatever else may be in question; let us see if we cannot get along without it. He gives reasons for holding that these things do not exist.

These reasons mainly take two different forms. One common line of argument is that the category in question is not ultimate; the things which fall under it have been mistakenly hypostatized; what really exists is something else. This leads to such assertions as that there are no material things but only sense-data, no numbers but only numerals, no universals but only sets of similar particulars, or alternatively no particulars but only sets of compresent universals, no propositions but only sentences, no mental events but only dispositions to behave in certain ways, and so forth. If the philosopher who takes this line is of an analytical rather than a metaphysical turn of mind, he will prefer to say, for example, that material things are logical constructions out of sense-data, or that numbers are reducible to numerals, rather than that material things or numbers do not exist, but this is only a difference of formulation. The motive for trying to get rid of these sets of entities may be that they do not fit in with a preconceived idea of what the world is really like: especially among analytical philosophers the tendency is to eliminate the abstract in favour of the concrete, but it may also go the other way. Or it may be just that certain types of entity, like numbers or universals, strike one as mysterious, and one wishes to explain them in terms of other sorts of entities which one finds less problematic. Epistemological considerations also play their part. If it is believed that one type of entity is accessible only through another, as, for example, it has been held that we can have no acquaintance with material things except through apprehending sense-data, or no acquaintance with propositions except through understanding sentences, then there may be an inclination to try to reduce the more remote entities to those which give us access to them. The vindication of these claims is that the entities whose removal is desired should be successfully explained away. But the trouble here is that we are not always given clear enough criteria for deciding when a successful explanation of this sort has been achieved.

The second line of argument is that the category, or concept, which is put in question, is somehow defective. A standard of intelligibility is set up which it is then argued that it fails to satisfy. This is the nerve of Parrmenides' attack on the concept of plurality, or that of the neo-Hegelians on the categories of space and time, or Ryle's on the concept of mind. Very often this line of argument is blended with the other. Thus Berkeley's reason for denying the existence of matter is principally that it is not verifiable. He takes over from Locke the requirement that for a concept to be intelligible it must refer to what could be experienced, and he argues that the physicist's conception of matter does not satisfy it. What we do experience, in his view, are what he calls sensible ideas, which correspond closely enough to what contemporary philosophers call sense-data; and he thinks it plainly contradictory to say of them that they exist when not perceived. At the same time, he maintains that any legitimate purpose which the conception of matter was designed to serve can be adequately fulfilled by talking only of immaterial percipients and their ideas. So he combines the view that the conception of matter is radically defective with the view that a different set of concepts, which are free from its defects, can be shown to be capable of replacing it. This is rather perplexing to his expositors, who are left in doubt whether to say that he rejected the concept of matter or merely offered an analysis of it.

As we shall see in a moment, this distinction is somewhat arbitrary, but the points on which it turns are important.

In any case, whatever one may choose to say of Berkeley, the general aim of this second line of argument is to disqualify the concepts against which it is directed. But this brings us back to the question with which we started. How can there be any hope of disqualifying a concept of which it is obvious that we make successful use? If it is a plain matter of fact that a concept has empirical application, then how can one think that it is radically defective, that it is meaningless or contradictory? Surely the metaphysician can proceed only by shutting his eyes to what he knows to be true.

This is again Moore's argument, and if the metaphysician's questions were internal, in Carnap's sense, it would be decisive. But once it is seen that these questions are external, it loses a good deal of its force. For now we have to distinguish between the practical operation of a concept and the theory which it carries with it. This distinction is not sharp, since it is arguable that the description of any phenomena incorporates some element of theory, but it can be made sharp enough for our present purpose. Thus there is a sense in which the concept of possession by evil spirits had empirical application. There were criteria for deciding when a person was so possessed; the malady had characteristic symptoms which differentiated it from any other: there was no doubt that these symptoms did occur. At a time when the belief in good and evil spirits was part of popular culture, to deny the possibility of demonic possession might have seemed to be flying in the face of common sense. Nevertheless we now find it perfectly easy to dissociate this concept from the phenomena to which it was taken to apply. We can dismiss the very notion of evil spirits as nonsensical, and still do justice to the facts which sustained it. We simply account for them in a very different sort of way.

But surely the notion of matter is not on a level with that of evil spirits. There is, indeed, an important difference in that it is very much more difficult in this case to distinguish between fact and theory. It is not at all clear that we can give an adequate description of the facts without bringing in the notion of matter. The notion of a sensible idea which Berkeley takes as primitive is itself problematic; and his notion of the immaterial subjects who are presented with these ideas may well be contradictory. Nevertheless it has not been shown to be impossible to construct a 'language of appearance' in which the empirical data would be described in such a way as not to presuppose the existence, or indeed the non-existence, of either minds or matter. This was indeed the aim of William James and, after him, of Bertrand Russell in developing their theories of Neutral Monism, and though they did not fully succeed in carrying it through, I see no reason in principle why it should not be feasible. In that case, the introduction of the concept of persistent physical objects, the existence of which is independent of their being perceived, may be represented as one means among others of systematizing our experiences. If, *pace* Berkeley, it still appears to us as the only genuine possibility, this is because we cannot conceive of any other procedure which would come anywhere near to matching it in efficiency.

If one holds an operational theory about the significance of concepts, one will attach no importance to the difference between rival conceptual systems, so long as they can equally be made to square with the facts; indeed one will be inclined to say that there really is no difference between them. From this point of view, even such a concept as that of possession by evil spirits should not be regarded as illegitimate if there are genuine phenomena to which it is used to apply. The only mistake that can be attributed to those who employed it is that of supposing that they were doing something more than merely describing the phenomena: they did not realize that all that they really meant by saying that people were possessed by evil spirits was just that they exhibited such and such symptoms. In the same way Berkeley was, from this point of view, mistaken in thinking that he was refuting the advocates of matter. For since they allowed that the statements which they made about physical objects were verified only by the existence of the observable state of affairs, which for Berkeley consisted in the perception of sensible ideas, this is all that they could really have been referring to. If Berkeley was right in his contentions, the only mistake which he could attribute to his adversaries was that of failing to see that when they talked about matter they really were talking about sensible ideas.

It is, however, debatable whether we ought to equate the meaning of concepts, in quite this straightforward fashion, with the states of affairs to which they are understood to apply. Perhaps it is not of very great importance what meaning we decide to attach to the rather vague word 'meaning', but it would be a mistake to insist on cutting concepts off entirely from their theoretical background. We are in something of a dilemma here because we want to reject a way of looking at the world which seems to us absurd or even unintelligible, but at the same time we do not want to say that everything which is asserted by those who take this point of view is false. Thus if the members of a primitive tribe attribute every natural occurrence to the moods of Mumbo Jumbo, we may have no doubt that they are utterly deluded: nevertheless we do not want to deny their ability to detect that it is raining, even though they see the rain as the expression of Mumbo Jumbo's grief. Accordingly, we distinguish the fact which they apprehend as well as we do from the ridiculous explanation which they give of it; and then if we are very tough minded we may go on to say that all that they really mean by their talk of Mumbo Jumbo's grief, though of course they do not know it, is just that it is raining. But any anthropologist will regard this, rightly, as a serious misrepresentation. We are imposing on them a distinction which it could never occur to them to make.

As we have already seen in the case of Berkeley, the way we react to this dilemma will very largely determine the view which we take of philosophical analysis. A very clear illustration of this is to be found in Hume's theory of causation. Hume demonstrated incontrovertibly that the relation of necessity which is supposed to obtain between cause and effect cannot be a logical relation, and he also saw that the idea that distinct events were somehow glued together by a relation of non-logical necessity was an empty fiction: it did not correspond to anything that one could conceivably observe. Accordingly, he placed the source of the supposed necessity in our mental habits of association, and for all practical purposes equated causality with regular sequence. Though his theory is open to objection on some points of detail, I have no doubt that on the central issues it is entirely right. But if we accept the theory, at least in its essentials, do we say that Hume has shown us what we really meant by causality, or do we say that he has demonstrated that our concept of causality was defective and shown us the way to replace it with something better? The reason against saying that the concept on which Hume set to work turned out to be defective is that we do not want to imply that it had no application; we certainly do not want to say that the world had to wait for Hume's theory before anyone was capable of making a true causal statement. And if we think along these lines, we shall be inclined to say that what Hume did was to make clear to us what we really meant all along; we shall look upon his achievement as a successful piece of philosophical analysis. On the other hand, there is a very good sense in which the concept which emerges from Hume's analysis is not the same as the popular notion which he set out to examine. It may do the same work, but it does not keep the same theoretical company. The popular notion was found to be infected with incoherent ideas of power and agency; and the fact that disinfecting it makes little or no practical difference does not, I think, entitle us to say that it makes no difference at all. In the same way, I suppose it could be maintained that the account which Einstein gave of simultaneity in his Theory of Relativity only revealed to us what we had really meant by the term all along: but it would in this case seem much more accurate to say that he replaced a defective concept with a better one. Yet once more we certainly do not want to hold that until Einstein produced his theory, no one ever judged truly that one event was simultaneous with another.

It appears from these examples that it is a fairly arbitrary question whether we are to regard the results of philosophical analyses as correcting our misapprehensions about the meaning of concepts, which are taken to be in good order because we employ them successfully, or as pointing out defects in the concepts themselves and thereby leading us to modify them. The salient point is that it is shown to be possible for a concept to be successfully applied even though it is embedded in a theory which does not withstand critical scrutiny. It follows that it is not automatically absurd for a metaphysician to condemn a concept which is in common use; he may indeed just be muddled, he may simply be talking nonsense, but he may be making a valid criticism of its theoretical background.

But while this sort of apology for metaphysics may cover philosophers like Berkeley and Hume whom we can regard as offering us an alternative way of representing the facts, which they believe, rightly or wrongly, to be superior to the conceptual machinery of common sense, it is harder to see how it applies to the more thoroughgoing metaphysicians who simply dismiss the concepts of space and time or motion or matter as self-contradictory and then make a bee line for the Absolute. In their case the impression given is not that they are offering us an alternative way of representing the facts but rather that they are altogether making light of them.

Here again, however, it will repay us to turn aside from the strange conclusions which these metaphysicians reach, and concentrate instead upon the arguments by which they reach them. How, for example, does Zeno prove that Achilles can never catch the tortoise? By pointing out that when Achilles reaches the point from which the tortoise started, the tortoise will have advanced some distance, however small, and that by the time Achilles has covered that distance the tortoise will have gone a little further and so *ad infinitum*. How does McTaggart prove that time is unreal? By pointing out that the characteristics of being past, present and future which every event is supposed to possess are mutually incompatible, so that if we are to avoid a contradiction we must assume that events possess them at different moments. So let us say that every event is past at a present or future moment, present at a present moment and future at a present or past moment. But then the same difficulty arises with respect to the moments. So either we relapse into contradiction or we are launched upon an infinite regress.

Now both these pieces of reasoning, given their premisses, are perfectly sound. If in order to traverse any given distance one had to occupy each member in turn of the infinite series of its parts, Achilles could not catch the tortoise, indeed he could not move at all, since he could never get started. If being past, present and future were non-relational characteristics of events or moments, their attributions to either would be logically vicious. Even so, we are disposed to say, all that this proves is that these conceptions of the nature of time and motion are mistaken, not that time and motion are unreal. But the problem for our metaphysicians was that they did not see how these consequences were to be avoided; they did not see what other account of time or motion could be given. And in this they were not so greatly to blame. It was only in the nineteenth century that mathematicians developed an adequate theory of continuity and even to this day there is disagreement about the way in which Zeno's arguments can most effectively be answered. Neither is there anything approaching unanimity among philosophers about the correct analysis of the passage of time. In my own view, the relation of temporal priority has to be taken as fundamental, and past, present and future defined in terms of it by reference to the temporal position of the speaker, this position itself being characterized by its temporal relation to other arbitrarily chosen events. But to a certain extent this vindicates McTaggart: for it leads to a 'static' spatial picture of the Universe as a four-dimensional continuum.

If we follow this approach, I think that we can even make sense of the metaphysical doctrine that things which are ultimately unreal are nevertheless real as appearances. We have seen that when this sort of talk is taken literally it can easily be made to seem ridiculous; the metaphysician is forced into the impossible position of maintaining both that some concept is self-contradictory and that it has application. But the explanation is, I suggest, that he is reacting in the same way to our ordinary system of beliefs as I supposed in my example that the anthropologist would react to the talk of the believers in Mumbo Jumbo. He would regard the idea of Mumbo Jumbo's grieving as nonsensical, but recognize that in their system it did correspond to a fact, namely the fact that he would describe by saying that it was raining. Similarly a metaphysician, like Bradley, wants to hold that our talk of space and time and matter is confused to the point of being implicitly self-contradictory and yet that it is an attempt to deal with genuine phenomena. Of course he cannot consistently allow that the phenomena, even just *qua* phenomena, are spatio-temporally ordered, any more than the anthropologist could consistently allow that Mumbo Jumbo was apparently crying; what they can both say is that these are misguided attempts to describe genuine facts. But here the parallel ends, to the grave disadvantage of the metaphysician. For whereas the anthropologist has an alternative way of describing the facts, which is not exposed to the same objections, a metaphysician like Bradley has not. He may assume that if *per impossibile* he were in the position of the Absolute he would have an entirely lucid view of everything that there is, but on his own showing he is not in this position, and never could be; and neither could we. So, having to his own satisfaction undermined our ordinary way of looking at the world, he not only leaves us with nothing to put in its place but also leaves himself with no firm standpoint from which to launch his attack. If our world collapses, he collapses with it.

In citing Bradley, I have taken an extreme case. There are metaphysicians, like Leibniz, who do offer us alternative conceptual frameworks. But the difficulty here is that it is not always clear how our observations are to be fitted into them. It may be that Leibniz's aim was fundamentally not so very different from that of Berkeley, in spite of the divergences in their outlook, but whereas I think I understand pretty well how Berkeley wanted us to conceive the world and why he believed that his system did greater justice to the phenomena, I cannot envisage what it would be like to conceive of the things around me as colonies of monads. Perhaps the analogy which Leibniz himself would have preferred is with a scientific theory of fundamental particles. But then, if the analogy is to be more than superficial, it has to be shown that this way of conceiving things is scientifically fruitful.

I think this would be hard to accomplish, but I do not want to say *a priori* that it is impossible.

It has recently become the fashion to claim in defence of metaphysics that even though it does not yield us any knowledge, in the sense of establishing true propositions, it can afford us valuable insights. It is, however, not very easy to see what these insights can be, or why they are valuable, if they are not expressible as truths. Perhaps what is meant is that it is illuminating to be made to look at the world in a radically different fashion from that to which we are accustomed, and with this I agree, provided that the alternative way of looking at the world can be shown to be viable. But this is a large proviso and I do not know of any metaphysical system in which it is adequately met. Even so, it does not follow that the labour of those who have constructed these systems has entirely gone for nothing. As I see it, the main service which they perform for us is to induce us to look critically at the theoretical background of the operations of science and of common sense. Puzzles are raised about the relation of subject and predicate, or the functioning of general terms, or the status of abstract entities, or the meaning of necessity, or the infinite divisibility of spatial and temporal extension, or the dualism of mind and matter, or about our justification for attributing experiences to other persons or believing in the existence of external objects. Except in the rare case where the problem has a scientific bearing, the solution of these puzzles will not increase our power to control our environment, or to predict the future course of events, but there is a sense in which it can add to our understanding of the world, by opening our eyes to the theoretical implications of the ways in which we describe it. I have no sovereign recipe for solving, or dissolving, philosophical puzzles, but in some cases at least I think that the solution may take the 'metaphysical' form of showing that some class of entities is eliminable, or that the character of some concept, or set of concepts, has been wrongly understood, or that some concept could with advantage be more sharply defined or in some way modified.

The fact that external questions can be raised allows us even to tolerate such metaphysical assertions as that it is we who bring time into the world. The implication is that reality is conditioned by our method of describing it and that it is open to us to decide what method to employ, so that in a certain sense we do not just discover but determine what the world is like. But here again if we are to speak of alternative methods of description, we have to make sure that they are viable, and it is hard to see how there could be any intelligible description of the world which did not include the category of time. Moreover it must not be forgotten that when we speak of ourselves as doing this or that we are already operating within a conceptual system. For what are *we*, if not physical bodies which occupy a position in space and time? But so long as we are operating within a conceptual system, we are committed to its criteria of reality; and then to say that we bring time into the world is to say that nothing happened before the appearance on earth of human beings, which is simply false, just as it is simply false, if one is operating within a system which makes provision for physical objects, to say that they do not exist when they are not perceived.

What the metaphysician would like to do is take up a position outside any conceptual system: but that is not possible. The most that he can hope to achieve is some modification of the prevailing climate; to find a way, for example, of eliminating singular terms or perhaps even to contrive to represent himself and the things around him as logical constructions out of their appearances. But if such a venture is even to be intelligible, let alone of any theoretical interest, it must have at least a rough correspondence to the way in which things are ordinarily conceived. Thus if a philosopher is to succeed not merely in involving us in logical or semantic or epistemological puzzles but in altering or sharpening our vision of the world, he cannot leave common sense too far behind him.

This does not mean, however, that he must tie himself strictly to its apron strings. The insistence that ordinary language is perfectly in order has been a very useful corrective to the wilder flights of metaphysical speculation but, if taken too literally, it can lead to our letting things go by which might profitably be questioned and mobilizing in defence of what does not need defending. It is indeed better to tabulate the milestones along the highway of ordinary usage than to rhapsodize about Nothingness or the Essence of Man; but it would be a mistake to forgo the more imaginative kinds of conceptual exploration, merely because of the greater risk of getting lost. In philosophy, nothing should be absolutely sacrosanct: not even common sense.

6

PHILOSOPHY AND SCIENCE

I

IN the sense in which astronomy or botany are sciences, philosophy is not a science. Philosophers have theories, but their theories do not enable them to make predictions; they cannot be empirically confirmed or refuted in the way that scientific theories can. But, it will be objected, this is not true of all the sciences. Palaeontologists do not make predictions: in pure mathematics there is no appeal to experience. But even if they are not predictive the propositions which figure in the historical sciences are at any rate empirically testable: and even if the propositions of pure mathematics are not confutable by observation, they are subject to recognized methods of proof. There are standard procedures for deciding whether they are true or false. But where in philosophy are such procedures to be found? If anywhere, in formal logic which has come very close to mathematics. Nowadays, indeed, it is hardly possible to draw a line between them. But by the very process of becoming a science, formal logic detaches itself from philosophy. Philosophers do indeed make use of formal logic. They employ deductive arguments; sometimes they are able to take advantage of the economy and precision of logical symbolism. But the premisses on which they reason, the propositions which the use of logical symbolism helps them to state more clearly, are not themselves drawn from formal logic. The truths which can be established by formal logic alone are not philosophical.

Formal logic is not the first science to grow up under the wing of philosophy and then emancipate itself. This had happened to physics by the seventeenth century, to biology by the nineteenth; more recently psychology has made its bid for independence. This is a particularly interesting case because the hold of philosophy upon psychology has been so strongly maintained. Thus it was the intention of Locke and his successors to achieve for the study of the mind what Newton had achieved for the study of inanimate nature. The hope, which was entertained by Hume, that even moral philosophy could be put upon a scientific basis, was kept alive by the Utilitarians and more recently by the Pragmatists. There has never yet been a time at which philosophers have not discoursed in their fashion about the activities of the mind; about perceiving, and thinking, and feeling, and willing, and the variety of concepts that are associated with them. The very notion of the mind itself is still a favourite subject for philosophical inquiry.

Nevertheless philosophy is not the science of the mind. The philosopher does not try, as the psychologist does, to account for the ways in which people feel and think. He does not advance theories about human behaviour which can be tested by experiment. He may examine mental concepts, but he makes no special use of them. They are not the tools of his profession. If so much attention is paid by philosophers to what is sometimes called the philosophy of mind, the reason is partly that mental concepts are not highly specialized. Psychology is not an advanced science. It has begun to develop a technical vocabulary, but it still has to rely to a great extent on concepts which are in common currency. With these the philosopher feels entitled and equipped to deal. When a science develops a proprietary language, the present tendency is for philosophers to leave it alone.

This is understandable, but hardly justified except on grounds of practical necessity. Whatever there may be about the use of a term that gives rise to philosophical problems, it can occur in any branch of language. If it is a philosophical task to exhibit the structure of a theory, to distinguish its logical from its empirical features, to define or explicate the concepts which it employs, to subject these concepts to critical scrutiny, there is as great a need for this in the physical sciences as in any other field of study. The problem of interpreting the quantum theory provides an obvious example. But the difficulty here is that we cannot altogether separate the business of interpreting a theory from that of working with it. The logical distinction is clear enough; a statement in which the terms of a theory are mentioned is of a different logical order from one in which they are used. In principle, therefore, the two functions might be separated, as that of an art critic is separated from that of a painter; the painter may not be a good critic even of his own work: the critic need not himself be able to paint. In this instance too the painter may not be a good critic; there are working scientists whose philosophizing about their own subject is muddled or naïve; but it does seem that in practice the critic must be something of a painter. Without experience in the handling of scientific theories, one can hardly expect to have the authority to interpret them. If anything is to be achieved in the philosophy of physics, it must come from the inside.

The upshot of this is that if philosophy were to be limited to the philosophy of science, it would not stand out as an independent discipline. Its work of criticism and elucidation could best be carried out within the sciences themselves. For this is the work of specialists. There is no room here for the general practitioner.

But this is to assume that the philosopher's work is purely analytical. Can he not fulfil a more constructive rôle? There is an old tradition that philosophy searches for first principles. Might it not still comprise a body of doctrine which would supply a common foundation for the special sciences; some set of propositions which would describe the workings of nature in terms of a higher generality?

Attempts have frequently been made to do this, but the fatal objection to them all is that the propositions which result are empty of factual content. A good example is the suggestion that the universe is teleological. Very often this is combined with a belief in the existence of a deity whose purposes it is supposed to serve. Now if the end which the universe was set to attain, on this view, were actually specified, the suggestion would have some significance. We could hope to establish, with some measure of probability, whether the course of events was tending towards this end or not; and if the evidence showed that it was not, we should regard the hypothesis as discredited. But in fact no such specific end is ever proposed. We are to regard the universe as teleological, irrespectively of what it contains and no matter what actually happens. On the theistic version of this view, any conceivable course of events would be in accordance with divine providence. But this means that the hypothesis has no explanatory power at all. For the force of any generalization depends upon the amount that it excludes. The greater the burden of conformity that it lays upon events, the more exposed it is to the risk of refutation. But a hypothesis with which everything is consistent runs no risk. It is not exposed to refutation because it does not exclude anything. It is, therefore, entirely empty. To be told that everything moves towards some unspecified end is to be told nothing, because it does not lead us to expect any one thing to happen rather than any other. Whatever were to occur the explanation would be the same, and this is its condemnation. Since it is not an explanation of anything in particular, it is not an explanation of anything at all.

A less obvious example of this sort is the so-called law of universal causation, the principle that every event must have a cause. Again, this can be given a factual content. It might, for example, be construed as implying the deterministic view of classical physics; the assumption that one could in principle know the exact position and velocity at a given instant of every material particle, and that this would enable one to calculate precisely the state of the system at any other instant. In this specific form the principle is exposed to refutation; and it is in fact commonly held to have been refuted by the observations which have led to the development of the quantum theory. What is not open to refutation, on the other hand, is the vague assertion that every event is subject to some causal law or other. If the laws in question are specified, their validity can be tested. But if no indication is given even of what is to count as a causal law, if we do not know what events are supposed to be related to one another and in what manner, we can make no use of the principle. Once more, there is nothing that it excludes.[1] One might indeed think that it at least excluded the possibility of events occurring completely at random, but this will not be so unless the prohibited degree of randomness is specified. Otherwise it will always be open to a defender of the principle to argue that what we take to be random events are governed by some undetected law. But this very act of making the principle secure divests it of content. It lays no charge upon the facts, if, whenever they seem to defy it, it is always permitted an avenue of escape.

The same objection, in my view, holds against the theory that the laws of dialectics are the governing principles of nature. To talk of one natural process as negating another, or of their being then resolved into a higher synthesis, or of changes in quantity producing changes in quality, is of no consequence at all unless the details are specified. We have to know what negation means in terms of physical processes, what counts as a synthesis, how differences of level are to be distinguished, what things are supposed to change and in what manner. Thus, if the word 'contradiction' is to be taken in its logical sense it is impossible that there should be contradictions in nature. Only propositions can be contradictory; and since all true propositions must be logically compatible, not only can the processes of nature not themselves be in contradiction, but the propositions which correctly describe

[1] In the last section of my essay 'Chance' (see below, pp. 113–14), I indicate a way in which the claim that every event is subject to causal laws may be given some empirical content.

them cannot be so either. But if such words as 'contradiction' or 'negation' are not to be taken in their logical senses, how are we to understand them in this context? Apparently as expressing something which would be better expressed by some such word as 'conflict'. The suggestion is that changes in nature are always the results, or manifestations, of conflict, a conflict in which the parties survive at the cost of being transformed. But then the character of this conflict, and the nature of the parties to it, require to be specified. If, as would often seem to be the case, the term is understood so liberally that every form of interaction is represented as a species of conflict, and every outcome of an interplay of forces is treated as their synthesis, then again it is not clear what the theory excludes. We can do nothing with it because it makes no specific demands upon the facts. No matter what were to happen it would still be satisfied.

The same lack of precision attends the idea of the dependence of change of quality upon change of quantity. The stock example is the condensation or evaporation of water as a result of varying its temperature. A continuous increase in temperature produces a discontinuous change, 'a sudden jump', from ice to water in its normal state and from water in its normal state to steam. But the force of this example largely depends on the fact that we happen to use a different word for water when it is solidified or vaporized, that we choose at these points to say that it changes into something else. This makes it easier to overlook the fact that the processes of condensation and evaporation are also measurable, and that the change in temperature could itself be represented as a change of quality, if we cared to introduce the necessary predicates. Neither is it clear how this example should be generalized. Perhaps the important idea which lies behind it is that all science can in the end be reduced to physics; so that all change can be represented as finally depending upon the numerically measurable properties, the mass, or energy, or velocity of homogeneous particles. But it does not appear that the fundamental laws of physics are dialectical in any interesting sense of this word; and it remains an open, scientific question whether this reduction can be achieved.

This is not to say that dialectical principles cannot be given a content which will make it possible to apply them in particular fields. Thus, whether or not it holds without exception, the theory which accounts for social change in terms of the conflicting economic interests of different classes is certainly significant: for here the vague idea of natural opposition is given a specific meaning. It is only when these principles are interpreted so loosely as to cover everything that they fulfil no function. Their unlimited tolerance makes them vacuous.

What emerges, I think, from these examples is that the conception of philosophy which they illustrate leads simply to its abdication in the face of science. The philosopher is set the impossible task of devising a set of principles which are to be both more general in their scope than any scientific theory, and at the same time endowed with explanatory power. But this is a contradiction: the two aims are incompatible. Certainly there could be explanatory theories which were more general in their scope than any scientific theory that we now accept: the success of an attempt to unify the theory of relativity with the quantum theory would furnish an example. But such a theory would still be scientific; it would be exposed to empirical refutation; it would be produced as the answer to a scientific problem. And this must be true at every stage of generality. If it is the mark of a philosophical theory that it is not empirically testable, in the way that scientific theories must be, it cannot do the work that a scientific theory does.

II

Nevertheless, it is true that one way in which philosophy differs from any of the natural sciences is in the greater generality of the questions which it raises. It is not, however, a matter of its attempting to give a more general description of the world, but rather of its being concerned with certain very general problems, problems which are not limited to any special branch of scientific inquiry. A good example is the problem of induction, which bears upon every form of factual argument. The grounds which sustain empirical theories are diverse; the way in which a historian handles his evidence is different from the ways in which a psycho-analyst or a chemist handle theirs. But what is common to all their reasoning is its going beyond its premisses. The conclusions which are drawn are not formally deducible from the data which support them. The problem of induction stems from the question how any argument of this sort is justified.

It is to be noted that this is not a problem that worries scientists themselves. A physicist may be doubtful about accepting the results of some experiment which goes against a well established theory: a psychologist may suspect that the report which a subject gives of his experiences is not to be taken at its face value: a historian may judge that one of his written sources is unreliable. But in all such cases bad or doubtful evidence is being contrasted with good. There are standards of evidence in all these fields, and if they appear to be satisfied, then the conclusion which they favour is accepted, at least provisionally. It never would occur to a physicist to distrust a theory, not on the ground that there was likely to be some error in the experiments which backed it, or that it conflicted with other theories for which there was stronger evidence, but merely on the ground that all experimental reasoning was logically suspect. For the problem of induction is not concerned with the question whether this or that particular piece of evidence is up to standard. By demanding a justification for any form of non-demonstrative argument, it puts the accepted standards themselves in question.

No doubt it is the sceptical aspect of this problem that prevents scientists from being interested in it. If they were being offered some better criteria of proof, some surer way of discriminating between good and bad theories, their attitude might be different. But if the best that they can hope to achieve in this way is to be regarded with the same suspicion, it is natural that they should regard the problem as academic. The most that they can obtain from its solution will be an official licence to do what they are doing already. But this does not mean that the problem has no interest. Philosophical questions are very often academic, in the sense that the answer to them makes no difference to our practical beliefs. But even if we are not disposed to abandon or modify these beliefs on philosophical grounds, we may be perplexed about their status; and once this perplexity is felt, it cannot easily be put aside. It becomes a matter of intellectual concern that the difficulty should be resolved.

I shall not attempt here to give a detailed analysis of the problem of induction. It is obvious that we can have no logical guarantee that a generalization which has held good in all the instances that we have been able to examine will also be found to cover any remaining instance. There must always be the possibility that nature will surprise us. The most we might hope for would be to prove that some hypothesis which we had come to accept on the basis of our past experience was at least more probable than its rivals; that in some cases we can have good reason to believe in the constancy of a specific set of relations between events. But even this proof eludes us. For the *a priori* calculus of probability is a branch of pure mathematics: it shows what is logically implied by a given distribution of chances, but by itself it can tell us nothing at all about the way in which the chances actually stand. We have to derive the actual probabilities from past experience. But then we are caught in a circle. For our right to base our estimates on past experience is just what is in question. Thus probability, in any sense in which it could be useful to us in this matter, presupposes induction, and therefore cannot serve as its ground. Because of this it is now fairly generally agreed that there can be no proof of the trustworthiness of any form of factual argument, if the demand for proof requires that induction be justified in terms of something other than itself. The fact is simply that we trust our empirical hypotheses so long as we find that they work. But this does not make a breach in the circle. For we are still assuming that methods which have been found to work in the past will go on working in the future.

It would seem then that there is no further progress to be made in this direction. But the problem does not end there. As often happens in philosophy, what starts as a problem of justification turns into a problem of analysis. What is it exactly that we are trying to justify? What do we mean by a law of nature? How does a law of nature differ from what is called an accidental generalization or a generalization of fact? If the difference is that the scope of the statement of law extends over possible as well as actual cases, how is the reference to possible cases to be interpreted? In other words, what is the analysis of unfulfilled conditionals? We regard a general hypothesis as having been confirmed when we find that it is fulfilled in particular instances; but it can be shown that these instances will also fulfil any number of other hypotheses which are incompatible with the first. Why then do we pick just the ones that we do? When confronted with questions of this kind, it is no use making some vague appeal to an alleged uniformity of nature. For however firm may be our belief in scientific order, none of us expects the future to be a carbon copy of the past. Our science commits us, not to a belief in regularity in general, but to a belief in certain specific regularities. They are in accord with our past experience but they are not dictated by it. There may be no call for us to justify our manner of selecting them. But what are the principles on which it operates?

This brings us to a larger question. How far can we sustain the distinction between theory and fact? The prevalent view is that we make observations on the basis of which we construct hypotheses; and then we test these hypotheses by means of further observations. If these further observations accord with the hypotheses, our trust in the hypotheses is confirmed. If they do not accord with them, we remodel the hypotheses so as to bring them into line with the new evidence. And so the process continues. When a theory has to be remodelled there are various ways in which this can be done. In selecting new hypotheses, in deciding which of the old ones to discard and which to retain, we have considerable freedom of choice. But this, it is held, does not apply to the observations. They do not allow us any such latitude. They simply make us acquainted with objective facts.

But do not the observations have to be interpreted? Let us take a very simple example. A doctor diagnoses a disease in such a way that if his diagnosis is correct the patient's temperature will rise. He takes the patient's temperature with a thermometer and his diagnosis is confirmed. Now it is a matter of theory that the level of the column of mercury in the thermometer corresponds to a certain degree of heat in the body with which it has been put in contact; but the reading of the thermometer, the coincidence of the top of the column with a certain figure on the scale, may be thought to be a straightforward matter of fact. But consider how much theory even this simple fact involves. The doctor's identification of what he sees as a physical object, let alone as a thermometer, implies that it occupies a position in three-dimensional space, that it can change its position without losing its identity, that it persists through time, that it is accessible to other observers, that it can exist when no one is observing it. To go further and say that this object is a thermometer, to identify the silver streak behind the glass as a column of mercury, is to bring in a great deal of physical theory besides. A physical object may be identified on the basis of its appearance; but in characterizing it as an object of such and such a kind, one is also putting forward an hypothesis about its behaviour.

For this reason some philosophers have come to the conclusion that the only purely factual statements are those that record the subject's private experiences. That the silvery streak really is a column of mercury is quite a far-reaching hypothesis for the doctor to make; it runs the risk of being confuted by further observation. But surely he runs no such risk if he merely says that it looks to him as if it were a column of mercury, or even more modestly that there now is a silvery streak at such and such a point in his visual field. For here he makes no claim about physical reality; his statement could still be true if he were dreaming, or undergoing an illusion. And this applies to all statements which are limited to describing the contents of experiences without attempting to fit them into any more general pattern, and without making any assumptions about the status of what they reveal. These statements are reached by stripping ordinary perceptual judgements of every element of physical theory; they are basic in the sense that it is by reference to them that all empirical hypotheses are tested.

But can this be so? It is certainly true that the test of any scientific theory consists in the end in someone's having some experience; in this sense, therefore, the reasons which any given person has for accepting the theory are to be found in the statements in which such experiences are recorded. But this does not mean that these statements express the facts on which the theory is based. For the experiences which they record are private and fleeting: this is the price that these statements pay for their security. But the events for which a physical theory is supposed to account are public. It may be held that they are analysable in terms of the contents of experiences, though this is a thesis to which there are known to be very serious objections; but even so these cannot be the experiences of any given person: for while it is required of the theory that it should be empirically testable, it is not required that it should actually be tested by this person rather than that. Consequently, even if a phenomenalistic analysis could be carried out, the statements with which it would leave us would be hypothetical. They would state that if ever such and such conditions were realized, such and such experiences would occur. But clearly at this level an element of theory still remains.

It is, indeed, hard to see how it can ever be eliminated. For even at the solipsistic level one's experiences must still be characterized: they must be brought under concepts if they are to yield any statements which we can regard as records of fact. But then the choice of concepts allows us a certain latitude. It is a contingent matter that we classify colours and shapes and sounds and textures in just the ways that we do. This is not to say that the things to which we apply these concepts do not in fact resemble each other in the ways in which we group them; but only that they resemble each other in any number of other ways which our language does not mark. We do classify things according to resemblances of various types; but it is also true that what is counted as a manner of resemblance depends upon our principles of classification.

If this is so, the realistic picture of the world as simply being there to be described and explained is in some respects too simple. For to ask what the world is like is to ask of any given empirical proposition whether it is true or false: and this means that what counts for us as the world depends upon our conceptual system. It is, however, at least conceivable that our conceptual system should be radically different, and in that case the facts would be different too. For the content and structure of the facts is determined by the content and structure of the propositions which they verify. But surely we can raise the question whether one conceptual system is not more adequate than another; we can decide that one or other of them is a better instrument for dealing with reality. In a sense, this is true. We may be able to show that one system is richer than another, or that in certain respects it permits us to discriminate more finely. What we cannot do, on the other hand, is to get outside language altogether, and from this point of vantage inspect the world in order to see which system best describes it. For in order to compare the two systems in this way we have to describe the world to which they are meant to be adapted, and this means bringing it under some conceptual system. We end therefore by comparing one such system with another.

At the same time we must not make the idealist mistake of concluding that nothing is true or false but thinking makes it so. For a proposition to be true it is not necessary that any one should believe, or even consider, it: there are countless facts that never will be known. No one knows, for example, how many fish there are in the North Sea at this moment, or how many human beings have been born and died in the last four thousand years, but certainly there is in fact a definite number in each case. There is indeed nothing which is logically dependent for its existence on being described. The stars pursued their courses before human beings ever began to think about them, and would have pursued the same courses even if no creatures with conceptual systems had ever come into existence. In this sense, the world and all the facts about it are there to be discovered. But what can be there to be discovered, the framework into which these facts must fit for it to make sense for us to talk of there being a world, does depend upon our conceptual system. To employ a simile which has been used independently by Wittgenstein and Eddington: we spread the net, but we have to wait and see what it catches. And while there is nothing that it is incapable of catching, there is much that is never actually caught.

This yields us a final illustration of the way in which the problems of philosophy may be more general in their scope than those of the natural sciences. For philosophy is concerned with what may be called the formal properties of the net, with the categorical concepts which dominate all our thinking. For example, we think of the world as consisting of a multitude of different things which have various properties and stand in various relations to one another. Exactly what does this imply? What are the grounds for the distinction between particulars and universals, or between substances and attributes, or between logical subjects and logical predicates? Do these distinctions coincide? And how is an individual thing to be identified? By its position in space and time? But our conceptions of space and time themselves require to be elucidated. So does the notion of a physical object, both as it is employed in science and at the level of common sense. Again, some physical objects are thought to exhibit consciousness. What is to be understood by this? What analysis are we to give of the concept of mind and its relationship to matter?

All these are philosophical questions and there are many others like them. The first step in searching for an answer to them is to give a careful and accurate account of our actual usage, to try to elicit the criteria that govern the ways in which these concepts are actually applied. This will not be found to be easy. With such pervasive concepts, it is hard to find a standpoint from which to inspect their working. One useful method of bringing it to light is to consider how far the same work could be done in a language of a different structure. Suppose, for example, that we had a language with no demonstrative expressions, so that we had to rely only on descriptions. How would this affect the problem of individuation? Or again, suppose that we had a language in which the criteria of identity for mental states and processes were such that they could be public, in the way that physical processes are now thought to be. What would remain of the distinction between mind and matter? Would there still be a problem of our knowledge of other minds?

This is not the only method. We can proceed more directly by asking ourselves how statements in which these concepts figure are empirically tested and then by redescribing the facts which make them true. But here there is the difficulty of finding terms in which to carry out the redescription. Neither need we confine ourselves to merely descriptive analysis. The philosopher's work is also critical; even our fundamental concepts are not sacrosanct: we can propose ways in which they should be revised. Thus there is after all a sense in which philosophy can change the world, not indeed materially, for that must be left to science, but formally, by refashioning the structure of language. In this way it may help to determine what facts there can be.

7

CHANCE

I THE CALCULUS OF CHANCES

THE word 'chance' is commonly used by us in several different senses, and one of the things which I hope to accomplish in this paper will be to disentangle them. In some of these senses, though not in all of them, it is a synonym for 'probability'. Thus such statements as that the chances of throwing double-six with a pair of true dice are 1/36, or that there is a slightly better than even chance that any given unborn infant will be a boy, or that there is now very little chance that Britain will join the Common Market, can all be regarded as expressing judgements of probability. It is, however, to be noted that the judgements of probability which these examples severally illustrate are of three different types. The first is an example of what is often called a judgement of *a priori* probability; it relates to the mathematical calculus of chances. The second is an example of a statistical judgement; it estimates the actual frequency with which some property is distributed among the members of a given class. The third is an example of what, for want of a better expression, I call a judgement of credibility; it evaluates the degree of confidence that we are entitled to have in the truth of some proposition, or in the occurrence of some particular event. Judgements of credibility may be based upon statistical judgements, and they may have statistical judgements for their objects, but they are not themselves statistical. It is, indeed, only by adopting some arbitrary standard of measurement that we can contrive to express them in numerical terms.

Though any of these judgements of probability can correctly be expressed as an estimate of chances, it is with judgements of the first type that the concept of chance is most closely associated. Thus it is characteristic of what are known as games of chance that their results are substantially in accordance with *a priori* probabilities. Our first problem is, then, to try to make clear exactly what this implies.

In dealing with this problem, the most important point to bear in mind is that the calculus of chances is a branch of pure mathematics: so that the propositions which it validates are necessarily true. This point tends to be obscured by the fact that statements like 'the chance of throwing double-six with a pair of true dice is 1/36' or 'the chance of throwing heads with an unbiased penny is a half' are open to more than one interpretation. A true die, or an unbiased penny, could be defined in physical terms, as one which was constructed of such and such materials and had its centre of gravity in such and such a place; and in that case these statements would be statistical. Their truth would depend on the actual frequency with which the results in question were obtained with dice or with coins which met these physical stipulations. More commonly, however, what is understood by a true die, or an unbiased penny, is simply one that yields results which match the *a priori* probabilities; and when they are interpreted in this way, our examples turn into statements of elementary arithmetic. It being presupposed that a penny has two faces, and that when it is tossed it will come down with one or other of them uppermost, to say that if it is an unbiased penny there is an even chance of its coming up heads is to say no more than that one is the half of two.

Not all our computations of chance are so simple as this, but the principle remains the same. For instance, when it is said that the odds against throwing heads with an unbiased penny three times in succession are seven to one, what is meant is that of all the possible ordered triplets of the numbers 1 and 2, such as 121, 211, 212 and so forth, the sequence 111 is just one out of eight. If we generalize this and say that the odds against throwing heads n times in succession are 2^n-1 to 1, what we are saying is that of all the possible ordered n-tuplets of the numbers 1 and 2, the sequence of n 1's is one out of a total of 2^n possibilities. Now clearly the value of $1/2^n$ diminishes as n increases, and just this is what is meant by saying that a long run of consecutive heads or tails, or a long run of either red or black at roulette, is highly improbable. In the case of roulette, the odds are slightly worse than $1/2^n$, because the number zero counts against both red and black, but this makes no difference to the argument. Whatever the initial fraction which represents the chance of a given result for any given coup, the chance of obtaining this result n times in succession will be represented by this fraction raised to the power of n, provided always that the successive coups are independent of each other. This is again a proposition of simple arithmetic. The only empirical assumption which is being made is that a game like roulette is in fact a game of chance;

or, in other words, that it is possible to construct and operate a thing like a roulette wheel in such a way that the calculus of chances is approximately satisfied by the results.

In applying the calculus to gambling games of this sort, the assumption that the coups are independent must not be overlooked. Otherwise one may find oneself committing the celebrated Monte Carlo fallacy. As we have just seen, the chances of throwing *n* successive heads with an unbiased coin, or having a run of *n* red numbers at roulette, are very small if *n* is at all large; for example, the odds against a series of as few as ten heads are over a thousand to one; and gamblers are tempted to infer from this that if *n* is a large number by these standards and heads has come up *n*–1 times in succession, the odds against its coming up again the *n*th time must also be large. So a roulette player who has watched red come up nine times in succession will for this reason bet very heavily on black. But his reasoning is fallacious. The very calculation which makes a long run of red improbable is based on the premiss that each spin of the wheel is independent of every other, so that the probability of red, or in the case of the coin the probability of heads, is the same in each instance, no matter what the results of the preceding spins or tosses have been. Even if a million tosses of an unbiased coin have yielded heads on every occasion, the odds against which are astronomical, the chance that it will come up tails on the next toss is still no better than a half.

Many people find this conclusion difficult to accept, because they do not realize that these estimates of chances are no more than the enumeration of abstract possibilities. To say that the odds against a million successive heads are astronomical is merely to say that if we were to list all the possible million-term sequences of heads and tails, the sequence consisting of heads a million times over is just one out of an astronomically large number of alternatives. To say that the chances of heads coming up on the million and first occasion are still no more than 1/2 is to say, quite correctly, that one is no less than the half of two.

But, it will be objected, if we put ourselves in the position of a gambler who has to place his bets, is it really so clear that 'the Monte Carlo fallacy' is fallacious? If the coin with which he is tossing is unbiased, it follows by definition that it comes up tails as often as it comes up heads. So if at some stage in the series of tosses a long run of either face of the coin disturbs the balance, the other face will come up more often in order to restore it. Surely then the rational course for the gambler to pursue would be to note the relative frequencies with which the two faces have appeared and support whichever of them has any leeway to make up.

The answer to this is that it would indeed be the right policy if the gambler were justified in making the assumption that there was some finite number of tosses, some number that he could in principle specify, within which equality would be reached. But this is not a proposition that can be derived from the calculus of chances or even from the assumption that the coin is unbiased. If he could know that the coin was unbiased, in the sense which is here in question, then he would know that any imbalance that had developed in the relative frequency of heads and tails would be corrected if the series of tosses were sufficiently continued. But so long as no limit is set to the number of further tosses which are allowed for this end to be reached, he can draw no conclusion about the way in which he ought to bet. All he can say is that if the existing ratio of heads to tails is $m : n$, then the result of the next toss will be to change it either to $m + 1 : n$ or to $m : n + 1$. No matter what numbers m and n may be, and however greatly one exceeds the other, there are then just two abstract possibilities; and, so far as the calculus of chances goes, there is nothing to choose between them.

An example which may bring this point out more clearly is that of drawing cards from an ordinary pack. Since the number of red and the number of black cards are equal and finite, it is obvious that the greater the preponderance of red cards that have been drawn, the greater is the chance that the next card will be black, provided that when a card is drawn it is not replaced. If, on the other hand, it is replaced, then it is as if the game started afresh with each drawing, so that no matter how great the preponderance of red cards has been, the chance that the next card to be drawn will be black remains even. The Monte Carlo fallacy may then be said to consist in treating the game in which the cards are replaced after being drawn as though it were on a level with the game in which they are not replaced.

It has to be remembered, however, that to talk about chance in this way is not in itself to say anything about what is actually likely to happen; it is not to make a judgement of credibility. In actual practice, the roulette player who observed that red numbers came up very much more often than black might very well conclude that the wheel was biased or that the croupier had discovered some means of spinning it unfairly; and then it would be rational for him to regard the odds on each occasion as being in favour of red. Whatever view he takes, he has to rely on some empirical assumption; for to suppose that the wheel is true, in the sense that its operations satisfy the calculus of chances, is as much an empirical assumption as to suppose that it is biased. These assumptions are empirical because they are concerned with the way in which some physical object actually behaves. The question is whether some particular roulette wheel, or coin, or die, or pack of cards, or whatever it may be, is constructed and manipulated in such a way that any one of a number of equally possible alternatives is realized about as often as any other. In the cases where the results have shown themselves to be unequal in the sense that one side of the coin, or one face of the die, or some group of numbers, or some distribution of the cards, has been particularly favoured, it is a matter of predicting whether this bias will continue, or whether it will be corrected: and this is not a question of abstract mathematics, but a question of fact. It is true that if there is no limit in theory to the duration of the game, the hypothesis that it is fair can never be strictly refuted. No matter how great the deviations have been found to be, it remains conceivable that they will subsequently be corrected, or at least that they would be corrected if the game were sufficiently continued. But although there is never any logical inconsistency in holding to this assumption, there may come a point at which it ceases to be credible.

II APPLICATIONS OF THE CALCULUS

It should be clear by now that no conclusions about any matter of fact can be derived from the calculus of chances on its own. There are no such things as the laws of chance, in the sense in which a law dictates some pattern of events. In themselves, the propositions of the calculus are mathematical truisms. What we can learn from them is that if we assume that certain ratios hold, with respect to the distribution of some property, then we are committed to the conclusion that certain other ratios hold as well. If each of a pair of dice has six faces, and in each case the faces are respectively numbered one to six, and in each case when the die is thrown any one face comes uppermost as often as any other, then the sum of the numbers on the faces which come uppermost when the dice are thrown together will be equal to eight on five occasions out of thirty-six. In other words, the chances of making a point of eight with a single throw of two dice are a little worse than six to one against. But these other words are misleading. For the proposition in question is merely a proposition about numbers. The references to dice, or to coins, or packs of cards, or roulette wheels, which occur in expositions of the theory of probability are entirely adventitous. These objects are dummies whose only function is to adorn the mathematical theory with concrete illustrations. The proof that they are dummies is that they exercise no control over the propositions which they serve to illustrate: the question is whether they measure up to the theory, not whether the theory measures up to them. Suppose, for example, that someone had brought himself to doubt whether the odds against making a point of eight with a pair of dice were greater than six to one, and decided to test this by experiment. And suppose that after recording the results of many thousands of throws he found that the proportion of times in which his pair of dice had yielded a total of eight was as high as one in five. What would he have proved? Perhaps no more than that his dice were biased: at most that tossing dice was not an affair of chance in the way that it had been taken to be: but certainly nothing which would have any bearing upon the theory of probability.

The fact that the propositions of the calculus of chances are not empirically testable does not, of course, entail that they have no factual application. What we require in order to be able to apply them successfully is to discover a set of possible states of affairs which satisfy the following conditions: first, that they are finite in number; secondly, that they are mutually exclusive; thirdly, that they are logically equal, in a sense which I shall explain; and lastly, that they come about with at least approximately equal frequency. When all these conditions are satisfied, the respective states of affairs may be said to be equally probable. It is, however, to be noted that this is no longer the same concept of probability as that which is employed within the calculus of chances. Since they refer to actual frequencies, the judgements into which it enters are not *a priori* but statistical.

What I mean by saying that the states of affairs in question must be logically equal is that each has to be treated as a unity on a level with each of the others. This does not preclude their being complex, in the sense of embracing a number of alternatives, but if any member of the set is represented as a disjunction of such alternatives, we must not allow these disjunctions themselves to rank as members of the set. Otherwise we shall find ourselves falling into contradiction. Thus it has been held by some writers that in a case where we have no evidence either for or against a given proposition, we are entitled to assume that it is equally likely to be true or false. Suppose then that I am playing a game of drawing marbles from a bag and that, relying on this principle, I take it to be an even chance that the first one to be drawn will be blue. This would be a foolish assumption to bet on, but it would not be contradictory, so long as I treat not-blue as a single colour on a level with blue. But if I follow the natural course of breaking down not-blue into a disjunction of other colours, and if, by parity of reasoning, I also take it to be an even chance that the first marble to be drawn will be black, an even chance that it will be red, an even chance that it will be green, and so forth, then I am involved in contradiction. If there are more than two possibilities, it is impossible that each of them should have an even chance of being realized. This is again a question of simple arithmetic. One is not the half of any higher number than two.

To avoid contradictions of this sort, we have to decide at the outset what possibilities we are going to regard as logically equal and then adhere consistently to our decision. As Carnap has shown,[1] such decisions can be taken on purely semantic grounds. We can construct a language with a limited number of primitive predicates and the power to refer to some finite number of individuals; we can then decide, in a more or less arbitrary fashion, that certain states of affairs, which are describable by these means, are to be counted as equally probable; and we can select our logical operators in such a way that the probability of any possible state of affairs within the selected universe of discourse can be calculated on this basis. But not only does this procedure have an unduly narrow application; there is also no reason to suppose that our judgements of equal probability will be at all conformable to anything that actually happens. On the other hand, if we follow a more liberal course by relying on *ad hoc* estimates of what it seems fair to regard as equal possibilities, we shall come upon situations in which what appear to be equally reasonable decisions will lead to incompatible results. I borrow a simple example from an article by Dr J. L. Watling.[2] Suppose that 'we are following a man along a road and reach a place where the road divides into three, two paths climbing the hillside, one lying in the valley'. Knowing nothing but that the man, now out of sight, will take one of the three paths, how are we to estimate the probability that he will take the path lying in the valley?

[1] In his *Logical Foundations of Probability*, 2nd ed. (1962).

[2] 'Confirmation Discomforted', *Revue Internationale de Philosophie* (1963), Fasc. 2.

If we follow the classical procedure of assigning equal probability to equal possibilities, and if we regard it as equally possible that the man will take any one of the three paths, we shall have to conclude that the chance of his taking the valley path is one in three. But we might just as well regard it as equally possible that he will go into the valley or go into the hills, and in that case it would follow that the chance of his taking the valley path was one in two. These conclusions are mutually incompatible; but, in default of further information, there is nothing to choose between them.

Dr Watling takes this as a proof that 'the classical interpretation' of probability is inconsistent. I should prefer to say, in cases of this kind, that it was inoperative. The calculus of chances is not inconsistent in itself; and so long as we have a consistent rule for deciding what states of affairs are to count as equally possible, it can be consistently applied. But if the application of the calculus is to be of any use to us, in the way of helping us to win our bets on what will actually happen, we cannot allow the assignment of initial probabilities simply to depend upon an arbitrary decision. In the example chosen, if we really knew nothing more than that the man would take one of the three paths, we should have no right to assume, either that it was equally likely that he would take any one of the three, or that it was equally likely that he would go into the valley or into the hills. Before we could make any such assumptions, we should have to have something further to go on than the mere arithmetical fact that one is the half of two or the third part of three. We should need some factual information about the man's habits or whatever, in order to supply the calculus of chances with a foothold in reality. In general, we cannot assume that any two states of affairs are equally probable, unless we have reason to believe that they occur with equal frequency. But pure mathematics cannot tell us anything about actual frequencies, neither can semantics. We have to rely upon empirical evidence.

The upshot of this is that when we come to apply the calculus of chances, our judgements of probability change their character; they become statistical judgements. To say that there is one chance in eight that a true coin will come up heads on each of three successive tosses may, as we have seen, be just a colourful way of expressing an arithmetical truism; but to say that the same applies to this penny which I have in my hand is to make the empirical statement that if it were tossed on a fairly large number of occasions and the results set out in groups of three, the sequence heads heads heads would be found to occur on the average once in eight times. This is, indeed, a consequence of the more general assumption that in a sufficiently long series of tosses with this penny each of the possible sequences of a given length would occur on the average as often as any other.

But here we are faced with the difficulty that unless some limit is set to the length of the sequence within which this equality is to be realized, the empirical evidence in favour of such an assumption is bound to be incomplete. And even if a limit were to be set, so that we could in principle run through all the members of the series to which our judgement of probability refers, it is only so long as we have not done this that a judgement of this kind is of any interest to us. When we already know that a given event has occurred, or that it has failed to occur, we do not speculate about its chances. The point of collecting statistics is to extrapolate them. In other words, we normally examine only a sample of the total class of events in which we are interested, and then if we find that the property about which we are inquiring is distributed in a certain proportion among the members of this sample, we infer that it would be distributed in much the same proportion among the members of a further sample, or throughout the class as a whole. Admittedly, if we were to toss our penny, say, fifty times and found that heads came up in the ratio of three to two, we should not feel ourselves bound to regard this as a typical sample. In default of physical evidence that the penny was biased, we might rather expect that if the series of tosses were continued, the balance would be redressed. But the reason for this would be that we were influenced by our knowledge that pennies which were physically similar to this one had been found to come up heads about as often as they came up tails. We should be drawing on a wider range of statistics, but we should still be going beyond our evidence. We should in fact be making a deduction from a general hypothesis about the distribution of heads and tails which had been derived from our knowledge of their distribution in a reasonably large sample. The question is how such a procedure can be justified.

The usual answer to this is that inferences from the character of a sample to the character of the total class, or population, from which the sample is drawn are logically justified, provided that the sample is large enough, by the Law of Large Numbers. I shall not go into the mathematical formulation and proof of this law, which is to be found in the standard text books. What it comes to is that if a proportion m/n of the members of some class possess the property p and we select from this class all possible samples of a given size, it must be true of the majority of these samples that the proportion in which *p* is distributed among their members also lies in the neighbourhood of m/n. Moreover, as the size of the samples increases, so does the extent of the concentration round m/n, with the result that, if the samples are made large enough, the frequency with which *p* occurs in practically all of them will differ only negligibly from the frequency with which it occurs in the parent class.

A common way of putting this is to say that it is very highly probable that the distribution of a property throughout a given class is almost exactly reflected in any large sample which is drawn from that class; and since if A matches B it must also be true that B matches A, it will follow from this that if a property is distributed in such and such a proportion among the members of a large sample, there is a very high probability that it is distributed in approximately the same proportion among the members of the class from which the sample has been drawn. It is in this way that the law of large numbers is thought to justify this very familiar type of inference.

There is, however, a point to be made here which is rather too often overlooked. When one speaks in this context of its being very highly probable that what is true of a large sample is also true of the parent class, this judgement of probability belongs to the first of my three types. It is not a judgement of credibility, but a judgement which relates merely to the distribution of logical possibilities. What one is saying, in fact, is that among all possible samples of the size in question the number of those which roughly match the parent class is very much greater than the number of those which do not. It follows that if one sample is seriously deceptive, with respect to the incidence of some property in the class from which it is drawn, it is highly untypical; and this is all that follows. Even to say that it is untypical does not mean that it deviates from most of the samples that are actually drawn, but only that it deviates from the vast majority of possible samples. This is the most that can be extracted from the law of large numbers.

But is it not very unlikely that our sampling of nature should be untypical? The trouble with this question is that it smuggles in a judgement of credibility, for which no basis has yet been assigned. If we make suitable assumptions about the constitution of the universe, we can supply ourselves with premisses from which to deduce that our sampling is fair. These premisses will, however, themselves need to be justified, and I do not see how this could be done except by an appeal to our experience. But then, as Hume saw, we are landed in a circle; for this appeal to our experience itself makes use of the assumption which it is required to justify. I am strongly inclined to think that this circle is unavoidable; but to develop this argument would lead me into the heart of the problem of induction, which I shall not here attempt to penetrate.

I have tried to show that while there is nothing wrong with the law of large numbers in itself, the support which it gives to arguments from inverse probability is much more precarious than has commonly been supposed. There is, however, one set of cases in which an argument of this type can be applied with complete safety. These are the cases in which the class with which we are concerned is finite and the unexamined portion of it is relatively very small. Suppose, for example, that we know what is the total number of births of children within a given area throughout a given period, but that our statistics with regard to their sex distribution are not quite complete. But then let the fraction of the class for which this information is lacking be comparatively small, say less than 3%. In that case, whatever the proportion of male births in our sample may be, we can be sure that the proportion in the whole class does not differ from it very much, just because there are not enough unexamined instances to make any great difference. By supposing all of them male, or all of them female, we can fix the fairly narrow limits within which the correct answer must lie.

But the very security of this conclusion robs it of any interest. It tells us no more than we know already. The prospective father who wants to know whether the child which his wife is carrying is more likely to be a boy or a girl learns nothing at all to his purpose from the information that the available statistics are such that the proportion of boys among the children born or about to be born within the relevant period is bound to be over 50%. All he learns is that the figures have now reached a stage where it is not going to make any appreciable difference to the final percentage which his child is. Not only can he deduce nothing whatsoever about the sex of his own child, since judgements of probability, in the sense of frequency, in any case refer to classes and not to individuals, but he can deduce nothing about the frequency of male births in the sub-class of so far unexamined cases to which his child belongs.

In fact, the ratio of male to female births has been found to be fairly constant, so that if the statistics had shown that slightly more female children had so far been born in the course of the year, the prospective father, knowing that there was normally a slight preponderance of males, might be encouraged to expect that his child would be a boy, as the result of a belief in what is popularly known as the law of averages. But if he did argue in this way he could easily be disappointed. What is not generally realized is that the law of averages only works deductively. If we already know, with respect to the incidence of some property in a limited series of events, what the final percentage is going to be and we also know what the percentage is in the part of the series which has already been traversed, we can calculate what the percentage will be in the instances still to come in order to make the sum come out right. But the consequence of this is that the law of averages can only be applied with any safety when it is backed by statistical laws which are very well established. We might perhaps rely on the Mendelian laws of heredity for the assurance that if a recessive character had already appeared in a given generation among the members of a certain family of plants or animals, the character of the kind in question which would be displayed in that generation by the remaining members of the family would be dominant. On the other hand it would be a very foolish man who argued that because the total number of road accidents in the current year had already risen to the average of previous years, he could drive as recklessly as he pleased, since the law of averages would keep him safe. And the reason why he would be foolish is not only that the incidence of road accidents is not known to fall under any very constant statistical laws, but also that for the most part these accidents, though they may be in some measure due to common causes, are causally independent of one another. The fact that a number of accidents have recently occurred in this neighbourhood does not make it any the less likely that another one will occur there today, unless, perhaps, the knowledge that they have occurred makes people more careful. But certainly it is not made any the less likely by the law of averages.

The same applies to our example of the prospective father, in spite of the greater constancy of the birth statistics. Whatever factors may determine the sex of his child, there is no reason to believe that the sex of other children who are not his kindred but merely happen also to be born in the current year has anything to do with it. Consequently, if there has been an unusual preponderance of female births, the inference which he should draw is not that there is any greater likelihood that his child will be a boy, but rather that it is a year in which, for some reason or other, the usual balance of the sexes has been altered.

III WHAT KINDS OF THINGS ARE DUE TO CHANCE?

We have seen that what is required for the application of the calculus of chances is that there should be a finite set of logically equal possibilities, which are fulfilled in the long run with equal frequency. It is because we suppose these conditions to be at least roughly satisfied in games which are played with coins or dice or cards or roulette wheels, that we characterize them as games of chance. Conversely, if we play one of these games and find in a particular instance that the different possibilities are not fulfilled with anything like equal frequency, we may decide that the results are not to be ascribed to chance: and then we look for some other explanation.

It is not only in gambling games that this procedure operates. Very often, when a statistical result is said to be significant, what is meant is that it deviates from chance in the sense that it fails to accord with the *a priori* probabilities. A good illustration of this is to be found in the experiments which are supposed to prove the existence of extra-sensory perception. The experiments are conducted with a set of cards severally numbered one to five, and another set of five cards, respectively symbolizing a lion, an elephant, a pelican, a zebra and a giraffe. Both packs are shuffled, the experimenter draws a card from the numbered pack and then draws from the animal pack the card which corresponds in order to the number which he has drawn. This procedure is repeated a hundred times, the cards being replaced after each drawing, and the packs reshuffled. The subject is required to say on each occasion which animal is represented by the card which has been drawn from the animal pack. It is assumed that if it were merely a matter of guesswork he would be right, on the average, twenty times out of a hundred. It sometimes happens, however, that a subject fairly consistently gets as many as twenty-eight right. This result is sufficiently improbable to be counted as statistically significant. It is therefore inferred that the subject's achievement cannot be put down to chance and he is credited with extra-sensory perception. Admittedly, to talk of extra-sensory perception is not to give any explanation of the subject's performance, but merely to stake the claim that an explanation is called for; but this does not matter for our present purposes. Our only concern is with the meaning and the implications of the statement that such things do not occur by chance.

Let us look into this case a little more closely. Why is it assumed that if the subject had no special power of divination he would pick the right card about twenty times out of a hundred? The answer is that if we take every possible sequence of a hundred drawings from this set of cards, and every possible sequence of a hundred guesses, then the proportion of cases in which the two selections match is twenty in a hundred, or one in five. And to say that it is rather improbable that as many as twenty-eight guesses should be right is just to say that out of the total number of possible parallel sequences of a hundred drawings and guesses, the proportion in which the two coincide in as many as twenty-eight places is rather small.

It is to be noted that both these calculations are *a priori*. They relate to the distribution of logical possibilities, and are in no way derived from the study of anything that actually happens. Why then should we regard it as a matter of no interest, as something only to be expected, that the series of guesses should match the series of drawings, in the same proportion as the total of possible matches stands to the total of possible combinations, but think it quite extraordinary that a subject should achieve a number of matchings which is 8% greater than the *a priori* average? Why should it be more remarkable that the proportion of actual coincidences should deviate from the proportion of possible coincidences than that they should be in conformity with one another? What we must be assuming is that the natural thing, in a card-guessing game of this kind, is for every possible combination of the members of the two series to appear with equal frequency. But what reason could we have for making such an assumption, antecedently to any experience? So far as I can see, none whatsoever.

If I am right about this, we are not entitled to assume that it is only a deviation from the *a priori* frequencies that calls for explanation. Conformity with them may equally have to be accounted for. And in fact there are many cases in which this seems to be recognized. If a coin, or a die, or a roulette wheel, yields 'improbable' results, if it favours one side or area at the expense of the others, we do indeed assume that some physical bias is at work: the coin is weighted; its centre of gravity has been displaced. But equally we think that there is a physical explanation in the case where such objects run true. It is quite an art to make dice and roulette wheels operate in such a way that each number comes up in a reasonably long run about as often as any other. There are physical reasons for this just as much as there are for the fact that one number, or set of numbers, comes up much more often than the others. In the sense in which chance is contrasted with design, or a chance event is one to which we do not assign a cause, it is not by chance that these operations obey the laws of chance.

Antecedently, then, to experience, we have no more reason to expect that the results of tossing coins or throwing dice will conform to the *a priori* probabilities than that they will deviate from them. The reason why we think that results which are very improbable in this sense call for a special explanation is that they are *empirically* abnormal. What is significant is not the deviation from the *a priori* frequencies but the deviation from frequencies which have been empirically established. The special interest which we take in the case where a die turns out to be biased stems from the fact that we have found by experience that most dice run true.

I believe that the same applies to the other cases in which we conclude, on purely statistical grounds, that such and such an occurrence cannot be ascribed to chance. Suppose, for example, that wherever I go in the course of a day I keep running across the same stranger; I may well conclude that this cannot be a matter of chance: the man must be following me. But my reason for this is not that our meeting so often is improbable *a priori*. Of course I could argue in this way. Starting with the assumption that we are both moving within a certain limited area, I could think of this area as divided into a finite number of equal squares, like a chessboard, and then make the assumption that each of us is as likely at any moment of the day to be in any one of these squares as in any other. My reason for concluding that we were not meeting by chance would then be that out of the total number of possible paths which we could severally follow, the number of those which intersected at several places was only a very tiny fraction. But not only is this line of argument not necessary for me to arrive at my conclusion; it rests on a premiss which is entirely open to question. If the assumption that each of us is as likely to be in any one square as in any other at any given time is merely a way of stating that the squares are equal, then it is true *ex hypothesi*, but nothing to the purpose: if it implies that over a certain period of time we are actually to be found in any one square as often as in any other, then, in default of empirical evidence, there can be no reason for accepting it. If I nevertheless conclude that these meetings do not occur by chance, my reason will be that experience has shown me that when two people are living independently in a large city with many different venues for business and for recreation, the occasions on which their separate pursuit of their affairs leads them to be in the same place at the same time are relatively few. Here again, what needs to be specially explained is the deviation not from an *a priori* but from an empirically established frequency.

This is also, in my view, the way in which we should interpret the card-guessing experiments. Antecedently to experience, there is no reason to believe that the degree to which any series of guesses matches any series of drawings will or will not reflect the distribution of the logical possibilities. What is known *a priori* is that any card which is drawn will be one of five possibilities, and that any guess which is made will also be one of five possibilities, but from this nothing at all follows about the number of matchings that will actually occur. We have to discover by experiment that certain methods of shuffling and selecting the cards do have the result that any one of them comes up about as often as any other. We have also to discover by experiment that the guesses which people make are evenly distributed; or if this is not true, as for psychological reasons it may very well not be in many instances, that their tendency to favour certain choices does not result in a number of matchings which is greater than the average. From these empirical premisses the standard conclusions about the results which would occur by chance do follow mathematically. But then if the results show a significant deviation, what is put in doubt is just the truth of one or other of the empirical premisses. The only thing that is remarkable about the subject who is credited with extra-sensory perception is that he is consistently rather better at guessing cards than the ordinary run of people have shown themselves to be. The fact that he also does 'better than chance' in itself proves nothing at all.

The same confusion is commonly found in discussions of the question whether the universe exists by chance. It is not, indeed, immediately clear what meaning this question could be given in terms of the *a priori* calculus of chances. But, if one can make the assumptions that there is a finite number of ultimate particles in the universe, and that the space in which they operate is also finite, then I suppose it could be said that the actual state of the universe is very improbable, in the sense that the actual distribution of the particles is only one of a fantastically large number of possible distributions. In this sense, of course, any other distribution of the particles would be equally improbable, but it might be argued that their actual distribution was more improbable than some others would be, on the ground that it exhibited a greater deviation from the *a priori* average. Alternatively, if we were able, by what would have to be a rather arbitrary procedure, to draw up a finite list of the simple properties which it was logically possible for anything to have, we might say that the actual state of the universe was improbable in the sense that the number of ways in which these properties were actually found to be combined was only a tiny fraction of the total number of possible combinations. In neither case, however, would anything of interest follow unless we had reason to believe that some different constitution of the universe from the one that actually obtains was antecedently more likely. But what reason could there possibly be for such a belief? What meaning can we attach even to this notion of antecedent likelihood? The most that we can say is that given the number of fundamental particles and the finitude of space, or given the number of primary properties and the range of their possible combinations, the number of possible universes in which the particles are more evenly distributed or the combinations of properties more various is greater than the number of those in which the particles are not more evenly distributed or the combination of properties not more various than they are in our actual universe. But why should it be supposed that a more probable universe, in this special sense, is more to be expected than the one in which we actually find ourselves? The answer is that there can be no reason at all for any supposition of this kind. The concept of *a priori* probability relates only to the counting of logical possibilities. How probable it is that these logical possibilities are realized, in a balanced or unbalanced way, can be estimated only in the light of our experience. But we can have no experience of a universe other than our own.

It is perhaps worth adding that the fact that our universe may be said to be improbable, in the senses which I have just defined, does nothing at all for the traditional argument from design. In order to give any force to this argument, it would have to be shown that we have good reason to believe first that the universe is a teleological system and secondly that it is the kind of teleological system which experience has shown us to be commonly the result of conscious planning. I take it to be sufficiently obvious that neither of these conditions is actually satisfied.

IV CHANCE, DESIGN AND CAUSE

WE are now in a position to distinguish the principal senses in which we commonly speak of the operations of chance.

(1) A chance event, as we have seen, may be a member of a series which exemplifies a game of chance. What is required of such a series is that it should conform to the *a priori* calculus of chances. If we take the simple example of a series of tosses with a coin, this would imply that in a reasonably long run there should be an approximate equality of heads and tails. It is, however, doubtful if this condition is sufficient. For instance, it would be satisfied by a series of tosses in which heads and tails regularly alternated: yet a series of this kind would not normally be regarded as typifying chance. What seems also to be required is that the series should satisfy a condition of randomness. I do not think that this condition need be so strong as the principle of indifference to place selection which has been adopted by some modern proponents of the frequency theory of probability. It might be enough that every possible sequence of some arbitrarily determined length should occur with approximately equal frequency.

To speak of a chance event, in this sense, is not to imply that the event is not caused, or even that it is not designed. The results of particular tosses of a coin, or throws of a die, or spins of a roulette wheel, are commonly not designed, but it is very often due to design that the series in which they occur conforms as a whole to the *a priori* calculus.

It is in accordance with this usage that when events of a certain kind occur with a frequency which deviates significantly from the *a priori* probabilities, they are said not to occur by chance. I have, however, tried to show that such a deviation does not, in itself, call for any special explanation. It is only when we have empirical evidence that the events are of a kind to which the *a priori* calculus normally does apply that their discrepancy becomes significant.

(2) Just as we look for a cause when we come upon an 'improbable' deviation in a series of a type which normally conforms to the calculus of chances, so conversely there are cases in which a deviation from an established law-like pattern is put down to chance. It is in this sense, for example, that biologists speak of chance mutations. What is implied here is not necessarily that the event in question is not susceptible of any causal explanation. It is enough that its occurrence should not be predictable in terms of the scientific theory with which we are operating. So, in our example, the theory of evolution provides for the occurrences of mutations only in a general way: it does not enable us to predict when and in what form they will occur. One could say that the theory made provision for them as chance events.

Examples of this usage occur also in historical discourse. 'For want of a nail the shoe was lost, for want of a shoe the horse was lost, for want of the horse the rider was lost, for want of the rider the battle was lost, for want of the battle the kingdom was lost, and all for the want of a horse shoe nail.' We say that the kingdom was lost by mischance, not for lack of a causal explanation but because its being lost in this manner is not something that any historical theory could have enabled us to foresee. It is not part of any recognized historical pattern that so trivial an event as a nail's falling out of a horse's shoe should have such far-reaching consequences.

(3) A third sense of chance is that in which it is contrasted with design. It applies to events which are brought about by human beings, or by other animals in so far as they can be said to have intentions. To attribute an event to chance, in this sense, is just to say that it was not intended by the agent in question. Here again, it is not implied that the event lacked a cause.

(4) We speak of a chance collocation of events when their concurrence is not designed and when, though we may be able to account for them severally, we have not established any law-like proposition which links them together. The ascription of such concurrences to chance is most often made in cases where something of especial interest to us follows from them, or in cases where the concurrence would normally be the result of design. Thus, if in the course of a journey I keep running into friends whom I had not arranged to meet, I am struck by the coincidence, though in fact it is no more of a coincidence than my meeting anybody else. This is on the assumption that the frequency of these encounters does not greatly exceed the average: otherwise, as we have seen, I am justified in suspecting design. If design is ruled out, our speaking of coincidence implies no more than that the events in question are not connected by any law-like generalization which figures in our accepted system of beliefs. It does not commit us to holding that no law which would connect them could ever be discovered.

(5) In one of the senses in which 'chance' is a synonym for 'probability', the chance that an event of such and such a sort will have a given character is equated with the frequency with which the character is actually distributed throughout the class of events in question. There are different ways in which these frequencies may be estimated: they may be extrapolated from recorded statistics, or they may be deduced from a scientific theory. In cases where they are deduced from a theory, it may or may not be assumed that the statistical laws which

figure in the theory are derivable, at least in principle, from underlying causal laws. Thus the assumption in classical physics was that everything depended on the state of individual particles the behaviour of which was rigorously governed by Newtonian laws. If, as in the kinetic theory of gases, one was content to rely upon statistical laws, it was because of the practical difficulty of tracing the movements of the individual particles. On the other hand, in contemporary quantum physics, the laws are fundamentally statistical; the individual particles are not represented as obeying causal laws: the states of the system are statistically defined. This does not exclude the possibility, in which some physicists believe, of finding a deterministic theory which would account for the same phenomena: but it would have to be a radically different sort of theory.

(6) Let us suppose that no such theory is forthcoming. It can then be said that these are chance events, in a stronger sense of the term than any that we have yet considered. A chance event, in this sense, would be one that was not subject to any causal law. If we are going to maintain that there are chance events of this kind, we must, however, be careful to formulate our position in a way that prevents it from being trivially refutable. The difficulty is that if we set no limit to the form of our hypotheses, then so long as we are dealing with a closed set of events, we shall always be able to find some generalizations which they satisfy. We, therefore, need to place some restriction on what is to count as a causal law. Perhaps the best course would be to stipulate that for a generalization to be a causal law it was necessary that it should apply to events which were not included in the set which it was already known to cover. In other words, one mark of a causal law would be that it was actually used to make successful extrapolations. To deny that phenomena of a given type were subject to causal laws would then have the force of predicting that however far our researches are pressed we shall never succeed in bringing them under 'workable' generalizations of a causal sort.

(7) Following C. S. Peirce,[1] I think that there is another way in which the course of nature may be held to exhibit an irreducible factor of chance. Even in a domain in which causal laws are well established, there is often a certain looseness in their grasp upon the observed facts. The phenomena which are taken as verifying them cover a certain

[1] See *The Collected Papers of Charles Sanders Peirce*, VI (1936), p. 46 *et al.*, and my *The Origins of Pragmatism*, pp. 103–12 (Macmillan, 1968), or 91–9 (Freeman, Cooper, 1968).

range: if they are quantitative, the values which are actually recorded may be scattered around the values which the laws prescribe. These slight deviations are not held to be significant: they are put down to errors of observation. But 'errors of observation' is here a term of art. Apart from the existence of the deviation, there is usually no reason to suppose that any error has occurred. Now it seems possible that this looseness of fit cannot be wholly eliminated or, in other words, that there are limits to the precision with which observable events can be forecast. If this were so, it might be said that anything which fell outside these limits remained in the hands of chance.

Admittedly, this cannot be demonstrated. Whatever limits are set, there can be no *a priori* reason for assuming that they will never be overstepped. The person who believes in chance, in any such absolute sense, can properly do no more than issue a challenge. He points to certain features of the world and defies anyone to show that they fall entirely, in every detail, within the grasp of causal laws. In the sense in which to speak of chance is to express what I have called a judgement of credibility, I think that there is a good chance that someone who takes this position will be able to maintain it. There is, however, a sense in which it can be said of anything not known to be logically or causally impossible that there is a chance that it will happen: and in this sense, however long the champion of absolute chance has remained in possession of the field, there must always remain the chance that his challenge will eventually be met.

8

KNOWLEDGE, BELIEF AND EVIDENCE

It is generally agreed that one condition of knowing anything to be the case is that the proposition in question should be true. To say that it was known that *p*, but that *p* was false, would be self-contradictory. What is more disputed is whether knowledge entails belief. Many philosophers assume that it does, but there are also those who reject the alleged entailment on the ground that to say only that one believes something to be true is implicitly to deny that one knows it; there are those who hold that the mental attitude of knowing is generically different from that of believing, and there are those who hold that even though there is no special state of mind which is characteristic of knowing, as opposed to believing, there can still be knowledge without belief; they would point to cases of self-deception, or cases where one has learned something which one cannot immediately call to mind, as showing that one's failure to believe a proposition does not prevent one from knowing it.

The first two of these positions are not defensible. It is indeed true that when someone limits himself to saying that he believes that such and such is so, we commonly infer that he does not think he knows it; but the reason for this lies in the convention by which a speaker does not make a weaker claim if he thinks he is in a position to make a stronger one. It clearly does not follow that the stronger claim excludes the weaker, in any other sense than that it goes beyond it. To come to know something that one has previously believed is not to cease to believe it, nor even necessarily to believe it more strongly, though this may happen in certain cases; it is rather that a further condition comes to be satisfied, a condition which we may provisionally describe by saying that it has to do with the justification of the belief. But if this is all the difference that there need be, apart from the fact that one can be said to believe but not to know what is not true, it must also be a mistake to characterize knowing as a distinctive state of mind. The idea behind this view is that the state of mind in question would be one that, as it were, guaranteed its object; but this is a delusion.

Whatever mental attitude one may have towards a given proposition, it must leave it open for the proposition to be false, except in the rare case where the proposition itself implies the existence of the attitude in question or states a precondition of it. This does not, indeed, refute the view that knowing and believing are different states of mind, though it takes away its point and interest; for it might be maintained that even though the state of knowing did not and could not guarantee its object, it was still distinctive. But the disproof of this is that when someone claims to know something which we think to be false we say that he does not know but only believes it; if we then find out that it is true we may allow that he did know it. There is no implication in either case that his state of mind has changed.

This third position, on the other hand, is not so open to attack. It is quite natural to describe a case of self-deception by saying that the subject refuses to admit what he really knows. The use of the word 'really' in this context indicates that this is not quite a standard case of knowledge, and it might also be argued that the refusal to admit something even to oneself is not inconsistent with one's really believing it, where again the use of the word 'really' indicates that this is not quite a standard case of belief. Because of these qualifications, this example is not conclusive; we are not obliged to treat situations of this kind as cases of knowledge without belief; at the same time if someone wishes to describe them in this way, it can hardly be said that his usage is incorrect.

Much the same applies to the case where a man is temporarily unaware of, or unable to recall, what he may nevertheless be said to know. I do not think that we should credit him with knowing the fact in question if he had forgotten it beyond recall, or if he were not sure even when reminded of it; but if it is a fact of which we ourselves have knowledge, we may be willing to allow that someone knows it if he has been apprised of it and has at least a latent disposition to be sure of it; we do not require that the disposition be actualized on every relevant occasion. It might indeed be argued that the man's knowledge was intermittent, in the sense that he ceased to know the fact in question for the periods during which he was not sure of it, or unable to recall it; but while this view can be maintained without absurdity, it puts a slightly stronger limitation on the use of the word 'know' than perhaps it ordinarily bears. However, it is also true that belief is dispositional, and in the case where someone has temporarily forgotten what he knows, there appears to be no stronger ground for saying that he has ceased to believe it than there is for saying that he has ceased to know it. On the other hand it may seem a little less strange to say that a man still knows something which he is unsure of than that he still believes it.

What emerges from these examples is that to insist that knowledge must entail belief is to put a slight but by no means unbearable strain upon ordinary usage. Whether it is worth paying this small price for the sake of greater neatness and uniformity is a matter for decision. It is in any case clear that knowledge is normally tied to belief and that even in the exceptional cases, if we admit them, there is at least a latent connection. We should not say of anyone that he knew a given proposition unless he had at some time believed it or was at the very least disposed to do so.

There would be a stronger motive for laying down the rule that knowing must entail believing if it were then possible to go on to identify knowledge with true belief. But notoriously this is not feasible. There is no contradiction in saying 'I fully believe that *p*, though I do not know it', even in a case where *p* turns out to be true. A further condition is required; the one to which we have already referred as having to do with the justification of the belief. The problem is to specify it more precisely.

It might seem that this presented no great difficulty. Why should we not say that a person *A* knows that *p* if and only if the following conditions are satisfied: first that *p* is true, secondly that subject to the possible exceptions which we have been reviewing, *A* is sure that *p*, and thirdly that *A* has good evidence for accepting *p*? And what would be meant here by his having good evidence is that he is able to justify his acceptance of *p* by adducing some other proposition *q*, or set of propositions *K*, which strongly supports it.

There are, however, various objections to this. In the first place it rules out the possibility of one's knowing propositions for which it is inappropriate to ask for evidence. If I were to say, truthfully, that I am not now in pain, it would be absurd to ask me what my evidence was for this; yet I should certainly claim to know that I am not now in pain. It has indeed been maintained, for example by Wittgenstein, that it is improper to speak of knowing that one is, or presumably that one is not, in pain, but I am convinced that this is wrong. It is true that we very seldom find occasion to use expressions like 'I know that I am in pain' or 'He knows that he is in pain', but the reason for this is not that it is improper to use the word 'know' in contexts of this kind, but rather that if we think that someone is in pain, we take it for granted that he knows it. There is, however, no need to press this point, since whatever we take to be the lowest level of empirical propositions, the same difficulty will arise. Thus a philosopher who rejects sense-data will think it absurd to ask what evidence he has for accepting such a proposition as that he sees a table in his room. Yet he would not want to deny that he knew such propositions to be true: or if he did he would be wrong.

A second objection is that we may want to say that someone knows a proposition for which he lacks evidence, even though it is not the sort of proposition for which it is inappropriate that evidence should be asked. An example which I have used elsewhere[1] is that of a man who is consistently successful in predicting the results of a lottery. I suggested that if his run of successes were sufficiently impressive, we might well come to say that he knew what the winning number was going to be, even though he did not reach this conclusion by any rational method, or indeed by any method at all. One might try to bring this case into line by saying that the man's evidence consists in the record of his past successes, but the point of the example is that his belief in his predictions is not based on this evidence. His having been consistently successful in the past is not supposed to be part of his reason for being confident that he has picked the right number, though it is our reason for trusting him, and our ground for saying that he knows what the right number is. It is, however, disputable whether this ground is sufficient; no matter how successful the man's predictions had been found to be, many people would still hesitate to say that he knew that they were going to be true.

The next objection is much more serious. It is that if we make it a necessary condition of knowledge that one has good evidence for what one knows, we fall into an infinite regress. For the question arises whether the evidence must be known in its turn. And the answer appears to be that it must, or else it would not serve its purpose. If I am asked how I know that a given proposition *p* is true, it is surely not enough for me to be able to cite some other proposition *q* which strongly supports *p*, even though it happens that *q* itself is true. If I do not also know that *q* is true, I may have given a reason for accepting *p*, but I have not given a reason for accepting my claim to know that *p*. But if I cannot ever know that a given proposition is true unless I have evidence which supports it, then I cannot know that *q* is true unless I know the truth of some further proposition *r* which supports

[1] In *The Problem of Knowledge* (Macmillan, 1956), p. 31.

q and I cannot know that *r* is true unless I know the truth of some further proposition *s* which supports *r*, and so *ad infinitum*.

There are various ways in which one might try to answer this objection. One of them would be to adopt the position which I take to have been that of C. S. Peirce: to admit the infinite regress but deny that it was vicious. It is clear, so one might argue, that if I try to set forth my reasons for claiming to know some proposition to be true, I embark on a process which I cannot in practice carry to infinity. If my pretension to knowledge is to be admitted, I must sooner or later succeed in adducing a proposition my claim to know which is allowed to go unchallenged. In such a case, however, it is possible that if I were challenged, I could justify the claim. It will then be a matter for decision when I choose, or am permitted, to bring this process to an end. The infinite regress, which is perfectly innocent, consists merely in the fact that at whatever point the process is brought to an end, it could have been continued further.

But the trouble with this answer is that even if I am not required to go on endlessly *giving* reasons in support of any proposition which I claim to know—reasons for accepting some proposition which supports it and reasons for accepting this proposition in its turn and so *ad infinitum*—I am, on this view, required to *have* them; and the idea that in every instance in which one knows that something is the case, one actually has this infinite chain of reasons is dubious to say the least. This is, indeed, a factual rather than a logical objection. It is not true, as has sometimes been suggested, that this argument shows the proposed definition of knowledge to be circular. There is no circle involved in saying that to know that *p* is to believe *p* truly on the basis of *q* which one believes truly on the basis of *r* which one believes truly on the basis of *s etcetera*. There is no circle because the infinite series contains no reference to knowledge. But the way in which the circle is avoided might itself be held to discredit the definition, on the ground that while the links in the chain support one another, there is nothing which supports the chain as a whole.

A way of escaping the infinite regress, which would avoid this last objection, would be to rely on the notion of incorrigible propositions. The regress would terminate when one arrived at a proposition which was, as it were, self-guaranteeing. The candidates for this rôle would be propositions which, as one used to say, recorded the subject's immediate experiences, propositions which described what he felt, or how things appeared to him, or what he seemed to remember. Here again it may be objected that we should fall into a circle, on the ground that these incorrigible propositions must themselves be known to be true; but again the charge would be unfounded. For we may characterize an incorrigible proposition as one which follows from the subject's believing it. Then the theory would be that for *A* to know *p* it was sufficient, and with certain reservations also necessary, that *p* be true, that *A* be sure that *p*, and that *A*'s confidence that *p* be based on his acceptance of a set of propositions *K* which satisfied the following conditions: first that *K* strongly supports *p* and secondly that *K* includes at least one proposition *s* which is such that *s* directly or indirectly supports the other members of *K*, that *A*'s acceptance of *K* is grounded in his acceptance of *s*, and that *s* follows from the proposition that *A* believes that *s*. Whatever else may be said about it, it is plain that this account of knowledge is not circular.

This does not mean, however, that our difficulties are at an end. For it is not at all obvious that there are any incorrigible propositions in this sense. Previously, when attacking the view that knowing consisted in being in a distinctive state of mind, I said that the truth of a proposition cannot follow from the fact that someone has a certain attitude towards it, unless the proposition is itself descriptive of that attitude or lays down a pre-condition of it. If this is right, since my believing that I am having some experience can hardly be a pre-condition of my having it, a proposition like 'I am in pain' can be entailed by the proposition 'I believe that I am in pain' only if it also entails it. In other words, the proposition that one is having an immediate experience of this kind and the proposition that one believes that one is having such an experience are taken to be equivalent. This is not manifestly false, but neither is it manifestly true.

A defender of incorrigible propositions could indeed avoid this conclusion by modifying the principle which forces it on him. He could argue that besides the cases for which we have already provided, the deduction of '*p*' from '*A* believes that *p*' is justified also in the case where it does not make sense to speak of *A*'s having a belief that *p* which is factually mistaken; and he could maintain, with some plausibility, that we do not attach any sense to such statements as '*A* believes that he is in pain, but he is wrong'.

Whether this view is tenable or not is a question which has been much debated, and I do not propose to examine it again in detail here. I am in fact inclined to think that the stock of incorrigible propositions which were furnished by these means would be too narrow for our purpose, if indeed it existed at all. It would often be difficult to devise examples which would provide a use for saying that a man was mistaken about the character of his present experiences, but I am not sure that it would ever be impossible. One might be able to dispose of these counter-examples by showing that the mistakes for which they provided were purely verbal, but it is doubtful whether this would always work, and in any case the distinction between a verbal and a factual mistake is not very easy to draw. In sum, I regard this as an open question, and consequently hold the notion of an incorrigible proposition to be at least problematic. But this being so, it is desirable to avoid having it play an essential rôle in our analysis of knowledge.

I conclude that to make it a condition of *A*'s knowing *p* that he should have good evidence for *p* is not satisfactory. The question is what to put in its place. A suggestion which I have made is that we should substitute the condition that *A* has the right, in the sense of being entitled, to be sure that *p*. But now the objection may be raised that this is no improvement. For what is it that gives *A* the right to be sure that *p*? Surely it can only be that he has evidence *q*, which strongly supports *p*. But this would not serve the purpose, unless he had the right to be sure that *q*, and so again *ad infinitum*. Even though we have refrained from writing a proviso about evidence into our definition of knowledge, we still land in the same infinite regress.

This is a plausible objection, but it depends on an assumption which I believe to be false. The assumption is that what gives one the right to be sure of a proposition can only be the fact that one believes some other proposition, suitably related to the first, of which one also has the right to be sure. Against this I want to maintain that in certain cases one acquires the right to be sure of a proposition not through holding any other beliefs, but simply because one is having or has had certain experiences. What for example, gives me the right to be sure that this is a sheet of paper? Well, partly my seeing what I now do, partly the fact that my past experiences have been such that I can identify sheets of paper when I see them. But for this it is not necessary that I should believe any propositions about the contents of my present visual field, other than what is entailed by my taking this to be a sheet of paper, or about the character of my past experience. It is enough that I am having the experience that I am and that I have acquired the necessary skill in identifying what I see. Of course I may go astray. I may on this basis come to hold a false belief. In that case my claim to knowledge fails, because the condition that what I claim to know to be true is violated, but it does not necessarily follow that I did not have the right to be sure. We are not demanding infallibility.

In the same way, if I am asked how I know that something or other happened in the past, very often the best answer I can give is that I remember it. Again, this does not exclude the possibility that I am mistaken: what I think that I remember may not in fact have happened. Even so, in normal circumstances, my seeming to remember that something happened does give me the right to be sure that it did happen. And here too what supports my belief that the event in question occurred is just that the belief arises out of the memory-experience rather than that I believe some further proposition which is descriptive of this experience. I should not, indeed, be able to formulate such a proposition otherwise than by just repeating 'I remember'.

If this view is correct, it explains why it seems improper to ask how I know such things as that I am not now in pain, or that I remember making a telephone call a few minutes ago, or that I see a sheet of paper in front of me. It is not that I don't know these things, or that it is meaningless, or a misuse of the word 'know' to say that I know them, but rather that the question 'How do you know?' is a request for evidence, a demand that you adduce some other proposition which supports the proposition which you claim to know, and in cases of this kind the request for further evidence is out of place, because your right to be sure of the proposition which you are advancing is based not on the truth of any other belief which you hold but just on your actually having the experience of which the proposition is an interpretation. If you are then asked to say what this experience is, your answer will indeed appear to beg the question. I can be confident of the truth of my belief that this is a sheet of paper because it arises out of an experience which I am now having. And what is this experience? That of seeing a sheet of paper. The appearance of circularity, so far as this example goes, would indeed be less striking if I were able to describe my experience in terms of sense-data; but whatever other advantages the introduction of sense-data might have, it would not affect the present issue otherwise than by making it necessary to change the example. The proposition of which my experience would give me the right to be sure would then be a proposition about sense-data; and the description of my experience in terms of sense-data would present the same appearance of circularity.

Nevertheless the circularity is only apparent. Though I may not be able to describe my experience otherwise than by reaffirming the proposition of which I am claiming that it gives me the right to be sure, I am not in fact using this proposition to justify itself. What justifies my belief in the proposition is the factual relation of the belief to the experience which the proposition describes. This relation is causal: the filiation of the belief is complex; it depends in part upon my having formed the habit of interpreting my experiences in a certain way, but the existence of the experience is a causal factor. It is not necessary, however, that I should be aware of this. If, in order to be justified in holding the belief, I had both to know that I was having the appropriate experience and know that the belief was causally related to it, we should again be embarked on an infinite regress. All that is necessary is that the experience should in fact occur and that the belief should in fact arise out of it, whether I am aware of this or not. In practice one generally would be aware of it, but the point is that this knowledge is not required for grounding the belief. The ground is furnished directly by the experience.

We can see now that the defenders of incorrigible propositions had the right idea. If they went astray, it was in thinking that they could not afford to forgo the demand for infallibility. And the reason for this was that they also made the false assumption that one belief could be justified only by another, and so were led to introduce infallible beliefs, as the only way of putting a stop to the regress. They were right, however, in that the propositions which they picked out as incorrigible were just those which are not supported by beliefs, not even by self-justifying beliefs in the propositions themselves, and still less by beliefs in other propositions, but draw their support directly from experience. Once this is seen, the question whether, and if so how, one can be mistaken about these propositions loses much of its importance. For the fact that one is justified in accepting a proposition because it is an interpretation of some experience that one is having does not exclude the possibility of its being a misinterpretation. As I said before, we are not requiring infallibility, though it is still open to anyone to argue that we are sometimes accorded it. One can turn out to be wrong and still have had the right to be sure.

An interesting question into which I cannot enter here is how to delimit the class of propositions which are in this sense directly known. It seems clear that a distinction has to be made between propositions which are to be accepted as interpretations of experiences, that is to say, propositions which the owners of the experiences which they interpret are entitled to accept just because of the occurrence of these experiences, and propositions which can be justified only as inferences from other propositions; but it is not obvious exactly where the line is to be drawn. I think it may turn out that this distinction is not sharp and that it is even to a certain extent arbitrary.

There is one final point which I should like to mention, because some people might regard it as a blemish in my argument. One consequence of accepting the definition of knowledge which I have proposed is that the question whether or not one knows something to be true depends not only on what might be called the objective features of the situation, that is, the truth of the proposition concerned, and the strength and grounds of the subject's belief in it, but also on the standards which are being applied. Two people may agree about all the factual items and yet disagree on the question whether this is to be counted as a case of knowledge, because one of them takes a stricter view than the other of what entitles anyone to be sure. A good example of this is provided by the case of propositions about the future. There are those who are reluctant to say that one can ever know, really know, anything about the future: however strong our evidence may be we are never entitled to be sure that God or nature will not surprise us. Others, of whom I am one, admit the possibility of surprise, but think that there are many instances in which it is negligible. I think that I know quite a lot about the future, though most of it is negative. I know, for example, that within the next few hours I shan't, like Alice in Wonderland, suddenly sprout to a height of more than six feet or shrink to one of less than six inches. At the same time, if someone insists that I don't know even this, I am not bound to hold that what he says is false. I may just recognize that he is employing a different standard and let him go his way, while still preferring my own standard and no doubt thinking that I have good reasons for doing so. One or other of us might try to claim that his position was more in accordance with common usage, that most English-speaking people, or most English-speaking people who had reached a certain level of education, used the word 'know' in accordance with his criterion rather than his opponent's. But in a case of this kind, I do not think that such an approach would be of much interest. The investigation would be difficult to conduct in a way which gave it any scientific value, and the result would not settle the issue. The loser might just take it as showing that the majority of his co-linguists were less enlightened than himself.

The conclusion that whether someone knows something is partly a matter for decision may disturb some people: it does not disturb me. For in the main what is interesting about the fact that someone knows something is not that we decide to give him his certificate, allow him the right to be sure, but that what he knows is so. If I am told that I have not the right to be sure that I shall not shrink to a height of six inches in the next hour, I may become worried. Perhaps there is a new drug which does these strange things to people; perhaps someone has slipped it into my food. But then if I learn that it is just on the general ground that one cannot know anything about the future, I relax again. Very well, if you are going to be so very strict, then by your standards I have not the right to be quite sure. All the same, I will bet you anything you like that it will not happen.

9

HAS AUSTIN REFUTED THE SENSE-DATUM THEORY?

In the series of lectures, entitled *Sense and Sensibilia*, which Mr G. J. Warnock has reconstructed from J. L. Austin's manuscript notes, Austin makes a sharp and witty attack upon the theory of sense-data. The texts which he singles out for criticism are Professor H. H. Price's book on *Perception*, Mr Warnock's study of *Berkeley*, and most of all my own *Foundations of Empirical Knowledge*. Though he says that he chose these books for their merits rather than their deficiencies, he sets about my book especially in a rather scornful way. It may even be questioned whether he is always scrupulously fair. I am not, however, now concerned to vindicate the honour of my self of twenty-seven years ago. My reason for taking up the subject is that it is widely believed that the sense-datum theory succumbed to Austin's attack. The purpose of this essay is to see how far this belief is justified.

The best way to achieve this will be to examine Austin's arguments in detail. I make them just seventeen in number and shall go through them very nearly in the order in which they occur in the book. As might be expected, they vary a good deal in their depth, and there is a certain amount of overlap between them.

(1) Austin's first objection to the sense-datum theorist is that the contrast which he tries to draw between perceiving physical objects, like chairs and tables, on the one hand and sensing sense-data on the other, is a typical philosopher's over-simplification. The plain man does not speak in such a way as to imply that what he perceives is always something like furniture. He talks of seeing, or, in the appropriate instances, feeling or hearing or smelling, people, people's voices, rivers, mountains, flames, rainbows, shadows, pictures on cinema screens, pictures in books, vapours, gases. Austin asks ironically whether all these are material things, the suggestion being that it is a mistake to lump them all under one heading.

He has a point here. Sense-datum theorists have tended to confine their examples to 'moderate-sized specimens of dry goods', as Austin characteristically calls them, perhaps for the reason that they do constitute the largest single category of things that we take ourselves to perceive. And the result of this has been that in drawing a distinction between material things of this sort and sense-data, they have not sufficiently considered how such things as shadows and photographs fit into their scheme. For instance, they have sometimes fallen into the inconsistency of both treating sense-data as private objects and citing mirror-images as instances of them. Nevertheless, I hope to show that the tendency of sense-datum theorists to rely on a limited set of stock examples has not made any serious difference to the validity of their arguments.

(2) Austin goes on to take exception to my quoting Locke's dictum that 'the certainty of things existing *in rerum natura*, when we have the testimony of our senses for it, is not only as great as our frame can attain to, but as our condition needs'. He says that it contains a strong *suggestio falsi*, which is that there is *any* uncertainty about the existence, say, of a chair when it is a few yards in front of me and I am looking at it in broad daylight. The plain man would say, quite correctly: 'Well, if that is not seeing a real chair, I don't know what is.'

This argument goes much deeper; indeed, it touches on the fundamental point at issue. The fact on which Austin is relying is that one would not ordinarily say that the existence of the chair was uncertain unless one had some *special* reason for supposing it to be so, such as that the light was very bad, or that one had something wrong with one's eyes, or that this would be a particularly odd place to find a chair, or whatever. But if one is going to say that the existence of the chair is uncertain even when the conditions under which one takes oneself to be perceiving it are normal in the sense that they give one no reason for suspecting anything to be amiss, then the distinction which we mark in this kind of context by contrasting what is certain with what is uncertain will cease to have any application.

This is true, so far as it goes. But if we consider the reasons which have led sense-datum theorists to speak of uncertainty in this connection, we shall find that they remain untouched. The most that is proved against them is that they have chosen a misleading way of expressing the point that they were trying to make. As I see it, this point is a purely logical one. It is that in any such situation as that described by Austin the occurrence of the experience which gives rise to the perceptual judgement is logically consistent with the judgement's being false. Even if we have a use for the word 'certain' which makes it proper to say, in these circumstances, that it is certain that the chair exists, its existence is still not logically deducible from that of the experience: the certainty in question is not based on a logical entailment. Of course, if the situation is described as that of someone's looking at a chair, the question is begged: it is then already implied that in supposing that he sees a chair the observer is not mistaken. But the point on which the sense-datum theorist takes his stand is that the situation does not have to be described in this way; indeed, he will argue that to insist on describing it in this way is to hamper any attempt to arrive at a satisfactory analysis of perception. The kind of description which is needed for this purpose is one that will uncover rather than conceal the fact that the observer could be having the experience in question even though the physical object which he takes himself to be perceiving did not exist: that the occurrence of the experience is consistent with his having been hypnotized or otherwise deluded. So, when the sense-datum theorist says, no doubt misleadingly, that even in the most favourable conditions of perception it remains uncertain whether the chair exists, what he must be understood to mean is that the statement that the chair exists does not follow logically from any statement, or indeed from any finite number of statements, which are limited to describing the content of the observer's experience.

Admittedly, this way of speaking also begs the question. It commits us to holding not only that in making even so simple a judgement as that this is a chair one is going beyond the evidence which is yielded by the senses on this occasion, but that it is possible to formulate a statement which does not go beyond the evidence, in the sense that it carries no implication about the status of what is seen. A statement of this kind, which I propose to call an 'Experiential Statement', will simply record the presence, say, of a visual pattern. It will leave it entirely open whether the observer is right in treating this pattern as a manifestation of the kind of physical object which he claims to perceive, or indeed of a physical entity of any sort at all. These are the assumptions that lie at the root of the sense-datum theory, and it is only by showing them to be unwarranted that the theory can be cut off at its source.

(3) In fact, Austin makes very little attempt to do this. The only argument which he brings forward is that we do not normally speak of verifying statements about physical objects through verifying statements of any other kind. Taking as his example the statement

'That is a pig', he roundly denies that there are or have to be 'statements of the form, "It looks...", "It sounds...", "It smells...", of which we could say straight off that "That is a pig" entails them'.[1] 'We learn the word "pig", as we learn the vast majority of words for ordinary things, ostensively—by being told, in the presence of the animal, "*That* is a pig"; and thus, though certainly we learn what sort of thing it is to which the word "pig" can and can't be properly applied, we don't go through any kind of intermediate stage of relating the word "pig" to a lot of *statements* about the way things look, or sound, or smell. The word is just not introduced into our vocabulary in this way. Thus, though of course we come to have certain expectations as to what will and won't be the case when a pig is in the offing, it is wholly artificial to represent these expectations in the guise of *statements entailed by* "That is a pig". And for just this reason it is, at best, wholly artificial to speak as if *verifying* that some animal is a pig consists in checking up on the statements entailed by "That is a pig". If we do think of verification in this way, certainly difficulties abound; we don't know quite where to begin, how to go on, or where to stop. But what this shows is, not that "That is a pig" is very difficult to verify or incapable of being conclusively verified, but that this is an impossible travesty of verification. If the procedure of verification were rightly described in this way, then indeed we couldn't say just what would constitute conclusive verification that some animal was a pig. But this doesn't show that there is actually any difficulty at all, usually, in verifying that an animal is a pig, if we have occasion to do so; it shows only that what verification *is* has been completely misrepresented.'[2]

And there he leaves it. He does not tell us what he thinks that verification is, but presumably he takes it to consist in carrying out certain familiar procedures, inspecting the object in question in various ways. His main point is that in a case of this sort, as opposed, say, to the case in which we are testing a scientific theory, the process of verification does not involve our checking the truth of statements which are deduced from the statement which we are verifying. And it is on this ground apparently that he concludes that 'it is not true of sentences about "material things" that *as such* they must be supported by or based on evidence'.[3]

Now it is perfectly true that when it is a question of an object which we have no difficulty in identifying, like the pig in Austin's example, we do not normally go through the process of saying to ourselves:

[1] *Sense and Sensibilia* (1962), p. 121. [2] Ibid. [3] Ibid., p. 123.

'It looks so and so, it feels so and so, it has such and such a smell, therefore probably, almost certainly, it is a so and so.' We just take it straight off to be a pig, or whatever. It is true also that in a situation of this kind it would sound odd to ask someone what evidence he had that he saw a pig. We should say this only if we had some reason to distrust his identification. Not that it is always incorrect to speak of having evidence for propositions of this type. If I detected the pig by its footprints, I could be said to be going on evidence: perhaps also if I detected its presence only by its squeak or by its smell. For these are indications that a pig is, or has been, in the neighbourhood. But seeing a pig in perfectly normal conditions is more than merely having an indication of its presence. So Austin elsewhere rebukes Professor Wisdom for speaking of perceiving all the signs of bread when one goes to the larder, sees a loaf in front of one, handles it, tastes it, and so forth. When one sees only a few crumbs, one sees signs of a loaf, but not when one sees the loaf itself. The point here is that seeing signs of x is to some extent *contrasted* with seeing x. In any normal case in which I am seeing or handling a physical object, it is an abuse of language to say that I thereby obtain evidence of its existence, especially if the implication is that the evidence is not conclusive.

All this may be accepted, as a comment on ordinary usage. As a general rule, when one speaks of having evidence for a proposition p, one expects it to be understood that one is not entirely convinced of the truth of p, that one does not answer for its being more than probable. If I think that I know that p, I am underplaying my hand, and so misleading my audience, if I say no more than that I have good evidence for p. It would, however, be rash to lay any weight upon this in the present context, since my knowing that p is certainly not inconsistent with my having good evidence for it. On the contrary, in very many instances it would not be proper for me to claim to know that p unless I did have such evidence. It is just that I am taken to commit myself more strongly to the truth of p by straightforwardly asserting it than by asserting that there is good evidence for it, and our habit is not to make the weaker claim when we are in a position to make the stronger one. But it does not follow from this that when I know that p I have not got evidence for it, any more than, from the fact that when I think I know something, it is misleading for me to say only that I believe it, it follows that if I do know something I do not believe it. Consequently Austin's example fails to prove his point. The fact that when one is looking at a pig, under normal conditions, it is not good usage to speak of having evidence for its existence, in no way entails that seeming to see the pig is not having evidence for its existence. The truth is that it is very strong evidence: and it does not cease to be evidence just because of its strength.

Against this it may be argued that to say that one has evidence for a proposition *p* is to imply that one's knowledge of *p* is indirect, in the sense that one is inferring *p* from some other proposition *q* which supports *p* but does not entail it. But surely my belief in the existence of the table in front of me is not the outcome of an inference. I may infer from its appearance that it is not a new table or that it is not an antique, but I do not have to infer that it exists. Since I see it and touch it no inference is needed.

This is the old argument about certainty, in a slightly different guise, and it is to be met with the same answer. Of course it would be absurd to suggest that the perception of familiar objects normally involves any conscious process of inference. On the rare occasions on which we are unable to identify an object, whether because it is of a kind with which we are not familiar, or because the conditions under which we are perceiving it are unfavourable, we may try to work out what sort of thing it is, but even in this case we do not have to work out that it is, for example, a solid three-dimensional object. There might be situations where even this was in doubt, but the point is that they are exceptional. The rare cases in which our judgements of perception do contain an inference stand in contrast with the normal case in which they do not.

Again the answer is that this is true, but not to the purpose. For those who say that even the most straightforward judgement of perception like 'This is a table' embodies an inference are trying to make exactly the same logical point as are those who say that all such judgements are uncertain. In both instances the contention is that the judgement goes beyond the data on which it is grounded, that it claims more than is contained in the experience which gives rise to it, that it makes assumptions which may be false, consistently with this experience. The question whether these assumptions are made consciously or unconsciously, hesitantly or spontaneously, is irrelevant.

But is this contention valid? Is one entitled to speak of 'the content of an experience' as distinct from the judgement of perception to which it gives rise? Some purists may object to this 'philosophical' use of the word 'experience' altogether, and even if this is allowed to pass, and such expressions as 'visual experience' are admitted as technical terms, it may still be said that my present visual experience just is the experience of seeing a table. How then can this kind of resistance be overcome?

The best way that I can think of overcoming it is to draw attention to the far-reaching implications of even so unambitious a statement as that this is a table. To begin with, it commits us to all the assumptions which are involved in asserting the existence of any physical object of this type. It is required of the object at least that it shall occupy a position in three-dimensional space, that it shall endure throughout a period of time, that it shall be accessible to touch as well as to sight, that it shall be accessible to different observers, and that it should continue to exist even when no one is perceiving it. Not all these assumptions hold of every type of object. Shadows and images, for example, are accessible only to the sense of sight, and there is a sense in which they do not occupy space, although they are spatially located; but in their case also it is required that they be accessible to different observers, and that they be capable of existing unperceived.

Now one way of looking at these assumptions is to regard them as setting the framework into which the results of our observations are to be fitted. For example, in dealing with Berkeley's contention that things cannot exist unperceived, I believe that we should interpret him not as raising a question of empirical fact but rather as denying the legitimacy of a fundamental element in this framework and also as suggesting an alternative to it. I do not here propose to consider whether Berkeley's position is tenable, or what other framework there might be into which our observations could consistently be fitted. I only remark that this is a proper question for philosophical discussion and that it cannot be settled merely by a study of the ways in which we habitually speak.

There is, however, another way in which these common-sense assumptions may be taken. In particular instances, they can be construed empirically as implying that some particular object passes the tests which the general scheme imposes. If this is a material thing of the kind I take it to be it must be tangible as well as visible; in the appropriate circumstances it must be perceived by others besides myself; it must satisfy the causal criteria of persistence; for instance, if the room is left empty and I return in a few minutes' time to find that the supposed table has vanished or been displaced, there must be some way of accounting for this; some explanation which will fit in with our general theories about the ways in which such things can happen.

But do I see that all this is so? There is indeed a sense in which I can be said to see that this thing is tangible, public and persistent. Namely, it looks like a perfectly ordinary table, and ordinary tables do have these properties. But, in making this judgement, I am drawing on my considerable past experience. I have found out that when things look like this, they normally do satisfy these further conditions. But surely this is an inductive inference. One starts with certain visual clues, and on the basis of these clues, one leaps to one's far-reaching conclusions. But the conclusions are not contained in the clues. If I may speak of a visual presentation in an entirely neutral sense, which carries no implication about the status of what is presented, then the existence of this visual presentation leaves it open whether the further conditions, of the object's being tangible and so forth, will be satisfied. In the vast majority of cases they will be satisfied, but sometimes they are not. For instance, I might have been hypnotized to see a table here, when there really was not one, or it might be a trick of the light. But then, it will be said, it would not look like a perfectly ordinary table. I shall deal with this objection later on.

So far I have been speaking only of the inferences which are involved, as I maintain, in taking this thing which I seem to see in front of me to be a physical object, as opposed, say, to an image or an hallucination. But when we make a perceptual judgement we do not normally content ourselves with assuming that we are confronted with a physical object of some sort or other. We identify it as a thing of some specific kind, and this brings in a number of further assumptions. For instance, in identifying something which I see as an apple, I assume not only that it is tangible but that it has a certain characteristic texture. I make assumptions about the way it smells and tastes and about the material of which it is made, for example that it is a fleshy fruit and not an object made of wax. I may also be assuming something about its origin, for example that it was grown on a tree, and about its causal properties. I assume further that it has other faces than the one which is turned towards me, that it has an inside, that it is not hollow. But can it seriously be maintained that I see all this? Of course it is perfectly correct for me to say that I see the apple: but this just proves the point that in making a statement of this kind I commit myself to the existence of much more than I do strictly see; some of what I claim to exist is visible in principle but not seen by me on this occasion;

and some things, like the taste and texture of the apple in our example, are not an affair of sight at all.

It should be clear from what I have just said that I am not suggesting that the fact that normally neither the whole of the surface nor the interior of a solid object is visible to a given observer at any one time invalidates his claim to see the object. For, as it is ordinarily interpreted, this claim is consistent with his not seeing the whole of the object. Or rather, when we talk of seeing the object as a whole, we do not mean that we see every part of it. There is perhaps some vacillation here in ordinary usage. As Moore puts it: 'In the case of any opaque object, that you are seeing it *entails* that you are seeing part of its surface: but that you are seeing some part of its surface does not entail that you are seeing it if the part is very small; we should often rightly say "Well, I see a little bit of your arm, but I can hardly say that I am seeing your arm".'[1] Moore goes on to argue that there are two different senses of the word 'see' at work here; so that when I say, truly, that I see the moon, even though part of it is hidden by cloud, or, in the case of the unobscured full moon, even though only one side of it is turned towards me, I am using the word 'see' in a different sense from that in which I use it when I say that I see only one side of the moon, or only a part of its surface. Whether he is right on this point will depend on the criteria which we use for deciding what is a single sense of a word like 'see'; and this is a question to which I doubt if an investigation of ordinary usage would return any clear answer. Neither, as I shall argue later on, is it of any great importance. Probably, what Moore's example should be taken to show is that we allow ourselves some flexibility, in ordinary usage, in deciding what is seen. It is a somewhat arbitrary question how much of an object we have to see in order to be able to say correctly that we are seeing it rather than just some part of it.

However this may be, the fact that we commonly do not see the whole of any object provides yet another ground for holding that our judgements of perception go beyond the data on which they are based. I have been referring so far only to visual perception, but exactly the same arguments apply *mutatis mutandis* to what we perceive by touch. In the case of the other senses it will hardly be disputed that our judgements are inferential. If I identify an object only by the noise which it makes, or by its taste or smell, then however quick and sure my identification, it embodies an inference from an observed effect to the existence of what may in this instance be an unobserved cause. The

[1] G. E. Moore, *Commonplace Book*, ed. Lewy (1963), p. 330.

part played by inference is more easily overlooked in the cases of sight and touch, largely because we habitually speak of seeing or touching physical objects themselves rather than their visual or tactual effects. This may be taken to prove that the inferences which we make in these cases are not causal. It does not prove that they do not exist. They are involved, as I have shown, first in the assumption that the things which we perceive by sight and touch are public and persistent, secondly in the assumption that they have parts which are not perceived by us on the given occasion, and thirdly in their identification as things of such and such a sort, in so far as this carries implications about their causal properties, their history and the materials of which they are made.

This being so, I do not see how it can reasonably be denied that our ordinary judgements of perception go beyond the evidence on which they are based. Another way of expressing this fact would be to say that they are the conclusions of inductive inferences. But if they are the conclusions of inductive inferences, it ought to be possible to formulate the premisses. It ought to be possible to make statements which are tailored to our experiences, in the sense that they offer a qualitative description of what is sensibly presented on a given occasion, without carrying any further implication of any kind whatsoever. I admit that this is not an easy undertaking, but I have yet to come across any arguments which convinced me that it was not feasible. At least I am safe in saying that if there are conclusive arguments against it, Austin does not produce them.

(4) What he does produce is a further argument against those who say that what we take to be the perception of a physical object never yields certainty as to its existence. This argument, which has also been used by Ryle, is that 'talk of deception only makes sense against a general background of non-deception'.[1] On the rare occasions when our senses do deceive us, we are able to discover this because we check the odd cases against the normal ones. It follows that there can be no question of our being generally deceived.

This argument has gained wider currency than it deserves. It is not even effective against the sceptic, since it establishes no more than that we arrive at the conclusion that some perceptual judgements are false because they conflict with others which we take to be true. But this gives us no guarantee, in any particular instance, that the judgement which we take to be true will not itself turn out to be false.

[1] *Sense and Sensibilia*, p. 11.

Moreover, so far from refuting the contention that perceptual judgements are uncertain, in the technical sense that they go beyond the evidence on which they are based, the argument tacitly admits it. For what characterizes the deviant case is just that the assumptions which are involved in the perceptual judgement are not corroborated by further experience, whereas in the normal case they are.

(5) After some further remarks about deception, in the course of which he makes the valid point that there are many different ways of being deceived, Austin goes on to criticize the use which philosophers have made of expressions like 'directly see'. He belabours the obvious fact that they are not using these expressions in any ordinary sense and then complains that they give no explanation or definition of the way in which they are using them. Although Austin does not mention him, the technical use of expressions like 'directly see' gained currency mainly through the work of Moore, and it is in fact a fair criticism of Moore that he did not lay down any definite rules for their use, perhaps because he did not sufficiently realize that it was technical. It is, however, reasonably clear that he intended these expressions to be understood in the same non-committal fashion as the designations of the sensibly 'given' to which they were meant to be correlative. To say of something that it was directly seen was to refer to it as a visual datum, without implying anything about its status. A statement of this kind would, therefore, be a version of what I have been calling an experiential statement, and the force of the word 'directly' is to make the point that these statements provide the evidence on which all our perceptual judgements are based. I do not think that this is an altogether happy usage, but, if I am right in what I have so far been saying, the point itself is valid.

(6) Moore was much concerned with the question whether the objects which we directly see are ever identical with the surfaces of material things. He was inclined to think that they could not be but was never quite certain of this. Austin complains, justifiably, that it is not at all clear what the question means. There may be a way of interpreting it which would leave the answer in doubt, but certainly, as I have construed expressions like 'directly see', it would be contradictory to speak of directly seeing material things, or any parts of them. The reason is that the reference to material things brings in assumptions which the use of these expressions is intended to exclude.

In *The Foundations of Empirical Knowledge* I made the true historical remark that what had led philosophers to deny that they were directly aware of material things was their acceptance of the so-called argument from illusion. This argument, which has played a very large part in the theory of perception, is based on four sets of admitted empirical facts. These are, first, the existence of hallucinations, mainly exemplified by cases of seeing objects which are not really there, such as Macbeth's dagger and the drunkard's pink rats; secondly, cases, like that of mistaking a wax figure for a flesh and blood policeman at Madame Tussaud's, where an object is misidentified; thirdly, the variations in the appearance of an object which may be due to perspective, the condition of the light, or the presence of some distorting medium, the stock examples here being the large tower which looks small when seen from a distance, the round coin which looks elliptical when seen from an angle, the straight stick which looks bent when it is immersed in water, and the white wall which looks green when seen through green spectacles; finally, the dependence of the way an object looks, or otherwise appears to us, on the nature of the physical conditions under which it is perceived and on the physiological and psychological states of the observer.

The main comment which Austin has to make upon these facts is that since they are not all of the same kind it is misleading to lump them all together. He also points out, quite correctly, that in many of the instances in question the word 'illusion' is a misnomer, since they are not cases in which the observer is deceived by the appearances or likely to be so. Except for certain cases of mistaken identification, they are not like the illusions which are created by a conjuror.

These points are unimportant. Let it be granted that the argument from illusion is infelicitously named. The question is whether anything of philosophical interest can be inferred from the facts which it assembles. Admittedly, some of the conclusions which have been drawn from them are very dubious. For instance, they have been taken to prove that strictly speaking we never perceive physical objects at all, or at least that we never perceive them as they really are. The facts which have been taken to justify this conclusion are principally those of my fourth class. It is mainly because of the causal conditions of perception that it has been thought necessary to draw a sort of curtain between things as they appear to us and things as they are in themselves. What exactly is meant by this distinction and how far it is necessary or even tenable are questions which need to be examined in some detail, and it is rather surprising that Austin makes no attempt at all to measure the force of any such causal arguments. Though it is clear that they cannot legitimately be used in the service of thoroughgoing scepticism, since their premisses themselves incorporate a good deal of alleged knowledge about the external world, they do create at least a *prima facie* difficulty for naïve realism.

What the argument from illusion, at least as represented in my first three sets of facts, does clearly establish is the humdrum conclusion that there is not a perfect coincidence between appearance and reality. It shows that if we were always to take appearances as it were at their face value we should sometimes go wrong and, what is important here, that we should go wrong predictively. When we misidentify an object, or misjudge its properties, or misperceive its status, taking it for example to be a physical solid when it is in fact an image, we issue a draft on our further experiences which they fail to honour. But this again implies that our judgements of perception are, in my sense, inferential.

It should be noted that in order to arrive at this conclusion we do not need to rely on the empirical fact that illusions, in this sense, actually occur. That is, it is not necessary for this purpose that we should ever actually be deceived by appearances or even that anything should ever actually appear in any way different from what it is. It is enough that these things be possible; and this possibility is already secured by the fact that our judgements of perception go beyond the data on which they are based. To the extent that they make the venture, they can also come to grief, and this would remain true even if they were never in fact mistaken. At the same time, by directing our attention to cases in which our judgements of perception diverge from the phenomenal description of what is sensibly presented to us, and also to cases in which the assumptions which are involved in them break down, the argument from illusion reinforces the contention that 'illusions', in this special sense, are abstractly possible, by adducing concrete examples of them. The argument, therefore, retains a certain usefulness, in spite of its unhappy title and in spite of the misconstructions which have sometimes been put upon it.

(7) In my exposition of the argument from illusion and elsewhere in *The Foundations of Empirical Knowledge*, I had used the words 'look', 'appear' and 'seem' more or less interchangeably. Austin protests that these words are not synonymous in ordinary usage and goes on to show that each of them is used in subtly different ways. He has some interesting things to say on this topic, but nothing that is relevant to the main argument. All that the sense-datum theorist requires is that the

purely phenomenal sense in which he employs words like 'look' and 'appear' shall be legitimate, and once this is granted, it does not greatly matter to him what word is chosen to mark it. Attempts have indeed been made to show that this sense is not legitimate, but they have not been successful. For example the suggestion that what we must mean by saying that something *looks* round is that we are inclined to judge that it *is* round is clearly unacceptable. For why should we be inclined to judge that the thing is round? Surely, in most cases, it is because of the way it looks, in just the phenomenal sense that is in question.

The most substantial point which Austin makes under this heading is that 'the way things look is, in general, just as much a fact about the world, just as open to public confirmation or challenge, as the way things are. I am not disclosing a fact about *myself*, but about petrol, when I say that petrol looks like water.'[1] This is true, but the fact remains that this most common dispositional sense of words like 'look' rests upon an occurrent sense. We determine how something of a certain kind would look to normal observers under normal conditions on the basis of the way things of that kind do look to particular persons on particular occasions. So once again, inevitably, the phenomenal sense is fundamental.

(8) We next come to a more central issue. Price and I had maintained, in my words, that 'there is no intrinsic difference in kind between those of our perceptions that are veridical in their presentation of material things and those that are delusive'. Having assumed from the start that there are sense-data, Price makes the same point by saying that 'there is no qualitative difference between normal sense-data as such and abnormal sense-data as such'. After recording his objection both to my use of the word 'perceptions' and to Price's assumption about sense-data, Austin queries the truth of our assertions. Could it be seriously suggested, he asks, that dreaming of being presented to the Pope is qualitatively indistinguishable from actually being presented to him? Seeing a bright green after-image against a white wall is not, he maintains, exactly like seeing a bright green patch actually on the wall; seeing a white wall through blue spectacles is not exactly like seeing a blue wall; seeing a stick refracted in water is not exactly like seeing a bent stick; seeing pink rats in *delirium tremens* is not exactly like really seeing pink rats.[2] Finally he accuses Price and myself of assuming that it must be the case that veridical and delusive experiences are not as such qualitatively distinguishable because if they were distinguishable

[1] *Sense and Sensibilia*, p. 43. [2] *Ibid.*, pp. 48–9.

we should not be deluded. And he replies to this that from the fact that we may be taken in by failing to distinguish *A* from *B* it does not follow that *A* and *B* are indistinguishable. It just may be that we are not good at distinguishing things or that we have not looked hard enough.

Much of this is true, but also, I think, beside the point. What Price and I were maintaining was not that it would never be possible to find any qualitative difference between experiences known to be veridical and experiences known to be delusive, in a sense of the word 'delusive' which did not necessarily imply that anyone was actually deluded, but only that appearances were in some way deceptive. It was rather that from a consideration of the experience alone it was not possible to tell to which category it belonged. No doubt, if I have both dreamed of being presented to the Pope and actually been presented to him, these experiences seem very different to me when I compare them in retrospect. But at the time when I am dreaming of being presented to the Pope is it obvious to me that this is not really happening? Is it always clear from the quality of the dream itself that it is only a dream? Plainly not, otherwise no one would ever suffer from nightmares. And the same applies to the other examples. Perhaps it is always possible to find some qualitative difference between the experience of looking at a blue wall in a good light and that of looking at a white wall through blue spectacles. The point is that if one did not know about this distorting factor, one could not infer just from the character of the experience that the wall was not the colour that it looked. Once one has learned about perspective, refraction and so forth one can, usually though not in fact invariably, discriminate between delusive and veridical experiences. But this is the result of a fairly elaborate process of finding out about the ways in which experiences of different kinds are normally connected. There is nothing in the character of any experience, considered by itself, which licenses the inference that it does not present things as they really are. Austin's arguments do not bear against this contention and I am not even sure that he would have disputed it.

(9) Austin goes on to protest that even if it were allowable to speak of sensing sense-data in cases like that of Macbeth's dagger or the straight stick which looks bent when seen in water, there is no warrant for extending this usage to cases of veridical perception. To justify this extension, Price had employed a rhetorical argument which I had accepted with some reservations. The argument appealed to considerations of continuity. If, for example, one is walking towards a distant

object, it is implausible, we said, to maintain that one begins by sensing a series of sense-data, and then suddenly at the point where the object looks to be the size and shape that it really is one starts directly seeing a physical object instead. Austin says that he can see no force at all in this argument. I should have thought that, for his purposes, he might have done better to allow it some force, but turn it the other way. It could be maintained that since it is implausible to say that one is not seeing the same kind of thing all along, then from the start one is seeing a physical object and not a series of sense-data. But in any case, whatever its force, this argument is not needed by the sense-datum theorist. For if he can make good his initial step, that in any case in which anything of whatever kind is perceived, something is directly apprehended, or, as I prefer to put it, that every statement which claims perception of a physical object is founded on an experiential statement, and if he chooses to use the term 'sense-data' to refer to the 'objects' which figure in experiential statements, he will already have established the conclusion that every case of perception, whether veridical or delusive, involves the sensing of sense-data. The proof that physical objects do not figure in experiential statements has already been given with reference to Moore's question whether they can ever be directly seen. It can be formulated succinctly by saying that whereas statements which refer to physical objects are always in some measure proleptic, experiential statements are not.

(10) The next argument is directed against me personally rather than against sense-datum theorists in general. My excuse for mentioning it is that it brings up a point of philosophical importance. I had maintained in *The Foundations of Empirical Knowledge* that what was at issue in the case of rival theories of perception, such as straightforward naïve realism on the one hand and, on the other, Whitehead's and Alexander's theory that things had properties from a point of view, was a choice between different forms of language. And I argued that if one found the naïve realist's way of talking unsatisfactory, one was not forced to adopt the sense-datum terminology. There might be other possibilities, such as choosing to deny the assumption that the real shape, say, of a penny remained the same when one changed the point of view from which one looked at it. Austin found this ridiculous. 'If we allow ourselves this degree of *insouciant* latitude, surely we shall be able to deal – in a *way* of course – with absolutely anything.'[1] But this misses the point. It overlooks the fact that I was not operating within our

[1] *Sense and Sensibilia*, p. 58.

ordinary conceptual scheme but considering a revision of it. Of course I could not, consistently with our present criteria, maintain that the penny changed its shape when it was observed from a different angle. I was not suggesting that people who were operating with these criteria might in fact be mistaken in supposing that the shape of things like pennies remained unaltered unless they underwent some physical change. I was suggesting that we might change our criteria, that we might employ a different method of determining what the shapes of such things really were. It might indeed be that the proposal which I mentioned was not viable, but this could only be decided when it had been worked out in some detail. It could not just be laughed off. I do not reproach Austin for failing to see this, since I did not put the point at issue very clearly. Probably at that time I was not entirely clear about it myself.

The only point of substance which Austin makes in this section is that I was taking it for granted that we were presented with a 'sensible manifold' which it was open to us to characterize in different ways, to organize in accordance with different conceptual schemes. And of course I did make this assumption, surely rightly. I am, however, willing to admit that even so it does not necessarily follow that there are no limits to the forms that this organization can take. It may, for example, be essential that some objects of perception be taken as public, for the reason that a language in which the rules of identity were such that no object perceived by one person could be identified with any object perceived by another would be incoherent. If this were so, as I now think it well may be, one form of phenomenalism could be shown to be untenable. This is, however, a conclusion which can only be reached by trying out such a language and seeing where it breaks down. Merely to point out that we do not ordinarily speak in such a way is nothing to the purpose.

(11) Having reproached me for my cavalier use of the word 'really', Austin proceeds to give an account of the ways in which the word 'real' is actually used. That this account is in some measure defective has been shown by Mr Jonathan Bennett in an excellent article on the same topic, which appeared in the October 1966 issue of *Mind*. Nevertheless Austin does achieve what seems to be his main purpose of showing how multifarious are the uses to which the word 'real' is put. We talk of real ducks as opposed to decoy ducks, real pearls as opposed to cultured pearls, a real sword as opposed to a toy one, and so forth. The fact remains, however, that we do also contrast what is real with

what is only apparent, as in the example 'the penny looks elliptical from this angle but it is really round' and that we do contrast what is real with what is illusory as in the example of the drunkard's seeing pink rats which are not really there. The sense-datum theorist concentrates on these distinctions because they are the ones that are relevant to his argument. The fact that he does not deal with distinctions which are not relevant is not a reproach to him.

(12) Having in view the cases, like that of the penny, in which we contrast the perceptible property, the shape or size or colour, which an object really has, with that which it may only appear to have, I had suggested that our procedure was to identify the object's real properties with those that it normally appeared to have under conditions which afforded the best basis for prediction; for instance, if we see something in a good light we can better predict how it will look in a bad light than *vice versa*. Austin points out that there are many cases in which this distinction is not clearly applicable. For example, we should be hard put to say what was the real colour of the sun or the real shape of a cat. This is true, but it does not prove that my explanation of the distinction was incorrect, in the cases where it does apply. I agree that it does not cover the case where we say of a woman 'That's not the real colour of her hair', on the ground that she has dyed it. I was not concerned with the distinction, also sometimes marked by the word 'real', between the natural and the artificial. Could Austin really (i.e. genuinely) have believed that I was?

(13) The next point is more serious. As I have already indicated, Moore set the fashion of distinguishing between different senses of words like 'see'. The sense in which I see the table was supposed by him to be distinct from that in which I see part of the surface of the table and from the sense in which I see, that is directly see, a sense-datum of the table. He also thought it probable, though not certain, that these two last senses were distinct from one another. To some extent following him, I had suggested that there were at least two senses in which such words were ordinarily used, one in which to say that something was seen implied that it existed but did not imply that it had the qualities which it appeared to have, and one in which to say that something was seen did not admit of its lacking the qualities that it appeared to have, but did not imply that it existed. And I suggested that the sense in which Moore wished to say that we 'saw' sense-data was a fusion of these two. Austin denies that there is any such sense of 'see' as the second of my alleged senses, the one which does not admit of the object's failing to

have the qualities it appears to have, but also does not imply that it exists. But surely, and most surprisingly, he is just wrong here on a question of linguistic fact. Indeed, he himself supplies an example of this usage when he speaks of the drunkard's seeing pink rats. When we say this, we do not imply that the pink rats exist, but equally we do not admit the possibility that the drunkard's pink rats were really green, though he was so drunk that they looked pink to him. It is his hallucination and what he says about it goes. Of course he may misdescribe the colour of the illusory rats, but that is a different question. A mistake of this sort is not of the same order as the mistake which he would be making if he saw what really were grey rats but because of his drunkenness saw them as pink: the criteria are different. Admittedly, my second sense of 'see' is uncommon, but that is because the occasions for employing it are so.

Since he holds that what Moore and others have mistaken for different senses of the word 'see' are at best differences in the nature of the objects seen, Austin goes on to reject an example which I had given of the use of 'see' in different senses. The example was that of someone's saying, in the same perceptual situation, both that he saw a large star and that he saw a silvery speck no bigger than a sixpence. In this instance, Austin denies even that there are different objects. One and the same object, he says, both is a large star and a small speck, just as one and the same object which I saw this morning both is a man shaved in Oxford and a man born in Jerusalem.[1] But here he has been led astray by a false analogy. If one is using the word 'see' in the sense which implies that what is seen exists, it is impossible that one should see an object which is both larger than the earth and no larger than a sixpence, because no such object can exist. Of course one may say with perfect propriety 'that small speck is a large star' but when one says this one is not implying that there *is* an object which is both a small speck and a large star; one is implying that something which from this distance *looks* very small *is* very large. So when one talks in this context of seeing a small speck, the word 'see' does not carry the implication that some small object exists, whereas when one talks of seeing a large star, the word does carry the implication that some large object exists. In this respect, therefore, the uses of the word are different. Whether it is proper to characterize this fact by speaking of there being different 'senses' of the word 'see' is immaterial.

The fact is that when we talk of seeing an object, like a star, we are

[1] *Sense and Sensibilia*, p. 98.

inclined both to attribute to it the properties which we believe that it really has, even though we do not see it *as* having them, and to represent ourselves as seeing whatever properties are phenomenally apparent to us. If these apparent properties are incompatible with those that we think the object really has, we bring in 'phenomenal' objects, like specks and dots and figures, to carry them. This is clearly a step in the direction of the sense-datum terminology, though not one that takes us all the way, since the size of the speck is a matter of how it would look to the generality of observers under normal conditions and not just a matter of how it looks to me on this occasion. For instance, if I suffered from double vision and seemed to see two specks, I should be undergoing an illusion. It is, however, quite natural for me to say, in a case of this kind, not that I seem to see but simply that I see two specks: and then we are admitting sense-data, if it is allowed that what I say is true.

One moral to be drawn from this example is that in dealing with locutions of this kind we must not be too quick to assume that the 'is' is the 'is' of identity. This comes out clearly in such instances as that of pointing to a photograph and saying 'That is my Uncle James' or pointing to a map and saying 'Those are the Pyrenees'. The case of the speck's being a star is more complicated because here there are not two objects, or at least not in the same sense as in the case of the photograph or map. To treat the speck as a representation of the star would be to insinuate a theory of perception rather than to analyse ordinary usage. For common sense, there is only the one object, the star. The puzzle then arises that the properties ascribed to it under one appellation are incompatible with those ascribed to it under another. This looks like an infringement of the law of identity, until it is realized that in talking of the speck we are not referring to an object which is identical with the star, but only to the way the star appears to us. If we go on to treat such appearances as objects in their own right, which we are not bound but may be entitled to do, we cannot consistently identify them with the things of which they are appearances.

(14) I come now to the question of incorrigibility. This is an important question for the theory of knowledge because the admission of incorrigible propositions puts a stop to what otherwise threatens to become an infinite regress.[1] If one holds that to know a proposition p to be true normally involves accepting it on the basis of some other true proposition q which strongly supports p, then it seems to be

[1] See above, pp. 119–23.

required that one should also know *q* to be true; and this leads to an infinite regress unless we come at some stage to propositions which are as it were knowable in their own right, propositions which do not require support from other propositions. If there were propositions with regard to which it made no sense to say that the person who accepted them might, in the circumstances in question, be factually mistaken about their truth, they would fill the bill. The obvious candidates are propositions in which a person refers to his present thoughts and feelings or to the way things currently appear to him. Austin maintains that not even these propositions satisfy the required condition. In particular, he argues that it is possible to be mistaken about the way things appear to one, and this not merely in a verbal sense.

On this point I am not sure whether he is right or wrong. There is no doubt that it is possible to misdescribe the way things appear to one, but it is not clear to me whether there are any cases in which a mistake of this kind ought to count as factual rather than verbal. Since I am on the whole inclined to think that there are, I do not wish to commit myself to the view that my experiential statements are incorrigible. On the other hand, I do wish to maintain the slightly weaker principle that the subject is the final authority with regard to their truth. The criterion for saying that his description was mistaken will be his own decision to revise it.

Even if this weaker principle could be shown to be untenable, it would not be fatal to my main contention that the truth of statements claiming the perception of physical objects is founded on the truth of experiential statements. It would, however, be a weakness in my general position if I were unable to give a satisfactory account of the criteria by which the truth of experiential statements themselves is to be determined.

(15) As I have already indicated, the support which experiential statements give to statements which imply the existence of physical objects never, in my view, amounts to logical entailment. This is sometimes said to have the consequence that statements which imply the existence of physical objects are not conclusively verifiable. Austin objects to this way of speaking, I think justifiably. Though it may be defended on the ground that it is no more than a picturesque way of making a valid logical point about the relation of different classes of statements, the idea which it gives of conclusive verification as an end which is pursued but never attained is anyhow misleading. The position which I now hold is that statements about physical objects are at a theoretical

level with respect to experiential statements. Like all theoretical statements, they are constantly subject to revision, but in any particular instance we always have some latitude in deciding what revisions we shall make.

(16) It may have been noticed that while I have spoken of perceptual statements as being necessarily founded on experiential statements, I have not spoken of their entailing them. The reason for this is that since there are no sharp boundaries to the range of experiences on which a given perceptual statement may be founded, it is impossible to say exactly what disjunction of experiential statements it entails. In *The Foundations of Empirical Knowledge* I made the same point by saying that one's references to material things were imprecise, or vague, in their application to phenomena. Austin takes exception to my speaking of vagueness and imprecision in this way. No doubt I could have expressed myself better, but I think that it was reasonably clear, in the context, what I was intending to say, and I also think that what I was intending to say was true.

(17) Finally, Austin reproaches Warnock for being too indulgent to Berkeley. His grievance is that Warnock concedes to Berkeley what is essentially the position that I have been defending. Warnock allows that, in the case of physical objects, statements about the way things are are founded on statements about the way they seem, and takes issue with Berkeley, as I now think correctly, only in denying that statements about physical objects are reducible to experiential statements. The arguments which Austin brings against him are with one addition a selection of those that I have already reviewed. The additional argument is that 'statements of "immediate perception", so far from being that from which we *advance* to more ordinary statements, are actually arrived at, and are so arrived at in his own account, by *retreating from* more ordinary statements, by progressive hedging. (There's a tiger – there *seems* to be a tiger – it seems *to me* that there's a tiger – it seems to me *now* that there's a tiger – it seems to me now *as if there were* a tiger.) It seems extraordinarily perverse to represent as that on which ordinary statements are based a form of words which, *starting from* and moreover incorporating an ordinary statement, qualifies and hedges it in various ways. You've got to get something on your plate before you can start messing it around.'[1]

This would be an effective argument if the thesis against which it is directed were that we in fact always go through a process of accumu-

[1] *Sense and Sensibilia*, pp. 141–2.

lating experiential statements before we venture to make a perceptual statement. I hope, however, that I have made it clear that in maintaining that perceptual statements are based upon experiential statements one is not implying that they are consciously inferred from them. They are based upon them just in the sense that it is necessary for any perceptual statement to be true that some experiential statement be true, but possible for the experiential statement to be true even though the perceptual statement is false. The thesis that experiential statements are primary, in this sense, is not in the least invalidated by the fact that their rôle is brought to light by what Austin calls the process of retreating from more ordinary statements. It is not invalidated even by the fact that the form of experiential statements is partly determined by that of the conclusions which they are thought to justify. No doubt, with sufficient ingenuity and labour, we could construct a purely sensory vocabulary, which would not draw on the vocabulary which we use to refer to physical objects. The fact would remain that the character of our experiences themselves is affected by our beliefs concerning the physical world, beliefs which are incorporated in the language which we first learn to speak. This is a fact of which too little account has been taken by sense-datum theorists. But while they may fairly be criticized for this, their logical thesis is not affected by it.

After this full and, I hope, fair review of Austin's arguments, I conclude that he has not disposed of the sense-datum theory. In particular, it seems to me that he has entirely failed to establish his conclusions that 'there is no *kind* or *class* of sentences ("propositions") of which it can be said that *as such* . . . they provide the evidence for other sentences' and that 'it is not true of sentences about "material things" that *as such* they must be supported by or based on evidence'.[1] There may be good reasons for accepting these conclusions but, if there are, Austin has not given them. It is, in my view, a tribute to his wit and to the strength of his personality that he was able to persuade so many philosophers that he had succeeded.

[1] *Sense and Sensibilia*, p. 123.

10

PROFESSOR MALCOLM ON DREAMS

I

In a book on *Dreaming*, which he has recently contributed to Mr R. P. Holland's series of *Studies in Philosophical Psychology*, Professor Norman Malcolm sets out to challenge the received opinion that dreams are conscious experiences which are enjoyed during sleep. His aim is to refute philosophers like Descartes and Russell, who draw sceptical conclusions from what they regard as the fact that our waking experiences are not intrinsically distinguishable from the delusive experiences that make up our dreams. Against them, Professor Malcolm argues that our dreams are not delusive experiences, because they are not experiences at all.

He begins by considering a remark of Aristotle's that the soul makes assertions in sleep. The example which Aristotle gives is that of a man who dreams that 'some object approaching is a man or horse' or that 'the object is white or beautiful'. But, says Professor Malcolm, if a man can make assertions in his sleep then he can presumably assert among other things that he is asleep. And since he is in fact asleep this assertion would be true. But the fact is that if he did make this assertion it would be bound to be false. For the expression 'I am asleep' does not have a use which is homogeneous with that of 'he is asleep'. 'He is asleep' can at any time be asserted, truly or falsely, of any man other than oneself; but 'I am asleep' can be asserted only falsely, since from the fact that someone makes an assertion it follows that he is awake. To say 'I am asleep' is like saying 'I am unconscious' or 'I am dead' in that the falsity of what is asserted is a necessary condition of the assertion's being made. But this means for Professor Malcolm that these are not genuine assertions; for he takes it to be the mark of a genuine assertion that it is at least theoretically possible that it should be made with truth.

This argument turns on the assumption that to make an assertion of any kind is logically incompatible with being asleep, and I shall argue presently that this assumption is false. But setting this aside for the moment, it is clear that Professor Malcolm has not refuted Aristotle. For what Aristotle meant, as his examples show, is that people make judgements during sleep. And even if Professor Malcolm were right in what he says about assertions, it might still be the case that a sleeping man could make judgements. And in that event might he not make the true judgement that he was asleep?

Professor Malcolm considers this objection and makes three answers to it. In the first place, he remarks that he does not see how one can be able to judge what one cannot assert. Secondly, he points out that in order to prove that one was asleep one would have to understand the use of the expression 'I am asleep' or some equivalent expression, and he thinks there is a difficulty in the question how the use of such expressions could ever be learned. And, thirdly, he maintains that if we are to credit a sleeping man with the ability to judge that he is asleep, we must ourselves have reason to suppose that he understands the content of this judgement; we must be able to verify the claim that he knows the meaning of such an expression as 'I am asleep'. But, Professor Malcolm argues, in order to do this we should have to be able to determine that the man applied the words to himself at the right time. For if he used them to say what 'was always or usually false one would have reason to think that he did not understand the words in the required sense'.[1] And since Professor Malcolm holds, for reasons which we shall presently examine, that there could be no way of discovering that a sleeper ever truly judged that he was asleep, he concludes that we are not entitled to assume that the expression 'I am asleep' is one that anybody understands.

The only comment that I wish to make at this point is that all three answers are easily rebutted. To say that it is impossible to judge what one cannot assert is in this instance to beg the question. For if we define 'assertion' in such a way that in order to make an assertion it is necessary to be awake, we thereby make room for the possibility of judging what one cannot assert; it may be held to be possible just in those cases where the person who makes the judgement is asleep. It may also be held that there could not be such cases; but this must then be established on other grounds. As for the argument that one could not teach another person the use of the expression 'I am asleep' or ever discover that he had succeeded in understanding it correctly, the fallacy should be obvious. For the argument assumes that the only way

[1] *Dreaming* (1959), p. 9.

in which we can teach someone the use of a sentence, and also be sure that he has learnt his lesson properly, is to train him to use it in the presence of the fact which it expresses. But to see that this is wrong we have only to remark that a great many sentences, which are successfully taught and known to be understood, are never used in the presence of the facts which they express, simply because there are no such facts: this happens in every case in which a sentence serves only to state what is false. But it would be absurd to suggest that there is no means of telling that sentences of this kind are ever understood.

What has misled Professor Malcolm here is the fact that one's using a sentence to state what is false may in certain circumstances be a sign that one does not understand it. For example, if someone kept on saying 'I am asleep', with every appearance of believing it, at times when he was manifestly awake, we might reasonably conclude that he did not understand what he was saying. But the mere fact that he failed to use this sentence during his waking moments would prove rather that he did understand it than that he did not. Neither can anything be inferred about one's understanding of a sentence from the fact that one fails to assert it when the assertion would be true. For there are a great many sentences which are perfectly well understood, and yet may not be asserted because the facts which they express are considered to be boring, or embarrassing, or obscene, or just because it never occurs to anyone to assert them. It may indeed be argued that the sentence 'I am asleep' falls into a special category, inasmuch as it does not merely happen not to be asserted when its assertion would be true, but logically could not be, since the making of the assertion would falsify it. But the answer to this is that it has yet to be proved either that the use of the sentence is in this way self-defeating or that if it were self-defeating it would not still make sense.

Returning to the main argument, let us now imagine that we are listening to someone who is talking in his sleep and that one of the things we overhear him saying is 'I am asleep'. Why should we not conclude that he was making a true judgement? Professor Malcolm's answer to this is that 'in order to know that when a man said "I am asleep" he gave a true description of his own state, one would have to know that he said it while asleep *and* that he was *aware* of saying it'.[1] But this, he argues, would be impossible, for 'whatever showed that he was aware of saying that sentence would also show that he was not asleep'.[2] But might there not be indirect evidence? Suppose that when

[1] Ibid. p. 10. [2] Ibid. p. 10.

the man wakes he tells us that he remembers thinking that he was asleep? Again Professor Malcolm has his answer ready. If the sentence 'I am asleep' has no legitimate use, there can be no such thing as thinking that one is asleep, and consequently no such thing as remembering that one had thought it. Neither, he adds, can one remember being asleep, for what would be the content of this memory? That one had one's eyes shut and was breathing stertorously? But such manifestations of sleep can be observed only by others, not by the sleeper himself.

Professor Malcolm concludes that there are no outward criteria by which one can determine that someone is aware of being asleep, and this leads him to contrast the sentence 'I am asleep' with sentences like 'I am in pain'. Both might be held to be reports of inner experiences, but only the second is so, for we have it on the authority of Wittgenstein that an inner process stands in need of outward criteria. And it is this same alleged absence of outward criteria that leads Professor Malcolm to conclude that there is no meaning in the suggestion that someone may be aware of saying to himself that he is asleep.

An obvious objection to the view that the sentence 'I am asleep' is meaningless is that its negation is unquestionably significant. But this does not worry Professor Malcolm. He gives as an analogy the example of a roll-call, where to answer 'here' is proper and significant, but to answer 'not here' would be an abuse of language. In fact, surely, it would be an abuse of discipline rather than of language. It would at worst be false and in the case of a powerful ventriloquist might even be true. In the same way, Professor Malcolm argues that to ask someone if he is asleep is not to put a genuine question but merely to make a noise to test his wakefulness, and *a fortiori* that it is impossible to put such a question to oneself. People are indeed known to say such things as 'Am I dreaming?' or 'I must be dreaming', but these are no more than exclamations of surprise.

It is now time to examine the whole argument, so far as it has gone. There are three different questions which Professor Malcolm does not sufficiently distinguish. The first is: Can one understand the sentence 'I am asleep'? The second: Can one correctly use this sentence to express a proposition which one believes? And the third: Can one correctly use it to express a true proposition? Since Professor Malcolm answers No to the first question, the second and third do not arise for him; but the least implausible of his reasons for answering No to the first question is, if anything, a reason for answering No to the third.

In fact it seems to me quite clear the proper answer to the first question is Yes. A simple proof of this is that someone who is feigning sleep may say to himself of those whom he is deceiving, 'They believe that I am asleep.' Now there is no question but that this sentence is intelligible. But in that case the sentence 'I am asleep' must also be intelligible; for, if it were not intelligible, how could one significantly credit others with believing the proposition it expresses? Against this, all that Professor Malcolm really has to urge is that it is unverifiable, in the sense that the subject himself cannot test it, if what it states is true. But this is to take an unduly narrow view of verifiability. For the proposition which the sentence expresses is one that other people can test, whether it is true or false: the subject himself can test it if it is false, assuming, that is, that he can know that he is awake; and he can subsequently test it even if it is true by relying, if not on his memory, at least on the testimony of others. Furthermore, it has yet to be established that its truth would prevent the subject from testing it at the time. It does sometimes happen that people wake with the memory of having dreamt that they were sleeping. Professor Malcolm would deny that this was any indication that they had been aware of being asleep, or indeed that they had been aware of anything. But in so far as this denial rests merely on the assumption that the sentence 'I am asleep' is unintelligible, we have seen that it is unwarranted.

The answer to our second question is also Yes. No doubt, as Professor Malcolm says, such expressions as 'I must be dreaming' are very often, perhaps normally, used as exclamations of surprise. But he is not entitled to infer from this that it is impossible really to wonder whether one is dreaming, and so asleep, or even to believe it. Consider the story of Hassan, the barber of Baghdad, who was taken one night by the Caliph and introduced to such phantasmagoric scenes of luxury that neither at the time nor subsequently was he ever sure that it was not a dream. In such a situation a man might very well decide, at the time that he was having these experiences, that they were dreams, and infer from this that he was asleep. His belief in this instance would be false; but this is not to say that he could not seriously hold it.

There remains the third and more difficult question. Given that it is possible to believe that one is asleep, might not the belief be true? The ground for saying that it could not be true is that its truth would be inconsistent with its being held. It is alleged that if I am really to believe the proposition that I am asleep, or indeed any other proposition, I must first be awake. But why need this be so? The criteria which Professor Malcolm gives for a man's being asleep are first his behaviour, the facts that his eyes are closed, that his breathing is regular, that he seems unaware of what is going on around him and so forth; and secondly his testimony, or rather the lack of it, the fact that he is unable later to report what was going on around him while he slept. Of these the first is the more important; indeed it is doubtful if the second should be included at all since there are cases, such as those of persons who have been hypnotized, where a man is able to give some report of what went on while he was sleeping and can still correctly be said to have been asleep. But now why should the fact that a man's eyes are closed, that he does not react in the normal way to his environment, and all the rest of it, make it impossible for him to be aware of anything at all, or to entertain any belief? A man who is lost in a day-dream may not react in the normal way to his environment; yet we do not for this reason say that he cannot be aware that he is day-dreaming, or know what he is day-dreaming about. Why should the question whether his eyes are open or shut, or the rate of his breathing, make so radical a difference?

But how could we find out that the sleeper was aware of anything? Well, how do we find out? Most commonly, by questioning him when he wakes. But then we should have no way of corroborating his report. Neither as a rule do we have any way of corroborating the day-dreamer's report; but this does not prevent us from attaching a meaning to it, or even from accepting it as true. Besides, there might be corroboration. People talk in their sleep; sometimes when people have fallen into trances they engage in automatic writing. I see no logical reason why someone should not acquire the habit of writing down his dreams, automatically, as they occurred. Suppose, then, we found that his waking report agreed with what he had written down or, to take the less fanciful case, with what we had overheard him saying in his sleep, would not this be corroboration? And might not one of the statements which was so corroborated be that he thought he was asleep? There is also the case where the sleeper has been hypnotized. We know little enough about the machinery of hypnotism. But surely we are not bound to say that the sleeper who obeys the hypnotist's orders does not hear them.

Professor Malcolm does consider these objections and his way of meeting them is to say that the sleeper who talks, or responds to the hypnotist, or in any way behaves as though he were conscious, is to that extent not fully asleep. But this is a mere evasion. Certainly, if you choose to define the state of being fully asleep in such a way that it is incompatible with any manifestation of consciousness, you can safely conclude that someone who is fully asleep will then give no outward signs of being aware of anything. But nothing is gained by this except the power to make a verbal point. It does not dispose of the examples in which the sleeper's subsequent report of what he thought or imagined in his sleep does receive corroboration; and if we are entitled to believe him in this case, why should we not also accept the similar reports that he gives us on waking from a less troubled sleep?

I conclude, then, that Professor Malcolm's argument fails on all counts. He does not show that the sentence 'I am asleep' is unintelligible; he does not show that the proposition which it expresses cannot then be believed by the person to whom it refers; and so far he has given us no sufficient reason for thinking that, when this proposition is so believed, it cannot be true.

II

Having proved to his own satisfaction that it is impossible for any sleeper to make the judgement that he is asleep, Professor Malcolm generalizes his argument to cover all judgements. He relies, as before, on a strict application of the verification principle. To talk of our making judgements during sleep must be meaningless because this involves two propositions which cannot be conjointly verified. The sleeper cannot observe that he is sleeping and others who can observe that he is sleeping cannot observe that he is then making any judgement.

But could there not be indirect verification? If the sleeper tells us on waking that such and such thoughts occurred to him during sleep, why should we not believe him? The answer, according to Professor Malcolm, is that no one, including the sleeper, can be in a position to know that when the thought occurred to him he really was asleep.

To this there are a number of possible answers which Professor Malcolm tries to deal with. For example, there might have been a storm while the subject was observed to be asleep, and he might report on waking that certain thoughts were occurring to him at the same time as he heard the thunder; but Professor Malcolm's answer to this is that if he heard the thunder he was not fully asleep. Or again, the subject may claim that he remembers making a certain judgement and remembers also that he did not make it either before he went to sleep or after he woke up. But perhaps, says Professor Malcolm, he only imagines that he made it; there is no independent way in which his claim to remember making it can be checked. In the same way, Professor Malcolm argues that the fact that people appear to solve problems in their sleep is no proof that their minds were working on them while they were sleeping. The facts may simply be that they fall asleep with the problem unsolved and wake knowing its solution, without any conscious process intervening. Finally, he considers the possibility of physiological evidence. It might be that a connection could be established between the occurrence of certain thoughts and some physiological condition of the thinker. If a sleeping person were observed to be in this condition, would this not be evidence that he was thinking the thoughts in question? Professor Malcolm's answer to this is that if such a connection could be discovered at all, it could experimentally be found to apply only to waking people: there would be no warrant for assuming that it also held good for those who were asleep.

This set of arguments adds nothing new. Professor Malcolm still relies entirely on Wittgenstein's dictum that an inner process stands in need of outward criteria, which he interprets as meaning not only that it is senseless to credit anyone with private thoughts or feelings unless they are in some way given public expression, but even that the man's own testimony, which is a form of public expression, is not to be accepted unless it can be independently checked; without this independent check the testimony is not to be regarded even as significant. Now I do not know whether Wittgenstein would himself have agreed with this interpretation of his oracular saying, but, whether he would or not, the result seems to me quite clearly wrong. If we have reason to think that a man is generally truthful, then we may be able to believe his word when he tells us what he has been thinking, even though in this instance his word is unsupported by any other evidence, and so far as this goes it makes no difference whether he claims to have been awake when the thought occurred to him or asleep.

Professor Malcolm's position is all the less defensible in that he admits that the subject's testimony may in fact be supported by other evidence. He tries, however, to neutralize this evidence either by the device of saying that it proves the subject not to have been fully asleep, or by explaining it away in some other fashion. Now the evidence is by its nature not demonstrative, so that if one has decided from the start that it is impossible for people to have thoughts of any kind while they are asleep, one may always be able to find some theory, however unconvincing, to dispose of the indications that they do have them. But this will be a highly arbitrary procedure. If the evidence is considered dispassionately it points the other way.

It is easy to see that the same technique can be employed to show not only that a sleeping man can make no judgements but that he can suffer no sensations, feel no emotions, and have no images. The conclusion being in each case supposed impossible, there can be no question of accepting any evidence which would tend to prove it true. In this way Professor Malcolm manages to satisfy himself that sleep is so effectively 'the death of each day's life' that it excludes our having any form of conscious experience.

III

What, then, are dreams? Surely if a man is dreaming, and it is not a day-dream, it follows that he is asleep. Professor Malcolm admits this, but meets the difficulty by denying that people are conscious of their dreams; or rather, to put his point more fairly, by denying that dreams come into the category of things of which one can be conscious. Dreams are connected with sleep, not as being experiences that we enjoy while we are sleeping, but simply in the sense that reporting a dream is somehow the result of having been asleep. 'The criterion of someone having had a dream', says Professor Malcolm, 'is that upon awaking he tells the dream';[1] and one test of its being a dream is that the events which make up its reported content did not in fact occur.

This is very like a suggestion once made by Professor Wisdom: we do not dream but only wake with delusive memories of experiences we never had; though Professor Wisdom meant it as a joke. Professor Malcolm does not in fact go so far as to identify dreams with such delusive memories; he does not give any account of what he thinks dreams are: no doubt he considers this an improper question. What he does say is that a person's conscious report of his dreams determines whether he dreamt or not and what it was that he dreamt. Thus dreams and the waking impressions which furnish the descriptions of dreams are said to be 'two different things but not two logically independent things'.[2] What this means is not made clear, but I take it to imply that the existence of the waking impression is at any rate

[1] *Dreaming* (1959), p. 49. [2] Ibid., p. 60.

a necessary condition for one's having had a dream, and further that if the subject's account of the dream is sincere, in the sense that it is a faithful record of his waking impression, there can be no question of its being either true or false. The reason for this is that there is nothing for it to be true or false of. On this theory a man who recounts his dreams is like a writer of imaginative fiction: we cannot significantly say of his story that it corresponds, or fails to correspond, with fact.

A consequence of this, which Professor Malcolm heroically accepts, is that dreams do not occur in physical time. We are naïvely inclined to think that people dream while they are asleep, but this is not true in any straightforward sense. Since dreams do not literally occur at all, they no more occur when the dreamer is asleep than when he is awake. It is, however, a convention that dreams are to be spoken of as though they occurred during sleep, and indeed on particular occasions of sleep. One says 'I had such and such a dream last night' or 'this afternoon', and what one is supposed to mean by this is that it is last night's sleep or this afternoon's sleep that has set up one's disposition to tell such and such a fairy story. At least this is the most plausible interpretation that I can put upon the theory. All that Professor Malcolm himself can find to say on this point is that it is improper to ask why people relate their fairy stories in the past tense: it is just the way in which this language game is played. But in the first place this is not even a correct description of the language game: it is not the events which make up the content of a dream that are assigned, in retrospect, to a particular period of sleep, but the process of dreaming about them. These are no more to be identified than are the dates of the events recounted in a history book with the date at which the book is written. And, secondly, it is not at all improper to ask why the language game, if you must call it that, takes the form it does. If saying 'I dreamed that . . .' were merely a way of saying that the story which follows is not to be regarded as a record of fact, why should we speak of dreaming as a process that occurs within a given period of time? To say that this is just part of the ritual is no answer at all.

In other ways, too, Professor Malcolm's account of dreams is stranger than he seems to realize. He treats them as though they posthumously masqueraded as waking experiences. Thus he says that 'to find out that one dreamt an incident is to find out that the impression one had on waking is false'[1] and this leads him to suggest that

[1] Ibid., p. 64.

statements of the form 'I dreamt so and so' are always inferential. 'If a man wakes up with the impression of having seen and done various things, and if it is known that he did not see and do those things, then it is known that he dreamt them'.[1] The objection that by no means every statement which helps to compose the story of a dream is false, that the persons and places about which one dreams may well be credited in the dream with properties which they really have, can perhaps be met by saying that the cardinal feature of the waking impression is that it purports to be a record of the subject's own experiences; so that, just as a work of fiction may contain true statements without thereby ceasing to be a work of fiction, the story of a dream is false as a whole because the subject did not have the experiences it attributes to him. Thus, in this special case in which the subject remembers, or rather seems to remember, dreaming that he was asleep, the statement to be considered is not the true statement that he was asleep but only the statement that he thought he was asleep; and we have seen that this statement is held by Professor Malcolm to be false, just because the other is true.

But even if this objection can be met, a more serious difficulty remains. It may be that children pass through a stage of being unable to distinguish dreams from waking experiences, and even when one has learned this distinction, there may be occasions when it takes one some time to realize that some incident of which one wakes with a strong impression was 'only a dream'; but in the normal way people do not fall into this confusion. When they remember their dreams they do not remember them as waking experiences. Yet this is what they are required to do by Professor Malcolm's theory. For if, as he holds, to tell a dream is to give a fictitious report of one's past experiences, and if, as he also holds, experiences can be significantly attributed only to those who are awake, it follows that the report of a dream is the report of waking experiences that one never had. But as an account of the ordinary run of dreams, this is simply incorrect. When I relate my dreams to my friends, or to a psycho-analyst, my intention is not to tell them falsehoods about my waking experiences: it is to tell them the truth about the experiences I had while I was asleep. Admittedly, I do not claim that these experiences were veridical, that I really did all or even any of the things that I dreamt that I was doing. But neither am I reporting that I woke up with the impression that I had really done them. What I am reporting is that it seemed to me

[1] Ibid., p. 66.

that I was doing them, and that I had this impression while I was asleep.

But this means, on Professor Malcolm's theory, that we are even more grievously deluded than he thinks. For, if I am right in my account of what dreams are taken to be, we constantly wake with the belief that we have achieved something which he holds to be impossible. That the process of emerging from sleep should produce in us a flock of illusions about our past would be mysterious enough; but that it should subject us to an overwhelming impulse to accept and assert meaningless statements is stranger still. Yet this is what Professor Malcolm's theory leads to when it is adapted to the facts.

Still, we must not be slaves to common sense. However odd a theory may seem, it may still be acceptable if it is supported by very strong arguments. It is disappointing, therefore, to find that Professor Malcolm has nothing better to offer us by way of argument than his old dogma that an inner process stands in need of outward criteria. We must be mistaken in identifying our dreams with experiences that come to us during sleep, because we must be mistaken in supposing that we have any experiences whose existence is not vouched for by physical signs. If dreams were inner states, says Professor Malcolm, how could one ever tell that different people meant the same thing by dreaming? In one's own case, how could one tell that the state which one called a dream-state was the same each time? Just as we acquire the concept of pain not just through feeling pain but through being told that we are in pain when we display the appropriate physical signs, so 'the concept of dreams is derived, not from dreaming, but from descriptions of dreams, i.e. from the familiar phenomenon that we call "telling a dream"'.[1] The dream itself is no more logically separable from the telling of it than is the pain in a sore foot from the behaviour which shows others that one has the pain. To assume in either case that there was an 'inner' phenomenon which was connected only factually with the behaviour which made it known to others would, in Professor Malcolm's view, be self-contradictory; for without physical criteria for the existence of the inner phenomena such empirical conclusions could never be established.

But even if it is true that the concept of a dream, or that of any other inner state or process, is acquired only through the association of what falls under it with certain physical events, it by no means follows that this association is not empirical; it does not follow that the

[1] Ibid., p. 55.

extension of the concept must comprise these physical events. One might as well argue that the concept of memory is derived from the physical process of relating one's memories, and that therefore no claim that one remembers anything can be either true or false. Neither am I impressed by the argument that if a word referred to an inner state, one could never tell that it was used with the same meaning by different people, or by oneself on different occasions. For how can one tell that this is true of a word which refers to a physical event? Only by noting that the different occasions of its use, by oneself or by others, are the same in the relevant respect. And how does one tell that they are the same? Only in the end by identifying some recurrent feature of one's experiences. And why should not pain be such a recognizable feature? Or, for that matter, the memory of a dream?

Thus, even if it were true that, apart from the reports of dreams, there was no physical evidence of their existence, I still should not regard Professor Malcolm's case as proved. But in fact it is not true: there is quite a lot of physical evidence. As we have already remarked, people talk in their sleep; and what they then say may be found to tally with the account they subsequently give of their dreams. When people have nightmares they may sweat and tremble and cry out in fear. Sometimes we can account for some detail of a dream in terms of the physical stimuli to which the sleeper has been subject; a familiar example is the way in which the sound of an alarm-clock may be woven into the last stages of a dream. There is even thought to be physical evidence that dogs have dreams, though they do not report them. Finally, there is the fact that, under hypnosis or when questioned by a psycho-analyst, people revise their accounts of their dreams; they recall incidents, perhaps entire dreams, which they had not previously been able to remember. This does not accord very well with the idea that there is nothing to which reports of dreams can correspond. Or are we to say that all that the hypnotist, or psycho-analyst, achieves is to cause the patient to remodel his fairy stories or to acquire a fresh set of delusions about his past?

Professor Malcolm makes an effort to deal with these facts, but the results are not happy. In the case where we hear someone talking in his sleep, and infer from this that he is dreaming, he says that our statement that the man is dreaming has no clear sense. The fact is that it has a perfectly clear sense, which cannot be accounted for on Professor Malcolm's theory. In the case where some reported detail of a dream can be connected with a physical stimulus, he falls back on his old device of saying that the subject cannot have been fully asleep. And when it comes to nightmares, he goes even further. The state of a man who is struggling in a nightmare is 'so unlike the paradigms of normal sleep that it is at least problematic whether it should be said that he was "asleep" when these struggles were going on'.[1] I leave this argument to speak against itself. As for dogs, their dreams have no content, which appears to mean only that they do not report them. But can Professor Malcolm allow that they dream at all? Perhaps he holds that they dream in some special sense, like the patients who go to psycho-analysts. For they too fall under the same blunt axe: their reaction in replying to the analyst 'is so dissimilar to the normal phenomenon of telling dreams that it is better, I think, to say that in psycho-analysis there is a different concept of dreaming, than to say that in psycho-analysis one finds out what one really dreamt'.[2]

But surely one of the main points about psycho-analysis is that it does not introduce a new concept of dreaming. The analyst tries to elicit and interpret the dreams that people normally have. What reason has Professor Malcolm for saying otherwise? The same as he has for doubting whether people whose sleep is troubled by nightmares are really asleep. He is convinced of the truth of his theory; so the facts which go against it must have been wrongly described. He sees it, therefore, as his duty to bring them into line.

There are times, however, when the effort is too much for him. Thus he remarks at one point that 'if I had a dream in which I heard a crash, and then found on waking that a vase fell in the night, I might make the conjecture "I must have heard the crash" meaning that the noise probably caused me to hear a crash in my dream'.[3] Now on the normal assumption that Professor Malcolm was literally dreaming at the time the crash occurred, this makes perfectly good sense. But what does it come to on his own theory? That the falling of the vase caused him, several hours later, to make the false report that he heard a crash, when in fact he heard nothing at all. Well, perhaps this could be explained physiologically, but if so Professor Malcolm does not try to tell us how. The truth is that he has forgotten his own theory and is using the expression 'hearing in a dream' in the way that I think it normally would be used: to imply that the dreamer does have an auditory experience, not that he does not.

A more striking example, perhaps, is to be found in a passage where he refers to Pharaoh's dream, as recorded in Genesis. 'Behold in my

[1] Ibid., pp. 62–3. [2] Ibid., p. 57. [3] Ibid., p. 99.

dream I was standing on the banks of the Nile; and seven cows fat and sleek, came up out of the Nile and seven other cows came up after them, poor and very gaunt and thin. . . .'[1] Professor Malcolm remarks, truly though perhaps not quite consistently, that if Pharaoh had really believed that he had gone to the banks of the Nile during the night and had there seen seven fat and seven lean cows, he would not, or at any rate should not, have used the expression 'in my dream'. But then he adds, suppose that instead of saying 'in my dream' Pharaoh had merely said that 'it seemed to him' during the night that he stood on the banks of the Nile and so forth, and suppose that there was independent evidence that this was so, that he talked aloud in his sleep, for example, and told the story about the cows; then, says Professor Malcolm, he would not have been dreaming but having an hallucination, and the statement which he made on waking that it had seemed to him that cows came out of the Nile and all the rest of it, would have been true.

Now this is surely very strange. For there might easily be a convention by which we always described our dreams by saying that it seemed to us during the night that such and such things were happening to us, and if these statements can be literally true when expressed in this form, it would appear that we are after all permitted to look upon dreams as conscious experiences, provided only that we do not describe them as dreams. This prohibition may seem a little arbitrary to Professor Malcolm's opponents, but it should not greatly worry them; for in allowing that we can have hallucinations during sleep he concedes the main point at issue. Admittedly, he would insist that a belief in the existence of such hallucinations must always be backed by physical evidence, and I suppose he would also say that when this condition is satisfied the subject is not fully asleep. But we have already met with these provisos at other stages of the argument and we have seen that they do not save his case.

But if we reject Professor Malcolm's theory, as it would now seem we must, does this not commit us to holding that reports of dreams are liable to error, and does not this raise difficulties? As Wittgenstein put it: 'Must I make some assumption about whether people are deceived by their memories or not; whether they really had these images while they slept, or whether it merely seems so to them on waking? And what meaning has this question? And what interest? Do we ever ask ourselves this when someone is telling us his dream?

[1] Genesis 16: 17–44. Quoted by Malcolm on p. 67.

And if not, is it because we are sure his memory won't have deceived him? (And suppose it were a man with a quite specially bad memory?)'[1] But the answer to this is that it has as much meaning as the question whether someone really had the thoughts or feelings that he claims to remember having in a waking state. And as for its interest, might not the fact that a person unconsciously, or even consciously, suppresses or distorts the recollection of his dreams be of great psychological importance? Neither does it seem at all absurd to suggest that people should be better or worse at remembering their dreams, as they are at remembering other things. There is in fact reason to believe that this is so.

But how could we ever find out that someone had given a false, or, for that matter, a true report of his dreams? Well, I have already suggested various ways in which this might be done. The most effective, in the present state of our knowledge, would be to compare his unsolicited report with that which he gave when under hypnosis or when questioned by a psycho-analyst. But supposing they are in conflict; why are we bound to accept the revised version? The answer is that we are not bound to accept it, but there might well be independent reasons for our doing so. For instance, it might have been established that his memory of events, which we could check, consistently improved when he was hypnotized. But perhaps this does not apply to his dreams. What reason is there to suppose that it does not? Or again, one version or the other might be in some degree corroborated by his behaviour during sleep. Or there might be physiological evidence. Of course there will be an enormous number of cases in which we have to allow reports of dreams to go untested; and our tendency will be to accept them in default of any reason why we should not. But this applies equally to the reports of experiences which people claim to remember having while awake. There is no reason, so far as this goes, for putting reports of dreams into a different category.

IV

I conclude then that Professor Malcolm's own account of the nature of dreams is not satisfactory, and that what he calls the received view can be defended against his and Wittgenstein's arguments. But this

[1] *Philosophical Investigations*, 1st ed. (1958), p. 184; quoted by Malcolm on pp. 55–6.

means that he has also failed in his object of providing a check to Cartesian scepticism. If we can have experiences while we are asleep, and if these hallucinatory experiences, which we call our dreams, are not intrinsically distinguishable from the veridical experiences which we have when we are awake, how can we ever be sure that we are not dreaming? How can we ever know that the experiences which we take to be veridical really are so?

The usual answer is that we make sure that we are not dreaming in exactly the same way as we make sure that some waking experience is not hallucinatory. The test which a perception has to pass in order to qualify as veridical is that the information which it seems to yield shall fit in with that which is obtained from the vast majority of our other perceptions. So the unreality of dreams is not due to their occurring while we are asleep but simply to their failure to satisfy this condition. As Russell succinctly puts it: 'Objects of sense, even when they occur in dreams, are the most indubitably real objects known to us. What, then, makes us call them unreal in dreams? Merely the unusual nature of their connection with other objects of sense.'[1] And again: 'It is only the failure of our dreams to form a consistent whole, either with each other or with waking life, that makes us condemn them.'[2] This principle of coherence, as Professor Malcolm calls it, was also adopted by Leibniz and Descartes.

He maintains, however, that as a method of finding out whether one is awake or dreaming it is open to 'a simple but devastating objection'. 'The objection', he says, 'that should occur to anyone is that it is possible a person should *dream* that the right connections hold, *dream* that he *connects* his present perceptions with "the whole course of his life". The coherence principle tells us that we are awake if we can make these connections and asleep in a dream if we cannot; but how does the principle tell us whether we are noting and making connections, or dreaming that we are? It seems to me that obviously it cannot and therefore the principle is worthless.'[3] His own solution is not that there is some better principle but that there is no need for any principle at all. For he holds that the question 'How can I tell whether I am awake?' is senseless.

Now I think Professor Malcolm's argument has this much force, that it is indeed possible to have a dream in which one raises the question

[1] *Our Knowledge of the External World*, 2nd ed. (1926), p. 85; quoted by Malcolm, p. 107.

[2] Ibid., p. 95. [3] Malcolm, op. cit., p. 108.

whether one is dreaming, applies the coherence test, and wrongly concludes that one is not. I do not think, however, that this makes the test worthless. What it does show is that it is not conclusive. Even if my present experiences seem to pass the test, it remains conceivable that further experiences will lead me to think otherwise. In fact I am quite convinced that I am not now dreaming, that I am really engaged in writing this paper; but this does not exclude the possibility that in the next moment I shall undergo the experience of waking up and, finding the paper still unwritten, conclude that I had only dreamt that I was writing it. Still, so long as this does not happen, the fact that my experiences continue to be entirely consonant with my having written these words may surely be taken as evidence that I really have written them. But suppose that I do have the experience of waking up. Might not that be the one which is delusive? Might not my finding the paper unwritten be part of an anxiety dream? Again, this is possible. And again, it is for further experience to decide. In taking it for granted that I am not now dreaming, I am taking it for granted that my present experience is in the main veridical; and the test for this is that further experience confirms it. In making this claim upon the future, I am indeed not betting on a certainty; but this is not to say that the claim has no support at all.

Apart from his objection to the coherence principle, Professor Malcolm's only reason for holding that it is senseless to ask for any sort of proof that one is awake is that he thinks it meaningless to say that one is not awake. 'Our investigation proves', he says, 'that nothing counts for or against the truth of "I am not awake" and so nothing counts for the truth of "I am awake". '[1] On his own principles, he ought to conclude from this that the sentence 'I am awake' itself is meaningless, instead of maintaining, as he mostly does, that it expresses a significant statement, which has no significant negation. He does, however, also make the suggestion that one uses this sentence not to report or describe anything but simply to show that one is awake. So Professor Malcolm says 'I am awake' and thereby reports nothing. He merely uses the sentence to show something which he describes by saying 'I am awake'. But 'I am awake' describes nothing. So nothing is stated by these means and nothing is shown.

Happily, Professor Malcolm's investigation does not prove even that it is meaningless to say 'I am not awake', and he himself tacitly acknowledges this. He remarks, for example, that someone who

[1] Ibid., pp. 115–16.

sought to prove that he was awake might try to use the following argument: 'I am perplexed as to whether I am awake or dreaming in sleep. But it makes no sense to suppose that I should be perplexed while asleep. Therefore I am awake.'[1] But this, he thinks, is open to the objection, which was suggested to him by Mr Warnock, that the man might be only dreaming that he was perplexed. If he really was perplexed then it would follow that he was awake; but because he can always invoke the possibility that he is dreaming, there is no way of forcing the sceptic to admit that he really is perplexed. But, whatever may be Mr Warnock's views on the subject, this is not a rejoinder that Professor Malcolm can accept. For if 'I am dreaming' makes no sense then 'I am dreaming that I wonder whether I am dreaming' makes no sense either. In allowing this refuge to the sceptic, Professor Malcolm implies, quite correctly, that these expressions do make sense. He makes a valiant effort to abide by the consequences of his misguided views, but now and again the truth breaks through.

The failure of Professor Malcolm's argument leaves us, so far as I can see, with no alternative to the classical theory. Dreams are experiences. They are mostly illusions and are found to be so by the same criteria as apply to illusions in general. Their peculiarity, by definition, is that they occur to us only when we satisfy the physical conditions of being asleep. But with respect to their status as illusions this is logically irrelevant.[2]

[1] Ibid., p. 17.

[2] In fairness to Professor Malcolm, I should add that he did not consider that this essay gave an adequate account of his views. His comments on it and my rejoinder to them are to be found in the *Journal of Philosophy*, vol. LVIII, no. 11.

II

AN APPRAISAL OF BERTRAND RUSSELL'S PHILOSOPHY

By the last quarter of the nineteenth century, British philosophy had fallen very largely under the spell of Hegel. The British Hegelians, of whom F. H. Bradley at Oxford and J. E. McTaggart at Cambridge were the most distinguished, were perhaps not very orthodox disciples of the master—Bradley in particular found it difficult to free himself entirely from the legacy of British empiricism—but with their belief in the absolute, their characterization of the material world as mere appearance, and their denial of the reality of space and time, they committed themselves to metaphysics in a way that British philosophers have fought shy of, both before and since. That the present century has seen a return to the older and sounder empiricist tradition, and its development in a more rigorous form, is very largely due to the work of Bertrand Russell. What is called the analytical movement in philosophy, which in one form or another has fashioned the philosophical climate at least in English-speaking countries during the last quarter of a century, is in a great measure the fruit of his ideas.

As he relates in *My Philosophical Development*, there was a period in Lord Russell's youth when he himself, under the influence of Bradley's writings, was a Hegelian idealist. He was, however, very soon converted by his Cambridge friend and colleague, G. E. Moore, to a form of Platonic realism. This conversion was made easier by the fact that Russell had first been led to take an interest in philosophy by his desire to find some reason for believing in the truth of mathematics; and he soon came to see that if he was to regard the propositions of mathematics as having objective validity, he would have to reject the fundamental idealist doctrine that the objects of knowledge are conditioned by their being known. Besides, Hegelian idealism looked askance on relational judgements which it regarded as incoherent; and Russell was convinced that the propositions of mathematics are irreducibly relational. For the same reason he rejected the view which is attributed to Aristotle and to Leibniz that all propositions are of the subject-predicate form. In the earliest of his philosophical books, *A Critical Examination of the Philosophy of Leibniz*, which appeared in 1900, Russell made a convincing attempt to show that the assumption of this logical doctrine can be made to account for the main features of Leibniz's metaphysics.

Two current explanations of the nature of mathematical propositions were the Kantian view that they were synthetic *a priori* truths, and at the other extreme the view of John Stuart Mill that they were empirical generalizations, which owed their security to their having been found to be supported by a very large number of instances. But neither of these explanations satisfied Russell. He did not then reject the notion of the synthetic *a priori*, as he came to do later, but the use that was made of it in this instance seemed to him not to explain enough; at the same time, the idea that the propositions of mathematics were empirical generalizations appeared to him untenable, because it implied the denial of their necessity.

Russell's own radical solution was to reduce mathematics to logic. In order to achieve this, he had to show that the fundamental terms of mathematics could be defined by means of purely logical concepts, but more importantly he had to transform logic itself. He had to elaborate a system of logic which would be rigorous and rich enough to allow the propositions of mathematics to be incorporated in it. The first part of this undertaking was carried out in the *Principles of Mathematics*, which appeared in 1903. The second led to *Principia Mathematica*, which extended to three large volumes, of which the first came out in 1910, the second in 1912 and the third in 1913. A comparatively untechnical account of the main ideas of these works was given by Russell in his *Introduction to Mathematical Philosophy*, which he wrote while in prison as the result of his agitation against the First World War, and published in 1919.

In his idea that mathematics could be reduced to logic, Russell had been anticipated by the German mathematician, Gottlob Frege. Though Frege's work had been published over twenty years before, it was very little known, and Russell arrived independently at very similar results. In their definition of the natural numbers, for example, both Russell and Frege made use of the concept of a one–one relation: that is, a relation which is such that if it holds between any two terms x and y, no other term but x is so related to y, and x bears the relation to no other term but y. Two classes are said to be similar if their members can be correlated by a one–one relation. Then the number of a class is defined as the class of all those classes that are similar to it, and a cardinal number is defined as anything which is the number of some class. This definition is not circular, as the notion of a one–one relation can be introduced in purely logical terms, without any reference to numbers. On the other hand, if the definition is to apply to every cardinal number, it seems to require that there be no upper limit to the number of things that can be classified; and it may be disputed whether this is a principle of logic.

At the time that he wrote the *Principles of Mathematics*, Russell was still very much of a Platonic realist. He spoke of 'whatever may be an object of thought' as a term, and maintained that 'every term has being, i.e. *is* in some sense'. This committed him to a belief in the reality not only of universals, propositions and classes, but of everything that was denoted by any substantival expression. His assumption was that if such an expression was meaningful, there must in some sense be an object to which it referred. This worked well enough in the case of proper names like 'Napoleon' or descriptions like 'the author of Waverley' which denoted objects which were known to exist: yet it hardly seems credible that there should in any sense *be* such objects as the present King of France, or the golden mountain, or the round square. At the same time, so far as the analysis of their meaning went, there appeared to be no justification for drawing a distinction between expressions like 'the present King of France' and expressions like 'the author of Waverley'. It was just a contingent, historical, fact that one of these succeeded in its reference and the other did not.

Russell's solution of this difficulty is to be found in his famous Theory of Descriptions. This theory was designed to show that even in their referential usage expressions of the form 'the so-and-so' do not function as names. It does not follow from the fact that they are meaningful that there is any object which they mean. Russell's way of showing this was to give a rule for translating sentences in which the definite descriptive phrase occurs, in such a way that the phrase no longer even looks as though it were a name. So, to take his own favourite example, the statement 'the author of Waverley was Scott' becomes in his translation a conjunction of the three statements: 'At least one person wrote Waverley': 'At most one person wrote Waverley': and 'It is not the case that anyone both wrote Waverley and was not identical with Scott'. To put it symbolically, as Russell himself preferred to do, the theory is that to say that something which has f has g, where f is the property concealed in the definite description and g is a property attributed to what it describes, is to say that there is an x such that x has f, and for all y, if y has f, y is identical with x, and x has g. Thus any description of the subject goes into the predicate, and only what Russell called a logical proper name, that is a pure demonstrative, can serve to designate the value of the variable x.

This theory, which the Cambridge philosopher, F. P. Ramsey, called a paradigm of philosophy, has recently had its critics. One objection to it is that there are many cases in which the literal application of Russell's rule yields unwelcome results. If I say 'The policeman on the corner told me where to go', I am surely not implying that there exists only one policeman or only one corner. The point about cases of this kind is that the definite description does not individuate the object to which it refers; it is assumed that the means of identifying the object are supplied by the context. Nevertheless the object will have a unique set of properties which could be specified: and if they are specified, then Russell's analysis will apply. Another objection is that the existence claim which is involved in the use of a definite description is not implicitly stated by it, as Russell assumes, but rather pre-supposed. It is alleged that we should not ordinarily say that a sentence like 'The present King of France is bald' was used to make a false statement: we should say rather that since there is no present King of France the question of truth or falsehood did not arise. It does not seem to me, however, that this is a question upon which the appeal to ordinary usage is at all decisive; and there are obvious advantages in construing sentences of this kind in such a way that they do make statements which have a truth-value.

A more serious criticism is that Russell starts from a false premiss. The theory is intended to show how it is possible for a descriptive expression to be meaningful, even though there is nothing which it denotes; and it does this in effect by maintaining that these expressions are not referential. The underlying assumption is then that the meaning of a referential expression is to be identified with its denotation; and it is argued that, even in the case of proper names, this theory of meaning is mistaken. I agree that it is mistaken, and, therefore, that the reasoning which appears to have led Russell to the theory of descriptions can be criticized. However, the fact that it was designed to meet an avoidable difficulty does not invalidate the theory itself.

It was not only in the field of the theory of descriptions that Russell came to be sceptical of the generous ontology which he had admitted in the *Principles of Mathematics*. In his later works he thought it unnecessary to attribute real existence either to classes or to propositions: he held them rather to be logical fictions, in the sense that they could be analysed in terms of entities of a more concrete sort. On the other hand, he has always felt bound to admit the existence of universals. He has allowed, it may be wrongly, that one can go so far in dispensing with universals as to reduce them all to the single relation of resemblance; but since he takes the view that resemblance itself is a universal, he does not think that the nominalists achieve their aim.

It is not possible, within the limits of a general sketch of Russell's philosophy, to assess the scope and originality of *Principia Mathematica*. There is in any case no doubt that it played a very important part in the development of mathematical logic. The break with Aristotelian logic consisted not so much in the use of a special notation as in the greater generality of Russell's and Whitehead's system, and above all in their attempt to make it rigorously formal. Other systems of logic have since been developed which lay claim to greater formal rigour, but they have in a large measure been inspired by Russell's and Whitehead's work.

One very important outcome of Russell's concern with the problems of mathematical logic was his invention of the Theory of Types. The need for this theory arose out of his discovery of a contradiction in the theory of classes: a discovery which made Frege say, when the news of it was communicated to him by Russell, that the whole foundation of mathematics had been undermined. This contradiction is fairly easy to set out. Most classes appear not to be members of themselves: for example, the class of men is plainly not itself a man. On the other hand, some classes do appear to be members of themselves. For example, the class of all the things that can be counted would itself appear to be a thing that can be counted. Now consider the class of all classes that are not members of themselves. Is it or is it not a member of itself? If it is, it is not, and if it is not, it is.

Similar contradictions appear in other fields. A notorious example is the paradox of Epimenides the Cretan, who said that all Cretans were liars. Another well-known paradox, which belongs to the same family as that of the liar, arises out of the fact that some, but not all, adjectives are predicable of themselves. For instance, the word 'short' is short but the word 'long' is not long. Let us call those that are so predicable 'autological' and those that are not 'heterological'. Then is the word 'heterological' predicable of itself? Once again, if it is, it is not, and if it is not, it is.

Russell's solution of these antimonies was to arrange objects into a hierarchy of types, with the consequence that what may be true or false of the objects of one type cannot be meaningfully asserted about those of another. In particular, if a given class is the extension of a given predicate, only nonsense results if the predicate is applied to that class. So, it is not false but nonsensical to say that the class of men is human: the question whether the word 'heterological' is itself autological or heterological is a meaningless question. Even when a predicate does appear to characterize objects of different types, it does not have the same meaning in each case. Thus a predicate like 'being countable' becomes, as Russell puts it, systematically ambiguous.

The theory of types, of which I have here given only an outline, has a certain *ad hoc* air about it. It is hard to maintain that all forms of self-reference are logically vicious: and there seems to be no sure method for deciding when it is legitimate and when it is not. For this reason attempts have since been made to find a less restrictive means of avoiding the paradoxes. All the same, the theory of types has had an important historical influence. It called attention, in a very striking way, to the fact that a sentence may be grammatically well formed and yet fail to express a meaningful statement. Among other things, it helped to set the stage for the Logical Positivists who rejected metaphysics on the ground that metaphysical doctrines were not even false but literally nonsensical. This is indeed a view that goes back to Hume, but Russell's work was taken as giving it logical support.

It follows from the theory of types that the statements which come lowest in the hierarchy refer to individuals; and it follows from the theory of descriptions that the individuals which, in Russell's phrase, make up the furniture of the world are designated by logically proper names. But, since logically proper names are pure demonstratives, it would appear that the only individuals which they can designate are those that are directly observable. In this way Russell's logic was integrated with his theory of knowledge.

The distinction between knowledge by acquaintance and knowledge by description, which is an outcome of the theory of descriptions, was developed by Russell in his *Problems of Philosophy*, which appeared in 1912. This book was written for the Home University Library and is still as good an introduction to philosophy as there is. It approaches the theory of knowledge from an empiricist standpoint; its guiding principle being that every proposition which we can understand must be composed of constituents with which we are acquainted. Thus Russell held that we are acquainted with universals. We are also acquainted with particulars, but only with a limited class of them; namely those which are directly given to us in experience. In their case, he took it to follow from the fact that one was acquainted with a particular object both that the object really existed and that it had the properties which it appeared to have. On this view, we can indeed surmise that particulars of other types exist: but we can only refer to them indirectly as objects which stand in certain relations to those with which we are acquainted. Thus, when an object is known by acquaintance, its existence is not open to doubt; but the existence of objects which are known only by description is problematic.

At that time Russell believed that the particulars with which it was possible to be acquainted were one's own self and one's own private thoughts, feelings, images and sense-data; these might be past as well as present, since he allowed memory to be a form of direct acquaintance. By 1921, when he published *The Analysis of Mind*, he had come round to the view that the existence of the objects, or events, which we claim to remember is not known to us directly but only inferred from our present memory-images; and he also rejected the idea that one could be acquainted with oneself, on the ground that the self did not exist as a separate entity. On the other hand, he has never given up the view that the objects with which we are directly acquainted in perception are our own private sense-data.[1] The sense-datum theory has indeed met with considerable opposition in recent times, as part of a general reaction against allowing the existence of private entities. If Russell still adheres to it, it is mainly because he thinks that the alternative of supposing that we are directly acquainted with physical objects is obviously untenable. His main argument against naïve realism is most succinctly put in the *Inquiry into Meaning and Truth*, which appeared in 1940. 'We all start from "naïve realism", i.e. the doctrine that things are what they seem. We think that grass is green, that stones are hard and that snow is cold. But physics assures us that the greenness of grass, the hardness of stones, and the coldness of snow are not the greenness, hardness, and coldness that we know in our own experience, but something very different. The observer, when he seems to himself to be observing a stone, is really, if physics is to be believed, observing the effect of the stone upon himself. . . . Naïve realism leads to physics, and physics, if true, shows that naïve realism is false. Therefore naïve realism, if true, is false; therefore it is false'.[2]

[1] This appears to contradict what Russell himself says in *My Philosophical Development*, p. 245. But his rejection of sense-data turns out only to be a rejection of the subject–object analysis of sensation. He continues to conceive of the immediate data of perception, which he now calls 'percepts', as private entities.

[2] Russell, op. cit., p. 15.

This implies a causal theory of perception, with which Russell began and to which he has reverted. There was, however, a period in which in obedience to the principle 'wherever possible substitute constructions out of known entities for inference to unknown entities', a principle which he has called the supreme maxim in scientific philosophy, he gave up the causal theory, at any rate in its conventional form, in favour of the phenomenalist position that physical objects are logical constructions out of actual and possible sense-data. This is a reformulation of John Stuart Mill's view that physical objects are permanent possibilities of sensation; the form in which it presents it is that statements about physical objects can be faithfully translated into statements about sense-data.

Russell developed this view in *Our Knowledge of the External World*, which was published in 1924, and in two of the essays collected in *Mysticism and Logic* which appeared in 1918. The materials out of which he tried to construct physical objects were not limited to the actual sense-data with which any single observer was acquainted. Russell also brought in the sense-data sensed by other persons and even unsensed sense-data, to which he gave the name of sensibilia. The only way in which a sensibilium was supposed to differ from a sense-datum was in its not being actually sensed. Roughly speaking, Russell's theory was that at any given moment each observer perceives a private three dimensional world with its own private space, or spaces, since Russell distinguishes the space of sight from the space of touch. He calls these private worlds perspectives. In addition to these perceived perspectives, there exists also an infinite number of unperceived perspectives, namely all those that an observer would perceive if he were in the appropriate state and in the appropriate position. The constituents of the unperceived perspectives are sensibilia. A physical object is then defined as a class of sensibilia, where sensibilia are taken as including sense-data; it is in fact identified with those sensibilia, or sense-data, which are commonly regarded as its actual and possible appearances. Since the three-dimensional perspectives are themselves arranged in a three-dimensional order, physical space is one of six dimensions. Russell does not work out this theory in full detail, but it is clear that it encounters very serious difficulties, even if one is willing to assume that sensibilia and unperceived perspectives literally exist.

In the 'Reply to Criticisms' which Russell wrote for *The Philosophy of Bertrand Russell*, a volume in the Library of Living Philosophers which was published in 1944, he remarked that he did not see why this theory should preclude him from regarding physical objects as causes of sense-data. His ground for this presumably is that the causal relations which are supposed to hold between physical objects and sense-data may themselves be capable of being analysed in terms of correlations among sensibilia. This is substantially the position which he took in the *Analysis of Mind*, where he develops a theory about mind and matter which is akin to the neutral monism of William James. The theory is that both mind and matter are logical constructions out of elements, primarily sense-data, which are themselves neither mental nor physical. Apart from the fact that certain elements, such as images and feelings, enter only into the constitution of minds, what chiefly distinguishes mind from matter, in this view, is the operation of different causal laws. Thus the same sense-data when correlated according to the laws of physics constitute physical objects and when correlated according to the laws of psychology help to constitute minds. In their mental aspect, they engage among other things, in what Russell called mnemic causation, a kind of action at a distance by which experiences produce subsequent memory-images. A consequence of this view is that Russell rejects the notion not only of the self, but also of consciousness, as a substantial entity. On the other hand, while he has dallied with behaviourism, he has never denied the existence of states of consciousness which are not definable in physical terms.

An interesting feature of Russell's more recent writings on the subject of perception is that he locates sense-data, or percepts as he now prefers to call them, in the percipient's brain. He does not mean by this that when we think that we are perceiving the world around us, we are, in any literal sense, really observing only our own brains. His argument is rather that an event's position in space-time is determined by its causal relations and that 'the causal and temporal connections of percepts with events in afferent and efferent nerves gives percepts a position in the brain of the observer'.[1] If this still sounds paradoxical it has to be remembered that for Russell the brain itself is a construction out of sensible events. It is one of the perspectives from which the world is viewed and it is via the perspectives which constitute their point of view, rather than the physical objects which are constructed out of them, that actual percepts acquire their own location in physical space.

[1] 'Reply to Criticisms', *The Philosophy of Bertrand Russell*, p. 705.

The view that the world consists in the last resort of sensible events is a feature of the doctrine of Logical Atomism which Russell, under the influence of his pupil Ludwig Wittenstein, put forward in the years following the First World War. It was expounded by him in some lectures which were first published in the *Monist* in 1918 and 1919 under the title of *The Philosophy of Logical Atomism*, and have since been reprinted in a collection of essays called *Logic and Knowledge*, which appeared in 1956; and there is also an essay called *Logical Atomism* which Russell contributed to the first series of *Contemporary British Philosophy* in 1924. While making a strong plea for the method of logical analysis, considered primarily as an application of Ockham's razor in accordance with the principle of substituting logical constructions for inferred entities, the lectures were largely concerned with the problem of truth. In his earlier writings on the subject of truth, at a time when he believed in the objective reality of propositions, Russell had taken the view that truth and falsehood were unanalysable properties by which propositions were simply characterized. Propositions, he held, were true or false just as roses may be red or white. It was not long, however, before he came, with reason, to regard this theory as obscurantist and he accordingly abandoned it in favour of a correspondence theory of truth.

In Russell's exposition of Logical Atomism, as in Wittgenstein's *Tractatus Logico-Philosophicus*, the correspondence theory is given a very literal interpretation. Russell conceived of sensible events as entering into what he called atomic facts; and these atomic facts were designated, as it were photographically, by elementary propositions. The truth of all higher-order propositions depended upon the truth of these elementary propositions and the truth of these elementary propositions consisted in their structural correspondence with atomic facts. Russell devoted much ingenuity to the elaboration of this theory, but it depends upon a pictorial theory of meaning which both he and Wittgenstein subsequently found to be untenable.

Russell has reverted to the problem of truth both in his *Inquiry into Meaning and Truth* and in *My Philosophical Development*, which was published in 1959. He still adheres to a correspondence theory in so far as he holds that propositions are made true by facts, but he no longer thinks that truth consists in a relation of structural correspondence, and he now prefers to regard the truth of propositions as derivative from the truth of beliefs. Roughly speaking, his view is that a belief is accounted tuue if the state of affairs which is taken as verifying it is found by observation to exist, and false if its 'verifier' is found not to exist. This is in line also with his rejection of a pictorial in favour of a causal theory of meaning.

Russell has remained a Logical Atomist in the sense of thinking that the world consists of a number of particulars. But in the *Inquiry into Meaning and Truth* he gives this position a new aspect by identifying these particulars with what are ordinarily called qualities. Here again his motive is one of economy, supported by the desire to eliminate the dubious notion of substance. Accordingly he follows Berkeley in treating the things of common sense as collections of qualities, which are united by what he calls a relation of compresence. There are some difficulties in this theory, which centre mainly upon the interpretation of the relation of compresence; but I think it quite possible that they can be overcome.

This view of the nature of particulars is retained in Russell's *Human Knowledge: Its Scope and Limits*, which was published in 1948. Otherwise, this book is of interest chiefly for its attempt to deal with the problem of induction. Russell takes the unfashionable view that inductive reasoning stands in need of justification, and he elaborates a set of principles which he thinks would be sufficient for this purpose. He does not, however, think that any of these principles can be known to be true.

There are many other aspects of philosophy to which Russell has contributed. He has written extensively on ethics, on political philosophy, on social philosophy and the philosophy of education, on the history of philosophy and the philosophy of history. But while this section of his work contains some of the best of Russell's writing, it has not the same theoretical interest as his work in the field of logic and the theory of knowledge. In moral philosophy, he began by sharing G. E. Moore's view that 'good' was an objective unanalysable non-natural quality, but he has since been persuaded that ethical judgements are not objectively either true or false, but are rather expressive of attitudes. Though he accepts this conclusion intellectually, he confesses to disliking it on emotional grounds. His own ethical standpoint appears to be mainly utilitarian. He believes that the proper concern of ethics is to find out what people want and how their ends can be attained. At the same time it is clear that he attaches an intrinsic value to such things as justice and liberty and the pursuit of truth.

While he has an extensive knowledge of history, of which he makes effective use, Russell's approach to social questions is more moral than historical. In the *History of Western Philosophy*, which he published in

1946, he did indeed set out to relate philosophical ideas to the social conditions under which they were produced, but for the most part the exposition of the ideas and the description of the social background proceed side by side: no very serious attempt is made to integrate them. As might be expected, his history of philosophy is most illuminating when it treats of the philosophers to whom he is most sympathetic; in particular, Leibniz and the British empiricists.

To my mind, the best of Russell's political writings is his book on the *Principles of Social Reconstruction*, which appeared in 1916 at the height of his campaign against the First World War. It is anarchist in temper and it reflects the distrust of institutions, and especially of the power of the state, that has always coloured his political thinking. Not only in politics, but also in the sphere of education, he has been a consistent advocate of liberty. Though he is more keenly aware of the irrational features in human conduct, his outlook on moral, political and social questions bears a fairly close affinity to that of John Stuart Mill.

In the course of his long career, Russell, as we have seen, has held quite a large variety of philosophical opinions. This has sometimes been used as an argument against him, especially by those who publish very little for fear of being discovered to be wrong. But the fact is that, while he has fairly often changed his views on points of detail, his approach to philosophy has been remarkably consistent. His aim has always been to try to find reasons for accepted beliefs, whether in the field of mathematics, natural or social science, or common sense. He has been a consistent sceptic, not in the sense that he denies our claims to knowledge, but that he questions them. He has adhered also to a single method, the method of starting with propositions which are the least susceptible to doubt, and trying to reconstruct the edifice of knowledge on this basis, with as few assumptions as possible. When he has changed his views, the reason has usually been either that he thought he could make do with even fewer assumptions, or else that he had pared them down too far, that the basis from which he was working was not adequate to the facts. The result of his using this method has been that his justifications usually take the form of analyses; it is thus that he has come to furnish so much of the inspiration for the analytic movement in contemporary philosophy. Even so, he himself has not been interested in analysis for its own sake, but only as a method of proof. In this, as in the power and elegance of his literary style, he continues the main tradition of British Empiricism. He is, and is likely to remain, its outstanding representative in the twentieth century.

12

G. E. MOORE ON PROPOSITIONS AND FACTS

In the third chapter of *Some Main Problems of Philosophy*, Moore sets out to explain what he means by a proposition. His method is to mention a couple of sentences and inform his audience that when they understood these sentences they were directly apprehending propositions. They were, of course, in Moore's view, also directly apprehending the sense-data which were conveyed to them by his utterance of the sentences; but he makes it clear that his use of the word 'proposition', unlike that of some other philosophers, is such that a proposition is not to be identified with any collection of words, whether the words be regarded as tokens or types, but only with the meaning of the words, with what a sentence is used to express. He does not attempt to define the relation of direct apprehension, beyond saying that it is the relation that one has to a proposition when one understands a sentence, and he confesses himself unable to decide whether, in speaking of directly apprehending propositions, as well as of directly apprehending sense-data, he is using the term 'directly apprehending' in the same or in a different sense.

Having given this account of what he means by a proposition, Moore goes on to list some of the most important characteristics which he thinks that propositions have. The first of these is that in addition to being apprehended, a proposition may also be the object of the mental attitudes of belief or disbelief, in any of their various degrees. Secondly, he says that while the most common way of apprehending a proposition is to understand some sentence which expresses it, we also often apprehend propositions without seeing or hearing or even having in mind any sentences which express them. Presumably he is referring here to the cases in which we cannot, or cannot immediately, find the words to express exactly what we are thinking. He notes also that even when propositions are verbally expressed, they need not always be expressed by whole sentences; for example, a man who calls out 'Fire' may be expressing a proposition. Conversely, he says that he is not sure that all whole sentences express propositions; for example, imperatives may not. His third point is that whenever we apprehend a proposition 'we always also apprehend things which are *not* propositions: namely, things which would be expressed by *some* of the words, of which the whole sentence, which would express the proposition, is composed'.[1] In the case where these words designate a concrete particular, other than a present sense-datum, Moore seems to have held that the relation was only one of what he calls indirect apprehension. We are said by him to apprehend a particular indirectly when we do not directly apprehend it but do directly apprehend a proposition which is about it. On the other hand, every sentence which expresses a proposition must also contain at least one word, or set of words, which stands for what Moore calls a general idea or universal: and he appears to have held that universals were directly apprehended. Finally, he remarks that propositions are 'a sort of thing which can properly be said to be true or false'.[2] They are not the only sort of things of which this can properly be said. For instance, it is also correct to say it of acts of belief. Moore says that the sense in which propositions are true or false is different from that in which acts of belief are, but that the two senses are inter-definable. We can equally well say that an act of belief is true when it has for its object a true proposition, or that a proposition is true when it is the object of a true act of belief.

The lectures of which *Some Main Problems of Philosophy* is composed were delivered in the winter of 1910–11, though the book was not published until 1953. Except for one important point, to which I shall come in a moment, Moore seems to have adhered pretty closely to the conception of a proposition which I have just set out. One very slight difference is that in his later writings he definitely commits himself to the view that the only sentences which are capable of expressing propositions are what he calls declarative sentences: and in an entry in the notebook which he began at the end of the year 1947, he defines a declarative sentence in the following way: 'An English sentence is "declarative" if and only if *both* it makes sense, when the words and syntax are used in accordance with good English usage, and also *either* (1) begins with "I know that", "I think that", "I feel sure that", "It's certain that" or any other of the English phrases which mean the same as one of these *or* (2) is such that the sentence formed by adding one of these before it makes sense.'[3] He does not comment on

[1] *Some Main Problems of Philosophy* (1953), p. 62. [2] Ibid.
[3] *Commonplace Book*, ed. Lewy (1963), pp. 357–8.

the fact that if we accept this definition we may be put into the position of having to say either that not every declarative sentence expresses a proposition or that not every proposition is either true or false. For instance, it is clear that both sentences which are used to express moral judgements and sentences like 'The present King of France is bald', which refer to non-existent individuals, satisfy Moore's definition: yet with regard to sentences of each of these kinds some philosophers have held that what they express is neither true nor false. In the case of sentences which refer to non-existent individuals Moore himself accepted Russell's theory of descriptions, which does assign a truth-value to what they express. On the other hand, in his reply to his critics in *The Philosophy of G. E. Moore*, he admits to being half-inclined to accept Professor Stevenson's 'emotive' theory of ethics, from which it would follow that sentences which expressed moral judgements were not used to assert anything of which truth or falsehood could be predicated.[1]

The distinction between propositions and sentences is maintained throughout Moore's writings on the topic. It is always clear to him that a proposition, in his usage, is not identical either with any token-expression or with any type-expression. There is, however, one passage in the printed selections from a course of lectures which he gave in the years 1925–6, in which he allows there to be a sense in which it might be true that some propositions, in his usage, were token-expressions. He explains that the sense in which this might be true is not one which would imply that any token-expression was identical with a proposition. In saying of some token-expression that it was a proposition, what one would mean would be that it had a certain predicate. The suggestion is 'that just as in "S made use of (uttered) the *expression*: It will be dark soon", what we are saying is *quite certainly* of the form "S made use of *some* token having this predicate"; so in "S was believing the proposition: it will be dark soon", what we are saying is of the form "S was believing *some* token which had this predicate"'.[2] In short, it is suggested that token-expressions may bear to propositions a relation analogous to that which they bear to the type-expressions of which they are tokens. Moore rather strangely speaks of this theory as one that might be expressed by saying that there are token-propositions. He does not say what predicate he thinks a token-expression would need to have in order to be a proposition in this sense, but appears at least to leave the possibility open that it could be described in some more

[1] *The Philosophy of G. E. Moore* (1942), p. 545.
[2] *Lectures on Philosophy*, p. 139.

illuminating way than simply by saying, as he does, that for someone to stand to something which has this predicate in some unspecified relation is, on this theory, a necessary condition of his believing a proposition. Neither does he commit himself as to the truth or falsehood of this theory. He says that he sees nothing against it, but also nothing for it. He does, however, add that if it were true it would point the way to the analysis of 'is believing the proposition that': and from this it might be inferred that he had given up the view that one can believe propositions which one cannot find words to express. His saying that it is only of some propositions that it might be true that they are token-expressions could still be accounted for by the fact that not all propositions are either believed or disbelieved.

Assuming that what he means by a proposition is made sufficiently clear by the explanation which he gives in the third chapter of *Some Main Problems of Philosophy*, Moore declares it to be certain that propositions are among the things that there are in the Universe. It may, therefore, come as something of a shock to find that when he devotes himself to the analysis of belief in chapter fourteen of the very same book, he reaches a conclusion which he expresses by saying that there simply are no such things as propositions, and that when, in the seventeenth chapter, he attacks the view that truths are to be identified with true propositions, he speaks of propositions as imaginary. Moore does not seem to have noticed this discrepancy at the time, but later, when he wrote the preface to the book, he remarked that there was at least a possibility that he had not contradicted himself, since it might be that when he said that there certainly were propositions he was using the sentence 'there are such things as propositions' in a different sense from that in which he was using it when he said that there were no such things. His point was that in the second case he was making the reality of propositions depend upon the correctness of a particular analysis of such sentences as 'I believe the proposition that the sun is larger than the moon', whereas in the passage in which he said that there certainly were propositions he thought it possible that he was 'using it in such a sense that the truth of what it expresses would follow from the mere fact that such expressions as "I believe the *proposition* that the sun is larger than the moon" are perfectly correct ways of expressing something which is often true'.[1]

But what exactly is this sense in which there being propositions is supposed to follow from the mere fact that sentences of the form 'I

[1] *Some Main Problems of Philosophy*, p. xii.

believe the proposition that so and so' can correctly be used to say something true? Moore can hardly be assuming that to receive a mention in a sentence which is used to express a truth is a sufficient title to reality. It is no doubt true that the average man does not believe in leprechauns; but Moore would surely not have held that it followed from this that there are leprechauns or that there is such an entity as the average man. Indeed, he himself remarks in his essay on 'The Concept of Reality'[1] that whereas from the proposition that lions are hunted it follows that there are lions, from the proposition that unicorns are thought of it does not follow that there are unicorns. The example is unfortunate in that hunting does not necessarily entail the existence of what is hunted; in reporting that an expedition had been organized to hunt abominable snowmen, I should not be committing myself to the assertion that there were such things; it would be enough that the members of the expedition should believe that there were, even if their belief were false. Nevertheless the point which the example is intended to make is sound. In some cases one can legitimately infer from the truth of what is expressed by a sentence of the subject-predicate form that there are things of the sort of which the subject is, in other cases one cannot.

But how are these two types of case to be distinguished? Could there be any means of deciding, otherwise than by a process of trial and error, whether a given predicate belonged to one class or the other? I do not know the answer to this question. I have not been able to discover any general criterion by which it can be satisfactorily determined in all instances whether a predicate admits of existential generalization or not. One point, however, which does seem clear is that the existential inference is never valid with respect to anything which is referred to by a proposition which is said to be believed. From the truth of 'A believes that S is P' it does not in general follow that there is such a thing as S. So, in the sense in which S, in this example, can be said to be an object of A's belief, the fact that something is an object of a belief is certainly not sufficient to prove that there is any such thing. The question is whether the position changes when the object of a belief is taken to be not something to which the proposition which is expressed by the subordinate clause refers but the proposition itself.

This question is difficult to answer, if only because it is not clear what is involved in casting propositions as the objects of beliefs. If the

[1] *Philosophical Studies* (1922), p. 216.

assumption is that a reference to propositions is required for the analysis of belief, we shall see in a moment that Moore himself gives a very good reason for holding that this is false. If all that is meant is that it is grammatically respectable to speak of believing propositions, it is hard to see why this fact about English philosophical usage should be thought to license any inference about what there is in the Universe, apart from the existence of some philosophers and the signs which they employ. What I think most likely is that Moore was making the assumption that something must be in order to be believed, but this assumption, in so far as it is intelligible at all, appears to presuppose the sort of analysis of belief that he himself was shortly to reject.

Another possibility is that Moore was led to the conclusion that there must be propositions not so much by any views that he held about the nature of belief as by his theory of meaning. From the innocent premiss that to understand a sentence is to apprehend its meaning, he inferred that there is something, the meaning of a sentence, in short a proposition, which one apprehends. But here again, if the conclusion of this inference is to be anything more than a mere repetition of the premiss, it must be interpreted as implying the correctness of a certain analytical position. The underlying assumption is that in order to give an analysis of what it is for a sentence to have a meaning, it is sufficient to postulate an abstract object which the sentence can be taken to signify. But once this assumption is brought to light, it becomes clear that what we are being given is not an analysis of meaning, but rather the result of a decision that no analysis is possible. To say that sentences signify propositions, and that is all there is to it, is merely a way of saying that the notion of signifying, as applied to sentences, and the notion of what is signified, are not further analysable. Now I do not know that any of the numerous attempts that have been made to give a further analysis of these notions has been entirely successful, but the difficulties are not such as to make it seem likely that success is unobtainable. I think, therefore, that Moore may simply have been mistaken in saying that propositions are directly apprehended, in so far as this is not merely a restatement of the fact that sentences are understood, but would also commit us to treating the meanings of sentences as objects. Not only is this an unwarranted denial of the possibility of a more informative analysis of meaning, but in suggesting, as it does, that what happens when one understands a sentence is that one contemplates an abstract entity, it is at least seriously misleading. I shall say a little more about this when I come to Moore's reasons for not treating propositions as the objects of beliefs.

In his paper on 'Facts and Propositions' which appeared as the second part of a symposium with F. P. Ramsey in the *Supplementary Proceedings of the Aristotelian Society* for 1927, and is reprinted in his *Philosophical Papers*, Moore remarks that he has not come across any argument which seemed to him to show conclusively that propositions were not genuine entities.[1] He did not say what sort of argument he would regard as conclusive, neither did he say what the assertion that propositions were genuine entities would be understood by him to mean. An indication of what he took it to mean may, however, be found in his treatment of the very similar question whether there are classes. He discusses this question in the 1925–6 course of lectures, and there makes the point that the proposition that there are classes can be taken in two different senses. The first of these senses is characterized by him as one in which the proposition that there are classes is not a proposition about symbols, the second as one in which it is. Of 'there are classes', in the first sense, he says that it seems to him 'something which is *logically equivalent* to saying that there are more than one proposition of a certain sort that are true: viz. "My fingers are a class", "The hairs of my head are a class". *If* there are classes, at least two different propositions of this sort must be true; and if *one* proposition of this sort is true then there is at least one class.'[2] Moore goes on to suggest that this can serve as a general explanation of this sort of existential statement. Whether, to use his own examples, it is a matter of there being men, or lions, or relations, or qualities, to say that there are things of the kind in question is to say that at least two propositions of the form 'x is a so and so' are true. In other words, the question of existence, in this sense, is settled by giving instances.

There is, however, still a difficulty about deciding when an existential statement comes into this category. If 'there are men' follows from the fact that the propositional function 'x is a man' is satisfied in at least two different instances, then, as Moore remarks, 'you might think similarly that (1) "There are imaginary beings" will follow from "Ariel is an imaginary being" and "Oberon is an imaginary being"; and that (2) "There are fairies" will follow from "Oberon is a fairy" and "Titania is a fairy".'[3] His answer is that you would be wrong in

[1] *Philosophical Papers* (1959), p. 76.
[2] *Lectures on Philosophy*, p. 122.
[3] Ibid., p. 123.

thinking this because 'x is an imaginary being' or 'x is a fairy' is not a function of the same sort as 'x is a man' or 'x is a class'. To say that Oberon is an imaginary being, if it is not to be taken as expressing the self-contradictory proposition that a certain set of predicates both belongs to one individual and to nothing at all, must be interpreted as saying that a certain set of predicates has been imagined as belonging to one individual, without in fact being attributed to anyone. To say that Oberon is a fairy is to say that the attribute of being a fairy is one of those that have been attributed to a particular imaginary character. Moore sees, however, that this gives no rule for determining when the existential inference is legitimate. You have first to decide whether the subject exists before you can decide whether the expression which appears to attribute a predicate to it is to be interpreted according to the model of 'Shakespeare is a man' or according to the model of 'Oberon is a fairy'.

In the case of propositions, it is safe to assume that Moore did consider the existential inference to be legitimate. If 'there are classes' is allowed to follow from 'my fingers are a class' and 'the hairs of my head are a class', and if 'there are qualities' is allowed to follow from 'red is a quality' and 'blue is a quality', then there is no reason why 'There are propositions' should not be allowed to follow from ' "Shakespeare wrote Hamlet" is a proposition' and ' "Queen Anne is dead" is a proposition' or from any other pair of different propositions that one cares to mention. The only thing that might make one hesitate to attribute this view to Moore is that he seems, in the paper on 'Facts and Propositions', at least to admit the possibility that propositions are not genuine entities, though he certainly cannot have been in any doubt concerning the fact that at least two propositions of the form ' "p" is a proposition' were true. But the probable explanation of this is that when Moore considered the possibility of its being demonstrated that propositions are not genuine entities, he was interpreting the expression 'there are propositions' not in a sense corresponding to his first sense of 'there are classes' but in a sense corresponding to his second sense, the one in which 'there are classes' is construed as expressing a proposition about symbols.

But what exactly is this second sense? The account which we are given of it in Moore's lecture notes is somewhat compressed and not at all points easy to follow, but its outline is reasonably clear. It is closely based on the treatment of classes which Russell adopts in *Principia Mathematica* and elsewhere. Russell used the word 'class' in such a way that every predicate can be said to determine a class. If nothing satisfies the predicate, it determines the null-class: if only one thing satisfies it, it determines a unit-class: and in general, for any number *n*, a predicate determines a class with *n* members if it is satisfied by just *n* things. In this usage, the concept of class is an extensional concept: if two predicates are co-extensive in their application, they determine the same class. So the class of unicorns is identical with the class of centaurs, the class whose only member is the author of Hamlet is identical with the class whose only member is the author of Macbeth. Moore regards this as a queer usage, not because of the extensionality, to which he has no objection, but because he thinks that, in ordinary language, it is contradictory to speak of a class with less than two members. We shall see in a moment that this is a point of more consequence to Moore than might at first appear.

To understand the next step, it is necessary to know the construction which Moore puts upon Russell's notion of an incomplete symbol. In *Principia Mathematica* Russell said that what he meant by an incomplete symbol was a symbol which was definable in use but had no meaning in isolation. So, according to his theory of descriptions, definite descriptive phrases are incomplete symbols. This definition does not satisfy Moore, both because he thinks it a mistake to say that expressions like 'the author of Waverley' have no meaning in isolation, and because he thinks that it fails to bring out the most important features of Russell's procedure. He first points out that what needs to be defined is not just '*x* is an incomplete symbol' but rather '*x in this usage* is an incomplete symbol' and then offers the following definition of Russell's use of this expression: 'In the case of *every* sentence, *p*, in which *x* occurs *with this meaning*, there can be formed another sentence, *q*, for which *p* is short, such that neither *x* itself nor any expression for which *x* is short, occurs in *q*, and *p* always *looks as if* the rest of it expressed a propositional function, such that the proposition expressed by *p* is a value of that function, whereas in fact it never does.'[1]

This may sound a little obscure, but it becomes clear enough when applied to Russell's theory of descriptions. Thus 'The author of Waverley went bankrupt' is taken in this theory to be equivalent to 'At most one person wrote Waverley, at least one person wrote Waverley, and it is not the case that anyone both wrote Waverley and did not go bankrupt'. The second sentence is more complex than the first; it does not contain the expression 'the author of Waverley'; the first sentence

[1] *Lectures on Philosophy*, p. 119.

is so constructed that it looks as if it supplies a value for the function 'x went bankrupt'; the translation shows, however, that this is not so; the descriptive phrase does not supply a value for the function but conjoins another predicate to it. This can all be summarized, for our purpose, by saying that what makes a symbol incomplete, in this sense, is that there is a special sort of way of translating it out.

Russell goes so far as to say that if anything is designated by an incomplete symbol, it follows that it is a logical fiction, but, as Moore points out, this cannot be correct, if only because it would have the unacceptable consequence that genuine entities could only be named and never described. For it to be true that there are no classes, in the sense in which this is a proposition about symbols, it is, indeed, necessary that symbols for classes should be incomplete, but it is not sufficient: a further condition is required, which is, according to Moore, that symbols for classes should not be descriptions. But now we run into the same difficulty as before. It seems that in order to decide whether symbols for classes are descriptions, one has first to decide whether classes are genuine entities. If symbols for classes are not descriptions, then, as Moore puts it, the expression 'determined by', in the sense in which classes are said to be determined by predicates, 'does not express any relation';[1] if they are, it does. Surprisingly Moore says that, in the sense in which Russell speaks of classes, 'hardly anyone would be disposed to question' that 'determined by' does not express a relation.[2] On the other hand, when it comes to classes in what he takes to be the ordinary sense of the term, he is disposed to go the other way; he inclines towards the view that 'having for a member' is an ultimate relation in which classes stand to their elements. But, so far as I can see, his only reason for adopting this position is that he just cannot bring himself to believe that there is such a thing as the null-class, or that there is an entity distinct from Scott, namely the class of which Scott is the only member, which is determined by the predicate 'wrote Waverley'; whereas he has no difficulty in believing that there are such entities as the classes constituted by the fingers on his right hand, or the pennies in his pocket. He fails, however, to explain what he thinks is meant by saying that these classes exist, over and above the fact that the predicates 'being a finger on Moore's right hand' or 'being a penny in Moore's pocket' at a given date are satisfied by such and such particulars.

All this applies *mutatis mutandis* to the question whether there are

[1] Ibid., p. 624. [2] Ibid., p. 626.

propositions. In this case also, the only substantial point at issue would seem to be whether propositions are designated by incomplete symbols. If it could be shown that in all cases in which we ostensibly referred to a proposition, the reference could be eliminated either by translation or at least by an adequate paraphrase, then it is not clear what motive anyone could have for continuing to assert that there were propositions; it is not clear even what his assertion could, at this stage, be taken to mean. I shall, therefore, assume that if we can find a way of eliminating propositions, in this sense, we shall have demonstrated that they are not genuine entities. What we are required to show is that the reference to propositions is not necessary for explaining how sentences have meaning, or for the analysis of belief, or for the theory of truth.

I shall begin with the analysis of belief, both because Moore devoted more attention to it than he did to the topic of meaning, and because the little more that I have to say about meaning arises out of it. As we have already remarked, it was Moore's rejection of his previous assumption that belief consists in having a proposition before the mind in a special sort of way that led him, in *Some Main Problems of Philosophy*, to conclude that there were no such things as propositions. His argument, though his exposition of it is elaborate, is essentially quite simple. I shall try to set it out as clearly as I can.

Moore takes as an example the false belief that anyone would be having if he believed that Moore and his audience were currently hearing the noise of a brass band. What would make this belief false, he says, would be the fact that they were not hearing any such noise, or to put it another way, the absence from the Universe of the fact which would make the belief true. He then points out that this conclusion can be generalized. What makes a belief true is the presence in the Universe of the fact to which it refers; what makes a belief false is the absence of this fact from the Universe. If we now ask what the fact is to which a given belief refers, the answer is that it is '*the* fact which has the *same name* as that which we have to use in naming the belief'.[1] To name a belief is to say that it is the belief that so and so, the belief that my scissors are lying on the table, the belief that unicorns exist, or whatever it may be; and the same verbal clause is used to name the fact, the fact that my scissors are lying on the table, the fact that unicorns exist, or whatever, the being or non-being of which renders the belief true or false. Moore makes it clear that he is not

[1] *Some Main Problems of Philosophy*, p. 256.

putting this forward as a definition of what is meant by the fact to which a belief refers: he is not suggesting that what we mean by saying that a belief is true is that the Universe contains a fact which has the same name. The identity of name expresses another relation which needs to be brought to light. But for this we require an analysis of belief.

Now the analysis which Moore had hitherto accepted was, as we have seen, that belief was a special act of mind which was directed towards an objective entity, a proposition; and the proposition was supposed to exist, or perhaps we should say, to subsist, whether the belief was true or false. It follows, as Moore now remarks, that in the case of a true belief there are two objective entities to be reckoned with: the proposition which is the object of the belief and the fact which makes it true. Though they are both named by the same name as the belief, these entities are identical neither with it nor with each other: the proof that they are not identical with each other is that the proposition is present in the Universe whether the belief is true or false, whereas the fact is present only if the belief is true.

This reduplication of entities is not regarded by Moore as a fatal objection to the theory, though he allows that it casts a suspicion against it. He thinks that the best line for an advocate of the theory to take would be to maintain that truth and falsehood were unanalysable properties of propositions and that the fact which made a given belief true simply consisted in the possession by the corresponding proposition of the property of truth. This would not be inconsistent with the definition of truth, according to which 'to say that a belief is true is to say that there *is* in the Universe *the fact* to which it refers'.[1] The sense of 'truth' in which propositions are true would, on this theory, be fundamental; and talking of the being of the fact to which a belief referred would come down to defining the truth of a belief in terms of the truth of the proposition which was its object.

Moore has two objections to this theory. He does not think that either of them is conclusive, but they are enough to make him give the theory up. The first, which is an objection only to the proposed analysis of the fact to which a true belief refers, is that he no longer finds it credible that such a fact can consist merely in the possession of some simple property by a proposition. Even if it be granted that there are propositions, their relation to facts must surely be something different from this. The second objection is more general; it puts in

[1] Ibid., p. 262

question the basic assumption that propositions are the objects of beliefs. In Moore's own words, 'it is that, if you consider what happens when a man entertains a false belief, it doesn't seem as if his belief consisted merely in his having a relation to some object which certainly *is*. It seems rather as if the thing he was believing, the *object* of his belief, were just *the* fact which certainly is *not*—which certainly is not, because his belief is false'.[1] But to say that the fact is not is only a clumsy way of saying that there is no such fact; and if there is no such fact, then no belief can have it for an object. Moore is therefore led to the conclusion that beliefs do not, in this sense, have any objects at all.

To develop this argument, Moore returns to his original example. He points out that the difficulty to which he is trying to draw attention does not arise only in the case of false belief. It is enough for his purpose that his audience should be able to conceive such a hypothesis as that they are now hearing the noise of a brass band. Here again it might be suggested that what they were conceiving was a proposition, and that this proposition had being, even though the fact which there would have been, if the proposition had been true, did not. But then, he goes on, in order to distinguish the proposition which is from the fact which is not, it is surely necessary to conceive both; and what can the object of the conception be in the case of the non-existent fact? It cannot be the proposition that they are not now hearing the noise of a brass band, for that has the same status as its contradictory; and anyhow what they need to distinguish is not a proposition from its contradictory but a proposition from the fact, the non-being of which makes it false. The only possible answer is that when they conceive of this non-existent fact, their conception has no object at all. But once it is admitted that there can be conceptions without objects, the motive for bringing in propositions disappears. In Moore's own words, 'if, in some cases, when we conceive or believe a thing, there really *is* no such thing as that which we *are said* to believe or conceive —if sometimes the words which we seem to use to denote the thing believed or conceived, are[2] not really a *name* of anything at all, I think there is no reason why we should not admit that this is *always* the case in false belief, or in conception of what is purely imaginary. We should then have to say that expressions of the form "I believe so and so", "I conceive so and so", though they do undoubtedly express *some* fact, do *not* express any relation between *me* and an object of which the name

[1] *Some Main Problems of Philosophy*, p. 263.

[2] The 'is' which occurs here in the text is presumably a misprint.

is the words we use to say *what* we believe or conceive. And since there seems plainly no difference, in mere analysis, between false belief and true belief, we should have to say of all beliefs and suppositions generally, that they *never* consist in a relation between the believer and something else which *is* what is believed.'[1]

What emerges from this argument is that propositions have no part to play in the analysis of belief. If they are treated as symbols, they gratuitously reduplicate the sentences which are used to state what is believed. It is, however, only if they are treated as symbols that it makes any sense to predicate truth and falsehood of them. To treat them as objects, on to which beliefs are directed, is to make it impossible to explain how anything comes to be true or false. Since an object, in this sense, does not refer beyond itself, the propositions simply cut off the beliefs from the actual course of events by which they are verified or falsified.

An objection of the same kind holds against the attempt to cast propositions in the rôle of the meanings of sentences. There is, indeed, no harm in talking of propositions, so long as it is understood that this is just a convenient device for referring to what is true not only of a given sentence but of any other sentence which has the same meaning. But to conceive of the meaning of a sentence as an abstract object is, as I said earlier, not only to fail to explain how sentences are endowed with meaning, but also to misrepresent the way in which they are understood. If one supposes that understanding a sentence simply consists in apprehending an abstract entity, one will be at a loss to explain how one ever succeeds in communicating any valid information about matters of empirical fact. Once again, if the proposition is not itself a symbol, it acts not as a bridge but as a barrier between words and things. If it is a symbol, it gratuitously reduplicates the words.

This argument does perhaps afford a sufficient justification for saying that there are no such things as propositions. We should, however, note that in saying this we shall be giving yet another sense to this existential negation. What we shall in effect be saying is that propositions need not be taken seriously, that they are incompetent to do the work to which they have been assigned. But clearly this is not the same as saying that propositions are designated by incomplete symbols. It leaves it an open question whether all the apparent references that we make to propositions can be translated out. I am in fact of the opinion that they can at least be paraphrased out and I have tried

[1] *Some Main Problems of Philosophy*, pp. 264–5.

elsewhere[1] to sketch a theory of meaning which could secure this result. I have, however, to admit that in common with all the other attempts that I know of to achieve anything like a formal elimination of propositions, my theory encounters difficulties which I cannot claim to have entirely removed.

Moore himself seems not to have been altogether satisfied with his proof that propositions are not the objects of beliefs. At least I can find no evidence that he ever subsequently relied on the argument which I have just been summarizing, and in his essay on 'Facts and Propositions', which appeared sixteen years after he delivered the lecture in which this argument is set out, he still wrote as if he thought it possible that a proposition should be what he calls 'the objective factor' in a fact of a certain sort. Since he explains that one condition for anything A to be an objective factor in a fact of the kind in question is that the fact should entail both that A is being believed and that if anything else is being believed it is contained in A, and since he goes on to say that only a proposition can satisfy this condition, and then only if it is a 'genuine entity', it is clear that in allowing this possibility he has gone back on his earlier position. To see how far he has gone back it will be necessary to examine his essay in some detail.

The first point to remark is that the facts with regard to which Moore says that he thinks it possible that they contain propositions as objective factors are facts of a peculiar sort. He defines them as facts which correspond in a certain way to another class of facts which he defines, as so often, by means of an example. The example is the fact which someone, who was at a given moment judging that Caesar was murdered, would express if he at that moment uttered the English words 'I am now judging that Caesar was murdered'. The class of facts which Moore uses this example to define consists of all those which resemble it in being correctly expressible by an English sentence of the form 'I am now judging that *p*'. Moore has no doubt that there are facts of this kind and he also has no doubt that they are all what he calls general facts. What he appears to mean by saying that they are general facts is that they are in some degree indeterminate. Thus, in the case of his example, he assumes that someone who judges that Caesar was murdered must be judging with regard to some description such as 'the author of *De Bello Gallico*' or 'the conqueror of Pompey' that the person who answers to this description was murdered:

[1] See *The Origins of Pragmatism*, pp. 173–9 (Macmillan, 1968), or pp. 162–8 (Freeman, Cooper, 1968).

but certainly this information is not conveyed merely by saying 'I am now judging that Caesar was murdered'. The answer to this might appear to be that if the description in question were substituted for the word 'Caesar', as it evidently could be, the resulting sentence would still express a fact which answered to Moore's definition; but I suppose he would have replied that even this would not remove the element of generality, on the ground that there were different ways in which the description might be thought to be satisfied. Again, he assumes that when one makes a judgement one must make it with a definite amount of precision, with a particular degree of conviction and so forth; yet none of this is stated in merely saying that one makes the judgement. Finally, he thinks it possible, in a fashion which he does not explain, that the use of the word 'I' in this context imports a further element of generality.

Now it is Moore's contention that to every general fact of this kind there corresponds one and only one non-general fact. The way in which it corresponds is that every one of the general facts 'is, or is equivalent to, a fact, with regard to a certain description, to the effect that there is one and only one non-general fact answering to that description';[1] the non-general fact in question is then the one which does so answer. It would seem that in order to express such a non-general fact, one would have to state, in a completely determinate way, exactly what happened on the relevant occasion to make it true that someone was then judging that Caesar was murdered or whatever it might be. Moore is, however, of the opinion that none of these non-general facts 'could possibly be expressed in any actual language', presumably on the ground that none of the sentences of any actual language which one might try to employ for the purpose would be sufficiently determinate; and he adds that 'perhaps even none could be expressed in any possible language'.[2] It is, then, with these inexpressible non-general facts that Moore believed that his co-symposiast, Ramsey, was really concerned when he wrote in his paper about analysing judgements; and it is of them that he asserts that they may contain propositions as their objective factors.

There is a good deal here that is puzzling. If we consider not the fact which someone might express by saying that he believed that Caesar was murdered, but simply the fact that Caesar was murdered, then I suppose that a case could be made out for saying that this was a general fact to which just one non-general fact corresponded. What

[1] *Philosophical Papers*, p. 69. [2] Ibid.

might be meant by saying that it was a general fact would be that there were a number of different possible concrete states of affairs which would make what is expressed by the sentence 'Caesar was murdered' true; and what might be meant by saying that just one non-general fact corresponded to it would be that there was just one state of affairs which did make it true, a state of affairs which consisted in a particular man's being killed at a particular time and place by such and such other men in such and such a particular way. But if this is an example of what Moore meant by a non-general fact, I do not find it at all obvious that non-general facts are inexpressible. To avoid any difficulties that there might be in pinning down their subjects, we could attempt to cast them in such a form that the only referential expressions of which we needed to make use in stating them were expressions which referred to places and times; and it would appear possible to make these references completely precise. In order to state what occurred at the place and time, we should then need only to use predicates; and these, I take it, would be qualitative predicates standing for observable properties: they might, for example, be predicates of colour or shape. But then, in view of the fact that there are limits to our powers of sensory discrimination, there would appear to be no reason in principle why these predicates should not be wholly determinate, in the sense that all the instances in which they were satisfied were qualitatively indistinguishable in the relevant respect. In the case of sentences which were designed to express the non-general facts which verified propositions about human actions there would, indeed, be special difficulties, since we might have to bring in predicates which were satisfied by mental images or by unspoken thoughts: but here again I see no reason in principle why a mental image should not be described with complete precision, or even an unspoken thought, to the extent that it consists not merely in the subject's having certain propensities to speak or act in certain ways, but in some actual state of his consciousness. Of course, no series of sentences of this kind would express anything equivalent to what is expressed by such a sentence as 'Caesar was murdered'; for one thing, they would not rise to the level at which causal relations can be formulated. Nevertheless they could still constitute a completely accurate record of the particular stretch of history in virtue of which the sentence with the greater generality of meaning could be held to express a fact.

This is, however, a simpler problem than the one with which Moore presents us. As we have seen, his example of a general fact is not the fact that Caesar was murdered, but rather the fact which someone would express by saying truly with reference to a particular time that he judged at that time that Caesar was murdered; and it is in the non-general facts which correspond to general facts of this sort that Moore thinks himself able to distinguish objective and non-objective or at least 'not merely objective' factors. We have seen that one sufficient condition which he lays down for anything to be an objective factor in a fact of this sort is that it be the one and only proposition which in asserting the fact in question one is asserting to be believed. A second sufficient condition is that it be something about which the fact entails that something is being believed, in 'some sense of the word "about"'.[1] A not merely objective factor is one that may or may not satisfy one of these conditions, but in any case also enters into the fact in some other way. Thus, in Moore's view, the time at which the judgement is made is an objective factor in the non-general fact corresponding to the fact of someone's judging that Caesar was murdered, since he assumes that anyone who made such a judgement would be judging with regard to the time at which he made it that the event of Caesar's murder occurred before that time. On the other hand, the time at which the subject made the judgement would also enter into the fact in another way 'since it would also be the time, with regard to which the fact in question would be a fact to the effect that he was making that judgement *at* that time'.[2] After the same fashion, the word 'I' might refer to a factor which enters into a fact of this kind in two different ways, if the judgement is one that the subject makes about himself. Because of this, Moore thinks it advisable to define what Ramsey calls a 'mental factor', in a fact of the kind in question, in such a way that something's being a mental factor is not inconsistent with its also being an objective factor. His proposal, given that F is a fact of the appropriate sort and B a factor in F, is that 'B will be a "mental" factor in F, if and only if both (1) B is not *merely* an "objective" factor in F and also (2) B is not the time (or whatever "factor" in F corresponds to this time) *about* which F is a fact to the effect that a certain judgement is being made at that time'.[3]

Having defined mental and objective factors in this way, Moore takes it for granted that every fact of the sort he is concerned with contains mental factors and he also thinks it unquestionable that

[1] *Philosophical Papers*, p. 70.

[2] Ibid., p. 71. [3] Ibid., p. 73.

every such fact contains more than one objective factor. Unfortunately, he does not say how factors are to be individuated. Thus, if we consider such a fact as that lions exist, we do not know whether to take lions and existence as factors, or the property of being a lion and the fact that it is satisfied, or some set of properties which together make up the property of being a lion and the fact that they are conjointly satisfied. Since the judgement that lions exist could, in some sense or other of the word 'about', be said to be about any of these things, it would seem that we have a pretty free choice.

There is, however, some indication that Moore held this choice to be subject to at least one serious restriction. From what he says about propositions, in this context, it may be inferred that he was not prepared to count anything as an objective factor unless it was a genuine entity. But, in that case, so far from its being certain that the facts of which Moore is speaking always contain a plurality of objective factors, it may very well be doubted whether they need contain any objective factors at all. The sort of counter-example which I have in mind would be one in which the judgement in question did not refer to any particular period of time or to any existent things. The most obvious instance would be judgements about mythical entities, like centaurs or unicorns. It might be argued that what such judgements were really about was the stories in which these imaginary creatures figured; but the answer to this would be that one can ascribe characteristics to such things as unicorns or centaurs, without knowing them to be imaginary. In face of this difficulty, the easiest line for Moore to have taken would have been to say that the objective factors, in such instances, were the properties in terms of which these imaginary creatures were defined. But then what ground would he have had for saying that properties were genuine entities? Here again, Moore's failure to supply any criterion for what is to count as a genuine entity makes this question impossible to answer. All that I can say is that just as one does not explain how sentences have meaning by saying that they stand for propositions, so one does not explain how adjectival expressions have meaning by saying that they stand for properties.

Having admitted, for whatever reason, that every fact of the sort he is concerned with has more than one objective factor, Moore considers whether this admission precludes him from holding that propositions are ever the objective factors in such facts. He thinks that it would so preclude him if the principle, which he attributes to Ramsey, that there cannot be two different facts, each of which entails the other, were true: but he says that he can find no reason for believing this principle to be true, and some reason for believing it to be false. Accordingly, his tentative conclusion appears to be that in the case of any general fact which consists in someone's making a judgement, there are two corresponding non-general facts. One of them consists in the holding of some relation or relations between some not merely objective factors and a plurality of objective factors, and the other consists in the holding of some relation or relations between some not merely objective factors and a proposition. In the second case, the constituents of the proposition are also objective factors which are contained in the fact, but the fact does not, as in the first case, consist in their standing in any relation to the not merely objective factor, but only in the proposition's doing so. These two non-general facts are equivalent, in the sense that they mutually entail each other, but they are not identical.

Apart from the unclarity of the notion of an objective factor, there are two further difficulties here. The first is that Moore does not attempt to explain, still less to justify, his mysterious distinction between what a fact consists in and what it contains. The second and more serious difficulty is that he fails to give any rules for individuating facts. He seems to have had no doubt that facts, both general and non-general, were genuine entities, but at the same time no very clear idea how one fact was to be distinguished from another.

One thing which we do know is that Moore was not willing to identify facts with true propositions. His proof that they are not identical is given in an entry in the first of his note-books, which was written in the year 1919 or thereabouts. It is shown, he says, 'by showing that "This is scarlet" is equivalent to "That this is scarlet is a fact" but is *not* equivalent to "The proposition that this is scarlet is a fact". "The proposition that this is scarlet is a fact" is nonsense, which shows that "is a fact" and "is true" are not interchangeable, although the sentences "That this is scarlet is a fact" and "That this is scarlet is true" have the same meaning.'[1] In short, the argument is that since the expressions 'is a true proposition' and 'is a fact' are not universally interchangeable, facts and true propositions cannot be identical. This would be a valid argument if its premiss were true, but the trouble is that the example, which is meant to show that the premiss is true, itself relies on the truth of the conclusion. If someone were convinced that facts were identical with true propositions, he would presumably

[1] *Commonplace Book*, p. 3.

not admit that the sentence 'The proposition that this is scarlet is a fact' was a piece of nonsense; he would accept it as an inelegant way of stating that the proposition that this is scarlet was true.

Moore's claim that his facts are not identical with true propositions might carry more conviction if he had been able to show how they could be separately identified. I shall suggest in a moment that this can be achieved in the case of Moore's non-general facts. On the other hand, when it comes to his general facts, I am unable to see any way of identifying them except through the true propositions which they gratuitously mirror, and ultimately, therefore, through the sentences by which these propositions are expressed. To the non-general fact to which the general fact that Caesar was murdered corresponds, there also correspond, if one is to believe Moore, the general fact that the author of *De Bello Gallico* was murdered, the general fact that Caesar did not die a natural death, the general fact that a great-uncle of Augustus did not die a natural death, the general fact that either Caesar or Napoleon was murdered, the general fact that either Caesar was murdered or Napoleon was an Irishman, and countless others of similar types. What distinguishes these facts from one another is just the differences in content of the propositions with which they are severally paired and the only purpose that is served by speaking of them is to make the point that these propositions are true. We have already had enough difficulty in attaching meaning to the thesis that propositions are real constituents of the Universe; there seems even less excuse for talking as if, corresponding to every true proposition, the Universe contained yet another sort of abstract entity, in the form of a general fact.

The case of non-general facts is different because here we are justified in thinking of facts, not as true propositions masquerading under a different title, but as the concrete states of affairs which make propositions true. Thus, all the propositions corresponding to the so-called general facts which I have just listed are made true by the non-general fact of Caesar's dying at the particular time and place and in the particular way he did. Even here, however, Moore shows his lack of concern for Ockham's razor. He distinguishes the fact that Caesar died from the event of Caesar's death, with the implication that they are both constituents of the Universe. But while it is true that facts are not identical with events, in the sense that we can say of one what we cannot significantly say of the other, the difference is no more than a difference of grammar: whichever way of speaking we find it convenient to employ, there is a sense in which the phenomena to which we are referring are the same. There is just one stretch of the world's history which Caesar's murder occupies, and whether we refer to it in terms of facts, or events, or states of affairs, or things and their attributes, or the instantiation of properties, or the satisfaction of predicates is a matter for our convenience. There is no reason indeed why we should not draw on all these forms of vocabulary: but it is neither necessary nor profitable to reify all the entities which figure in them.

One motive which Moore may have had for upholding the reality of facts was that he thought that this was required for his correspondence theory of truth. The relation of correspondence on which this theory depends is one which is supposed to hold between a fact of the form '*A* judges that *p*' and the fact which the *p* in question expresses, if it does express a fact. Moore maintains that in some uses of the word 'true', the meaning of this word can be defined by reference to this relation, and that '*all* our usages of "true" are such that a proposition expressed by the help of that word is *equivalent* to some proposition in which this relation occurs'.[1] For instance, he thinks that, in one of its meanings, '"It is true that *p*" means the same as "If anyone were to believe that *p*, then the fact which consisted in his believing that *p* would correspond to a fact"'.

This theory is not objectionable in itself. It avoids the mistake into which some other correspondence theories fall of trying to cash 'correspondence' in terms of resemblance or structural similarity. All the same it achieves nothing that is not achieved more clearly and simply by the semantic schema '*S* is true in *L* if and only if *p*', where it is understood that the expression which is put in the place of '*S*' designates a sentence of the language *L* which has the same meaning as the sentence which is put in the place of '*p*'. In both cases, the interesting philosophical problems still remain to be tackled. We need an informative account of meaning; we need a clear specification of the forms of sentences which are used to record the empirical states of affairs which finally determine the truth or falsity of everything that we say about the world; and we need an exact analysis of the ways in which the truth or falsity of what is expressed by sentences of other types depends upon the truth or falsity of what is expressed by sentences of this basic sort. If we had satisfactory answers to all these questions, we should, I think, be left with only a stylistic motive for speaking of propositions or of any but what Moore calls non-general facts.

[1] *Commonplace Book*, p. 83.

In a recent review of Moore's *Commonplace Book* and his *Lectures on Philosophy*, Mr G. J. Warnock has remarked on the lack of sophistication which went with Moore's extraordinary critical acumen.[1] I think that this remark is just and that it particularly applies to most of Moore's writing on the topic of facts and propositions. The lack of sophistication is shown in his approach to the question whether these are genuine entities. He treats it as a much more straightforward question than it turns out to be. Only in the chapter on 'Beliefs and Propositions' in *Some Main Problems of Philosophy* does he bring out the connection between the belief in the reality of propositions and the acceptance of a particular, unsatisfactory, theory of meaning and truth. It is strange that having had this insight he never again attempted to develop it.

[1] See *Mind*, vol. LXXVII, no. 307, pp. 431–6.

13

REFLECTIONS ON EXISTENTIALISM

THE philosophy of Existentialism is hardly a body of systematic doctrine. The contemporary writers who are looked upon as its leading representatives are Heidegger, Jaspers, Gabriel Marcel and Jean-Paul Sartre, but there are so many points on which they disagree that it is doubtful if any one of them would regard himself as belonging to a movement which included all the others. Nevertheless they do all have something in common, if not a coherent body of doctrine, then at least a fairly similar attitude to philosophy and to life: to use a fashionable expression, they have a family resemblance, which I shall try to bring out. The method which I shall follow will be to discuss certain themes which seem to me, rightly or wrongly, to be characteristic of existentialist thought. I shall devote particular attention to the views of Heidegger and Sartre, but even in their case I shall make no attempt to give a complete account of their philosophy. Thus my comments on Heidegger will be based on only two of his works: the pamphlet *Was ist Metaphysik?* and his most substantial, but early, book *Sein und Zeit*; my comments on Sartre will be confined almost entirely to his major philosophical work, *L'Être et le Néant*. I shall also have something to say about the position of Kierkegaard, who may be regarded as the founder of the existentialist movement, and about the views of Albert Camus, who would never indeed consent to be called an existentialist, but still put forward an interesting version of what I would regard as an existentialist standpoint on one of my central themes.

I shall begin with the elementary question: Why is the movement to which these writers loosely belong called Existentialism? Because they are thought to maintain that existence is prior to essence. But what does it mean to say that existence is prior to essence? In one sense, this is obviously true. A thing cannot have properties unless it exists. But in another, more interesting sense, one might argue that essence was prior to existence. For as Professor Quine has pointed out,[1] the

[1] See W. V. Quine, 'On What There Is', in *From a Logical Point of View* (1953).

tendency of Russellian logic is to show that the question of ontological commitment, the question of what a body of statements, let us say a scientific theory, assumes to exist, depends upon the predicates that the theory contains. Essence is prior to existence, then, in the sense that it is the properties attributed to a thing, its defining properties at least, that determine whether it is a candidate for existence. The thing has to be described in some way before the question of its ontological status can significantly be raised: but to describe it is to classify it as a thing of a certain sort.

Existentialist philosophers are keenly interested in questions of ontology, but they do not approach them in this technical fashion. Their reason for saying that existence is prior to essence is that they think that essences are housed in concepts and that concepts, being necessarily abstract, can never be adequate to, can never sufficiently pin down, the concrete, colourful, pulsating reality. F. H. Bradley expressed the same feeling when he talked of his 'unearthly ballet of bloodless categories'. Putting it in more sober language, we may say that the existentialists are concerned, as many philosophers have been from Aristotle onwards, with the fact that no set of descriptions necessarily individuates. It may in fact be the case that only one individual satisfies them, but this is a contingent matter. It remains logically possible that the class which is defined by these predicates has other members; so that if the possession of these predicates is taken as constituting the essence of the individual, his essence will not necessarily be his alone. From this it is inferred that language can never capture the particularity of the things to which it is intended to refer. Once again this comes out in Bradley who maintained that demonstrative words like 'this', 'here' and 'now' all stood for universals. The point is not so much that existence precedes essence as that it escapes it.

This makes it intelligible that the existentialist movement should have started with Kierkegaard's rebellion against Hegel. Kierkegaard had a strong sense of his own individuality, which was combined with a sense of his personal relation and responsibility to God, and he objected to being swept up, along with everything else, into the impersonal heights of the Hegelian system. He could not find himself in it; he felt that it did not do justice to him. His emphasis on Existence was a protest against Hegel's attempt to intellectualize everything, to refine it all away into abstract concepts, taking as his starting point the most abstract of all: Being and not-Being. It was in fact part of Kierkegaard's grievance that Being should be treated as an abstract concept, for he took this to imply that his own concrete existence was somehow being denied to him.

Now there is certainly a difference between undergoing an experience and merely understanding a description of it: a true statement is to be distinguished from the fact which makes it true; one does not dine off the bill of fare. This is not to say, however, that there is any other way of thinking about reality than by bringing it under concepts. There may be other means of gaining illumination; but if we ask *what* is discovered by these means the answer must be expressible in conceptual terms. The idea that concrete reality must elude the grasp of abstract thought leads to the untenable position that nothing that we think is ever true. For what would be an instance of concrete thought? The proof that our concepts are adequate to reality is just that they are very frequently satisfied.

Nevertheless the feeling that thought and language are somehow too anaemic to come to grips with reality is not confined to existentialists. We have seen it exemplified in Bradley, for all his Hegelian sympathies, and there is at least a touch of it in William James as in the famous passage in which he mocks the Hegelian 'through-and-through' philosophy as seeming 'too buttoned up and white-chokered and clean-shaven a thing to speak for the vast slow-breathing unconscious Kosmos with its dread abysses and its unknown tides'.[1] There is even an echo of it in Wittgenstein: 'We feel that if *all possible* scientific questions be answered, the problems of life have still not been touched at all. Of course there is then no question left, and just this is the answer. The solution of the problem of life is seen in the vanishing of this problem. (Is not this the reason why men to whom after long doubting the sense of life became clear, could not then say wherein this sense consisted?) This is indeed the inexpressible. This *shows* itself; it is the mystical.'[2] However, this strain in Wittgenstein's thought was not acceptable to most of those who were influenced by him in other ways. Thus Neurath's comment on the famous last sentence of the *Tractatus* 'Whereof one cannot speak, thereof one must be silent' was that 'One must indeed be silent, but not about anything' and Ramsey pointed out, in another context, that 'What you can't say, you can't say and you can't whistle it either.' In reading the works of existentialists, one does indeed sometimes get the impression that they are vainly trying to whistle what they cannot say. They come to this point,

[1] W. James, *Essays in Radical Empiricism* (1912), p. 278.

[2] L. Wittgenstein, *Tractatus Logico-Philosophicus* (1922), 6. 52 ff.

however, not so much through taking the metaphysical view that there are realms which lie *beyond* the limits of language as through the belief, which I have tried to show to be mistaken, that language is too abstract an instrument to do justice to our concrete experience.

The problem of individuation applies to things as well as to persons. If there were a difficulty about reproducing the particularity of fact in language, it would be a general difficulty. Physical objects would be as hard to pin down as anything else. But for the most part existentialist philosophers refrain from drawing this conclusion. Physical objects are thought, as Sartre puts it, to exist in themselves (*en-soi*): they are what they are; their properties can be listed; the laws which govern their behaviour can be discovered and formulated: any difficulty of principle that there might be with regard to individuating them is overlooked. The reason for this is that existentialists are not much concerned with physical objects, except as things which resist our will. It is true that they are apt to regard the physical world as somehow dependent on our consciousness, but to the extent that we bear this responsibility we cannot do anything about it; whatever we may contribute to the nature of physical objects, we still have to take them as we find them. Human beings, on the other hand, are in a special category, oneself most of all. In Sartre's terminology, they exist not in themselves but *for* themselves (*pour-soi*). They exist for themselves both in the sense that they are self-conscious and in the sense that they make projects. They always have in view something that they *have* to be. They are perpetually trying, as it were, to catch up with themselves, a situation which Sartre describes rather too cryptically, by saying that they are what they are not and are not what they are.[1]

In metaphysics Sartre closely follows Heidegger, and since Heidegger also develops themes to which there are parallels in the work of Jaspers and Kierkegaard, there is some profit in treating him as the central figure of the existentialist movement. I shall do my best to expound the principal ideas which emerge from the obscurity of his *Sein und Zeit*.

His main purpose, he says, is to inquire into Being, a topic which he thinks has been neglected, or at any rate mishandled, by all philosophers since the Ancient Greeks. But what, we may ask, would such an inquiry consist in? What can be meant by talking about being in general, or even about the being of different sorts of thing, or the

[1] See *L'Être et le Néant* (1943) passim (published in England. as *Being and Nothingness*, tr. Helen Barnes, 1957).

being of a particular individual? When something has been described, what can remain to be said about its being? Heidegger himself says that the concept of being (*Sein*) is indefinable but he thinks that it can be explicated. To begin with, he distinguishes it from the concept of the existent (*Seiendes*). Thus, he is not doing ontology in Quine's sense: he is not merely asking what there is. He is concerned rather with the question why things should be as they are; in his own words, he wants to investigate the ontological structure of existence. My interpretation of this is that the question of being is the question of the status of different types of entity.

Now among the sorts of existent things there is one that is sharply differentiated from the rest. Its peculiarity consists in the fact that it alone poses the question of its being. So the study of being in general must begin with, and be based on, the study of the being of this type of existent, for without it there would be no question of being at all. There would be no question, in the rather trivial sense that the question would not otherwise be raised. Heidegger calls this existent *Dasein*—etymologically Being-there, a word which is said to be untranslatable, and I shall leave it untranslated. It refers of course to mankind, or perhaps just to oneself. There is an ambiguity here which Heidegger never honestly faces; his outlook is always anthropocentric, but sometimes it is solipsistic. *Dasein* is defined as 'that existent that we ourselves always are and which has among its other possibilities the possibility of raising the question of its being'; or again as the existent which in its being conducts itself understandingly towards its being. In short the peculiarity of men is that they can be philosophers and ontologists into the bargain. I do not suppose that even Heidegger would claim that this was in fact true of all men, but he might claim that they all had this potentiality.

What then are the main features of the *Dasein*? First, that its essence is subordinated to its existence. Secondly, that it has the property of *Jemeinigheit*—always being mine. Next it is thrown into the world which it in a sense also creates. The world is indeed alien to it and appears independent. Considered in itself the existent is inaccessible to our intelligence. It dwells in an original chaos (*Grundverborgenheit*). It is the being of the existent that allows it to be understood and interpreted into an organized world. And this is the work of the *Dasein*. It operates in the same way on itself. Thus, the world as we know it, the world that alone we can talk about, is our creation. For this reason the *Dasein* is said to be constitutive of truth. It brings truth into the world by making it intelligible. One may note the very close parallel with Kant.

The parallel is further extended in so far as the mode of being of the *Dasein*, and so derivatively of all existence, is being in time. Time is said to be the sense (*Sinn*) of the being of the existent. But not time as we ordinarily conceive it. According to Heidegger, the time which passes, the time which is the framework of events, if it exists at all, is not original time. Original time is the fruit of our preoccupation (*Sorge*). It is the unity of three incompatibles, past, present, future, but again not past, present or future in any ordinary sense. The present is a *presence* in the order of preoccupation, not a pure 'now' which is a myth. Our preoccupation is said to create the now. Similarly the past is what it is no good being preoccupied about. The future is the domain of our possibilities—the possibilities which at one point it is said that we are: but at another point it is said that the *Dasein* is its past. I do not, I confess, make very much of this but it seems to me that any attempt to derive temporal concepts from psychological ones, even psychological concepts with metaphysical frillings, *must* fail. If it appears to succeed, it is only because it is covertly circular. Thus the *presence* in the order of preoccupation (*Sorge*) by which the present is supposed to be defined has in fact to be understood as a *temporal* presence. And indeed *Sorge* itself is defined as 'being in advance of oneself already in a world' (sich-vorwegs-schon-sein in einer Welt)—the interpretation being, I take it, that one is placed willy-nilly in a situation where one has to start worrying about what one has to do, or become. The point here is that 'in advance of' and 'already' are themselves temporal words.

From *Sorge* it is only a short step to *Angst*. The difference is that whereas one worries about particular things, *Angst* has no specific object. It is never provoked by anything determinate. Just for this reason, it is held to be metaphysically illuminating. As the foundation of *Sorge*, and so the ultimate source of time, it enters profoundly into the being of *Dasein*. Put succinctly, it is our capacity for *Angst* that makes us what we are, and so makes the world what it is. I shall explain this further when I come to Heidegger's account of negativity.

The feeling of *Angst* is also involved in our capacity to live authentically. The idea here is that each of us has a set of possibilities—possible lines of development, possible courses of conduct—that are his own possibilities. These are possible ways of existing concretely. And since it is said that the *Dasein* is its possibilities, this may be the ground for saying that its essence is subordinate to its existence. But how one can discover what these possibilities are is not made clear. To the extent that one chooses to realize them, one is oneself. This is a common existentialist theme. The main part of Jaspers's philosophy, for instance, is devoted to the duty of being oneself—not a critical discussion of it but an invocation, a piece of preaching. To common sense it might seem that one could not avoid being oneself, so that this preaching must be supererogatory. But this is not the existentialist view. One can choose not to be oneself, the *Dasein* can refuse itself to itself, it can make an inauthentic choice. It does this precisely in so far as it succumbs to *common* sense, in so far as it follows the tune of the average man. We live inauthentically when we accept the standards and opinions that are prevalent in our society; when we do the done thing, or think the thought thing, we then become subervient to the impersonal 'One', '*Man*', '*On*'. This is a real mode of being of the *Dasein*, but it is a mode of being itself which consists in not being itself.

In order to live authentically, it is not enough, however, that one should form one's own opinions irrespectively of what other people are thinking, it is not enough even that one should be a rebel against accepted standards. Not sufficient and perhaps not even necessary. What matters is one's inner attitude, one's general view of things, which will of course to some extent reveal itself in action; and above all one's attitude towards death.

The significance of death is that it is the most personal of our possibilities—the least exchangeable, in the sense that no one else can die for me: he can die in my place, but he cannot die my death. I have to die my own. But equally no one else can smile my smile, or cry my tears, or even suffer from my cold (he can catch my cold of course but the one he then has is not mine but his—not *both* mine *and* his. 'How is our cold today?' is a bad joke.) There is nothing, therefore, peculiar about death in this respect. What might be thought to be peculiar about death is that it is inescapable. But other things are inescapable—everything if you accept complete determinism. Getting old, for example, and by this I mean not just having lived more years, but the physical and psychological processes of ageing. But someone might discover a drug which would keep one young in this sense. Well, I suppose someone *might* discover a drug which would keep one from dying, or at least from dying what is called a natural death. I take it to be a contingent fact that we cannot live for ever. The story of the Wandering Jew, however queer a fantasy, is surely not self-contradictory.

Anyway, if you want to be authentic, you have to look upon death in its full significance; and this means accepting its ultimate inevitability and recognizing it as a pure negation. In the light of death, the *Dasein* understands itself as nothingness, just for the reason that all its possibilities are subject to death. Each one of us, therefore, is isolated in his own negativity. There is no means of overcoming it. There are just two attitudes open. Accepting the fact, facing it resolutely, assuming the burden of one's negativity: that is the authentic way. Or shutting one's eyes to it, distracting oneself, having a good time, or even a bad time, but anyway attending to *life*, and to a life not consciously lived in the shadow of death. That is inauthentic. It is the fact that this choice is sometimes offered him that according to Heidegger gives man his only freedom. It is offered only sometimes, or rather only to some men, because the others are so plunged in inauthenticity, so caught up in the world of the average man, so subject to the impersonal 'one', that the possibility of this unique free choice is never seriously presented to them.

Important consequences are held to follow with regard to morals. The moral conscience implies for Heidegger and also for Jaspers and Kierkegaard—I do not think this is true of Sartre and Camus—that we are to regard ourselves as guilty. Guilty existence is defined as that which is the foundation of some negativity. The *Dasein*, therefore, being guilty, is itself affected with negativity, and this negativity consists in the restriction of its possibilities, in its finitude. Because of death, it can never be the absolute master of its existence. Agreeing to exist as finite, we become responsible for our finitude. We consent to an imperfect existence. And this is our guilt. Authentic or resolute existence then consists in the silent, *Angst*-ridden concentration upon one's own state of guilt.

This dismal conclusion has a parallel in the thought of Jaspers and Kierkegaard. Thus for Jaspers 'to act is necessarily to limit oneself, to limit oneself is to sin because it is to will finitude'. Neither is there any refuge in quietism. For not to act is still a form of action and so commits one to sin. Similarly Kierkegaard held that men attained freedom and independence only through *Angst* and Sin. In willing myself, I deny God, but God reveals himself to me in the moment that, asserting myself against him, I reject him. The solution for someone who believes in God, and so presumably does not want to reject him, would seem therefore to be that he should avoid this form of self-assertion, but that is not allowed. It is only the will to be ourselves that makes us be at all; and in willing ourselves, we necessarily sin. To will ourselves to be unlimited, if that were possible, would be just as bad, for then we should be willing ourselves divine, so sin has it either way.

What are we to make of this? It is quite true that most people do not live constantly in the shadow of their own deaths. They know that they are going to die but they know it in a detached sort of way. For much of the time they behave as if they were immortal, or rather, less positively, as if the question of their mortality did not arise. The prospect of their death—not their dying but their not being—is not real to them. One says 'I shall be dead in fifty years', and believes it, but it is hard to envisage. When one thinks of what will be happening after one's death, one still tends to put oneself in the picture, if only as an invisible spectator. The reason may be that what one looks forward to, with pleasure or apprehension, are events in one's life of one sort or another, and as Wittgenstein put it 'Death is not an event in life. Death is not lived through.'[1] It is noteworthy that we do not have the same difficulty in envisaging the existence of events before our birth. And yet logically there is no difference. There is a short stretch of time t_m to t_n which is occupied among other things by events which constitute my personal history. There is a very long, perhaps an infinite stretch of time (infinite if the world had no beginning) t_m to t_{m-x} which contains no such events, and another very long, perhaps infinite stretch of time (infinite if the world has no end) t_n to t_{n+y} which also contains no such events. If I cheerfully accept the existence of t_m to t_{m-x}, there seems no good reason why I should boggle at t_n to t_{n+y}. But there it is: people do feel strongly about survival, whereas, with a few notable exceptions, such as Plato and the late Professor Prichard, they do not usually stake a claim for pre-existence.

But granting that we most of us do not live *sub specie mortis*, is it at all clear that we should? What is the virtue in being obsessed by death and seeing the skull beneath the skin? Of course if someone believes that all sorts of interesting things are going to happen to him afterwards, that he is going to be called to account for his behaviour in life, and rewarded or punished, then he will have a motive for taking death seriously, in a sense. But it is a loose sense; for what he will be taking seriously is not death but the alleged continuation of life. For someone who does not believe any of this, death does indeed become more significant; it is not indefinitely put off. But why should it be his duty

[1] *Tractatus Logico-Philosophicus*, 6. 43ff.

to dwell upon the prospect in guilt and *Angst*? It is not as if his life would thereby become more agreeable or useful. Quite the contrary. The suggestion is that not to be obsessed with death is somehow cheating. But it is not clear why it is cheating. And if it were, perhaps this is a case in which cheating is allowable, even one in which we ought to cheat.

As for this doctrine of original sin, it seems to be as stupid and malign as the religious doctrine which it echoes. Stupider even, if that is possible. We are said to be guilty because we consent to an imperfect existence, imperfect because of its finitude: we have only a limited number of possibilities—there is a limited number of things that any one of us can do or be—and they are all circumscribed by death. All of which is true. But why should this make us guilty? What would it be like not to consent to a limited existence? We have no choice so long as we live at all. There is the alternative of suicide: of which indeed Camus says in the *Mythe de Sisyphe*, that it is the only serious philosophical problem; but even he does not conclude that we all ought to commit it, at most that there is no good reason why any of us should not. There is also the suggestion, implied in Kierkegaard, that we should will ourselves as unlimited, that we should aspire to be divine. But even if this were possible, it would be condemned as blasphemous, so here again there is no deliverance from sin. There can be no deliverance because the view taken is that we are *necessarily* sinful. It has nothing to do with our conduct. It is part of the human condition. Now this might make some sort of sense—not much but some—when combined with the idea of a vindictive deity who is going to make things unpleasant for us just because we are human. And then John Stuart Mill's attitude seems to me much the more noble, not to accept one's guilt and all the rest of it, but to say 'I will call no being good, who is not what I mean when I apply that epithet to my fellow creatures; and if such a being can sentence me to hell for not so calling him, to hell will I go'.[1] In its religious context assuming this to be intelligible, the idea of original sin is morally repugnant: taken on its own it makes no sense at all.

And what are we to understand by this talk of negativity, of nothingness, *das Nichts*, *le néant*? It is a subject on which the existentialists have a great deal to say, but the purport of what they say about it is very hard to grasp. Consider Heidegger again in that extraordinary pamphlet *Was ist Metaphysik?* 'What interests us in our relations with the world',

[1] *Examination of Sir William Hamilton's Philosophy* (1865), p.129.

he writes, 'is the existent itself and apart from that—nothing. What all action takes its direction from is the existent itself and besides that—nothing. What scientific inquiries make inroads into is the existent itself and beyond that—nothing. The existent alone must be explored and apart from that—nothing; only the existent and besides that—nothing; uniquely the existent and beyond that—nothing.' 'Erforscht werden soll das Seiendes nur und sonst—nichts; das Seiendes allein und weiter—nichts; das Seiendes einzig und darüber hinaus—nichts.' And then splendidly 'What about this nothing?' 'Wie steht es um dieses Nichts?' What has it been up to? And a good many pages further on we get the answers 'Die Angst offenbart das Nichts', '*Angst* manifests the nothing' and 'Das nichts selbst nichtet', 'The nothing itself nothings': in Sartre, 'le néant se néantise'.

Carnap has made play with this. He cites it, not unreasonably, as a good specimen of metaphysical nonsense, and he suggests that it all comes from a simple grammatical mistake, the mistake of taking 'nothing' to be the name of something. Compare Lewis Carroll, 'I am sure nobody walks faster than I do. He can't do that or he would have been here first.' But it is not quite so simple as that. Heidegger admits that it does not make sense to talk of nothing as though it were something. He allows that logically his assertions about *das Nichts* make no sense at all. But (and here is the rub) he insists that this is a field in which he has the right to go beyond logic. In this inquiry into nothing, not logic but the understanding is master (how the understanding can dispense with logic—how it can go against the rules of logic is not explained: but this is a favourite existential gambit: and alas there is again a parallel with Wittgenstein's *Tractatus*, the cheerful admission that his own statements are nonsense, with the implication that nevertheless they are important and ought to be taken seriously: but if they really *were* nonsense, then they would not be saying anything and could have no claim to be taken seriously).

But to return to Heidegger. His defence of going beyond logic is that logic makes the nothing depend upon negation, whereas it should be the other way round. The nothing is primary. We may characterize it provisionally as the out-and-out denial of the totality of the existent. But this requires that we should be able to conceive of the totality of the existent. Heidegger appears to maintain that we can think it but we cannot lay hold of it (*erfassen*) conceptually. But this does not put it beyond our reach. *Boredom* gives it to us: not just boredom with this or that but boredom in general with no specific object, the mood of

Mallarmé's 'La chair est triste hélas et j'ai lu tous les livres' (compare Sartre's *nausée* which plays the same rôle). This, as it were, gives us the nothing negatively, inasmuch as to see the world as a whole is to see it as limited—by what? by nothing!—but it does not give it to us positively. To get it positively we have to have *Angst*. *Angst* reveals the nothing, in that it makes it slip away with the being which it encircles and thereby somehow enables the existent to stand out. I quote: 'In the clear night of the nothingness of *Angst* there first arises the original manifestation of the Existent as such: that it is existent and not nothing.' And later 'The essence of the original nihilating nothing consists in this: that it first of all confronts the *Da-Sein* with the Existent as such.' From this it is inferred rather startlingly that unless we apprehended nothing, we could not apprehend anything; could not therefore stand in any sort of relation to the existent (this is surely a non-sequitur) and so could not exist. Therefore we exist only so long as we are in a constant state of *Angst*. But surely we are not all of us in a constant state of *Angst*. The answer given is that we are, but we are not always aware of it. Finally it is argued, on the basis of a piece of bad philology, that metaphysics is the study that goes beyond being and so deals with nothing. And the treatise ends with the splendid question: 'Why is there anything at all and not rather nothing?'

This is rather sad stuff; and it is distressing to think that over much of the continent it still passes for the last word in philosophical profundity. I have gone through it at such length mainly because it so well illustrates the existentialists' technique. They take a genuine problem, like the problem of negation, perhaps make a valid point, as that you cannot (as for example Bradley tried to do) define negative statements in terms of the activity of negating (for the so-called positive statement is just as much a negation of the so-called negative one as the other way round), forsake analysis for the description of some psychological condition, preferably an abnormal one, generalize this psychological condition, sometimes even to the point of making it a logical necessity, and then transfer the whole concoction to the metaphysical plane, and treat the metaphysics as a background to some literary conclusion about the tragic state of man.

Sartre is not so ponderous as Heidegger, but his method is basically the same. On the subject of time and negation he follows Heidegger closely, though without the extravagancies of the 'clear night of the nothing'. But he has some views of his own—for instance, his doctrine of insincerity—*mauvaise-foi*—which explains, or goes some way to explain, the cryptic statement I quoted earlier that human beings, who exist *pour-soi*, are what they aren't and aren't what they are. The object of sincerity is to recognize what one is and so to be what one is; the object of *mauvaise-foi* is to conceal what one is and be what one is not. But, argues Sartre, the mere fact that sincerity, the being what one is, is posited as an *ideal* proves that one is not what one is; for an ideal is essentially something that has to be attained and consequently is not already realized. Again, the man who is *de mauvaise foi* must somehow be aware of himself as being so, since every conscious state is self-conscious. But how then can he really be so? How, for example, being cowardly and being conscious of being cowardly, can he pretend to himself that he is brave, and being aware that he is pretending yet deceive himself? Sartre's answer is that if he were a coward 'in the way in which this ink-pot is an ink-pot' there could be no question of *mauvaise-foi*. But this is where the *pour-soi* comes in. The man who feels afraid is conscious that he feels afraid, but this means for Sartre that the feeling of fear is put in question because of the Void (*das Nichts, le néant*) that subsists between it and the consciousness which necessarily accompanies it. The man believes that he is a coward but since 'to believe is to know that one believes and to know that one believes is no longer to believe' the fact that he believes it is supposed by Sartre to entail that he does not. If one could be what one is, in the way that a physical object is what it is, insincerity would not be possible, but the divided nature of consciousness, the intrusion of the *néant* into every conscious state (consciousness is separated from what it is conscious of—by what? by nothing!) prevents this, in Sartre's opinion, from ever being the case. All that one can do, according to him, is to *play* at being what one is. The waiter, for example, *is* a waiter in the sense that he performs the office of a waiter rather than some other. But inasmuch as he is conscious of himself as being a waiter, he thinks of it as something that he has to make himself be, as a part that he has to act, and therefore, according to this argument, it becomes something that he actually *is not*. For if he *were* it, there could be no question of his *having* to be it, in this sense. Accordingly the waiter, like everybody else, is what he is not, and is not what he is. It follows that the aim of sincerity, wholly to be itself, is unattainable. And inasmuch as sincerity is conscious of being bound to miss its aim it is itself *de mauvaise foi*. Generalizing these conclusions, Sartre then finds that an essential characteristic of what he calls 'human reality' is *le manque*, an incompleteness which by being conscious becomes frustration. *Le pour-soi* strives incessantly to be wholly and self-identically *en-soi* in the manner of a physical object, but without sacrificing the self-consciousness which distinguishes it from *l'en-soi*, and the achievement of this, according to Sartre is a logical impossibility. *Hinc illae lacrimae.*

Here again we start with a genuine problem: the analysis of insincerity. And as a contribution to it, we are given quite a good account of a psychological condition. Some people do play-act most of the time, perhaps all of us some of the time. What is objectionable is only the sophistry by which Sartre reaches the conclusion that this psychological attitude is not only universal but necessary, that it is logically impossible for anyone not to be insincere. For the effect of this is to rob the concept of sincerity, and therefore the concept of insincerity as well, of any empirical content.

The same technique is used in Sartre's gloomy account of human relationships. He takes as his starting point the special relation in which one person wishes to dominate another or be dominated by him (Hegel's master–slave relationship, or the sadist and the masochist) and he then shows how these may fail. A wishes to dominate B, but this is of no interest if B has no will of his own, if he is like an inanimate object: there is no satisfaction, or not the right sort of satisfaction, in dominating things that have no will to resist you. A wishes to dominate B as an alien power: but to the extent that A succeeds in dominating B, B ceases to be an alien power, he loses his will to resist, and so ceases to be worth dominating. In other words, this enterprise is self-defeating. Similarly, if B wishes to be dominated by A, he is still imposing his will on A inasmuch as he is getting A to dominate him, so that this too does not work. This perceptive analysis of certain rather special human relationships is then represented as an account of them all. It is inferred that all emotional relationships are doomed to frustration. Love, for instance. To love someone is to want them to love you. But their loving you is, by definition, a matter of their wanting you to love them. So to love someone is to want them to want you to want them to want you *ad infinitum.* One might suspect at this point that there was something wrong with the definition, or at least with the way it was being used. But not Sartre. He is happy to draw the conclusion that the attempt to love is necessarily self-defeating.

Sartre is dependent on Heidegger for his metaphysics, but not to anything like the same extent for his moral philosophy. He is not, for example, so greatly obsessed with death. In morals, he takes the line that since there are no absolute values, one has to set up one's own.

We have to assume the responsibility of choosing how to live, and this responsibility is inescapable; even if we allow ourselves to be guided by others, we assume the responsibility of letting them speak for us; we make their standards our own. Moreover we do not choose simply for ourselves; a moral standard is *posited* as holding universally. In this way we become responsible for others also; we do not become responsible for their actions, but we commit ourselves to a view of how they ought to live. We legislate for them as well as for ourselves.

All this seems to me very sound. My only quarrel with Sartre here is that he makes a sort of grievance of the fact that there are no absolute values. He seems at times to imply that if the world had been rather different, if there had been a God for example, then there would have been absolute values, and we should not have had to make these moral choices, at least not in the way we now have to. There would have been no occasion for the heroism we now display. But if it is true that there are no absolute values, it is necessarily true; it does not just happen to be so. It is that the expression 'absolute values' is being used in such a way that there could not be such things, as for example if it were taken to imply that 'ought' statements were derivable from 'is' statements. And there does not seem to be anything especially heroic about accepting the consequences of a necessary truth.

It is characteristic of existentialists to violate the distinction between necessary and contingent statements as well as that between descriptive and normative statements. It is not that they reject or question these distinctions, like Quine and his associates, but rather that they treat contingent propositions as though they were necessary, that they feel that normative judgements somehow ought to be descriptive. Among other things this blurs Sartre's celebrated doctrine of *engagement* (commitment). It is never quite clear whether we are necessarily *engagés*—through the mere fact of being alive—that is, that we have to take some line, even the line of taking no line, or whether it is supposed to be our duty to take an *active* line, to do something about the political and social problems of our time. Sartre's arguments on the whole favour the first interpretation, but his practice the second. Thus his reason for allying himself with the Communists, to the extent of saying in *La Critique de la raison dialectique* that Marxism is the only serious philosophy for our times, is basically that history is on the side of the working class, which means presumably that this class is going to come to power anyway (but what sort of reason is this for supporting it?) and that the Communist Party objectively represents the working class, no matter what policy it actually pursues. This is Hegel taking his revenge on Kierkegaard.

The dramatization of necessary truths, which we have seen to be a feature of Sartre's morals, comes out very strongly in Camus. Camus thinks that the problem of suicide (whether or not to commit it) is *the* problem of philosophy, because it is a startling way of putting the question what attitude we are to take in face of the tragic fact that life is meaningless. But when we come to consider why he thinks that life is meaningless we find that it is because statements of fact are contingent. There is in the end no reason why things are as they are: they just happen to be so. But that empirical statements are contingent is itself a necessary fact; if they were necessary they would not do the work they do. There is no tragedy here. Only, if we want existence to have a meaning, we have to put it there. Camus himself is in favour of putting it there. He admires those men who choose to live intensely while recognizing that everything is ultimately futile, men whom he absurdly calls absurd men, and he cites Don Juans, conquerors and artists as examples. In his book *L'Homme révolté*, the sequel to *Le Mythe de Sisyphe*, he continues to recommend an attitude of heroic defiance of the fates. Now there is nothing wrong with his recommendations as recommendations: personally I find them sympathetic. One can take the attitude that everything is futile, one can take the attitude that, though everything is ultimately futile, one should behave as though it were not, or one can take the attitude that certain things are not futile. Camus seems to favour the second position. I on the whole should opt for the third. Where he is wrong is in assuming that his position is in some way closer to the facts.

A comparison is sometimes drawn between existentialist and so-called linguistic philosophers to the advantage of the existentialists. It is said that they are dealing with real problems, whereas the others are only doing verbal gymnastics. But this turns out not to be true (as regards the existentialists at least: I do not now want to go into the question of the verbal gymnastics). Existentialists do discuss philosophical questions, such as solipsism, negation, the analysis of time, but in a very confused and uninstructive way. For the rest, they describe certain psychological states, fascinating enough in some cases but of a rather special character, and they make some general recommendations as to conduct. But their recommendations are so general that not much can be extracted from them. To be told to live authentically is not really to be told how to live.

14

MAN AS A SUBJECT FOR SCIENCE

> 'Oh, the monster!' exclaimed the Reverend Doctor Folliott, 'he has made a subject for science of the only friend he had in the world.'
>
> PEACOCK, *Crotchet Castle*

THOSE who catch the allusion in my title may remember that the science in question was anatomy. The devotees of science, to whom Peacock was referring, were body-snatchers who provided medical students with corpses for dissection; for in 1831, when *Crotchet Castle* was published, it was still thought improper, mainly on religious grounds, to treat even lifeless human beings as subjects for experiment. But the march of mind, of which these criminals were supposed to be the camp-followers, had far more ambitious aims than that which they were serving. It was the belief of the positivists and utilitarians who gave its progressive intellectual tone to the first half of the nineteenth century that the science of nature which Newton had established was due to be completed by a science of man. This was not merely a question of supplementing physics with biology: the empire of science was to be extended to every facet of man's nature; to the workings of men's minds as well as their bodies and to their social as well as their individual behaviour; law, custom, morality, religious faith and practice, political institutions, economic processes, language, art, indeed every form of human activity and mode of social organization were to be explained in scientific terms; and not only explained but transfigured. For Comte and Bentham and their followers, no less than for the Marxists, the point of understanding society was to change it; there was a rational way of ordering human affairs, and it only required the application of scientific method to discover and put it into operation.

It is not an underestimate of what has been achieved in the social sciences to say that these hopes have not been fulfilled. Auguste Comte died in 1852, just a year after the opening of the Great Exhibition, which expressed a faith in the power of science that has indeed been justified; we have since had more than a century of astonishing scientific progress. But the progress has been in the physical, and to a rather lesser but still very considerable extent, the biological sciences; the social sciences have not kept pace. Admittedly they began this period in a very much less favourable position; neither would it be fair to say that they have made no progress at all. How great this progress has been is not very easy to assess. A large body of economic doctrine has been built up, but the deductions which are made from it appear still to fit rather loosely to the facts; the emergence of psycho-analysis, particularly in its Freudian version, has had important social and literary effects; it would not be too much to say that our ideas of human nature have been transformed by it; even so the charge that psycho-analytical theories are not testable has not been effectively met, and so long as this is so their scientific value remains in doubt; in anthropology the reaction against the rather too facile acceptance of far-reaching theories has led to a puritanical distrust of generalization; the theoretical contribution of Marxism to the study of history, though not entirely negligible, falls a long way behind its practical influence. All in all, the stock of generally accredited and well tested theories that the social sciences can muster is comparatively small. The social scientist may well look on the garden of the natural sciences as an intellectual paradise from which he has lamentably been excluded.

But why should this be so? Is it just that the factors which govern human behaviour are unmanageably complex? Is it that for moral and practical reasons there are rather narrow limits to the type and number of experiments that can be carried out on human beings? Have the wrong methods been pursued? Have the right questions not yet been asked? Are the social sciences merely waiting for their Galileo or their Newton? Or is there some more fundamental reason, some reason of principle, why the kind of success that the natural sciences have had is here unattainable? This is the first question that I wish to examine.

In whatever other ways they may differ, the various special sciences at least have this in common that they contain a set of what are anyhow provisionally taken to be valid generalizations. These generalizations may be more or less abstract; they may be causal or statistical in form;

they may or may not be capable of being organized into a deductive system; they may be valued primarily for their own sakes or for the particular inferences which can be made from them, according to the character of the science and the view which is taken of it: all that I am now concerned with is that they must exist. Now it is characteristic of the social sciences that their stock of generalizations is relatively poor. For the most part the generalizations which they do claim to have established are lacking in precision and scope; and in some fields at least they are not very well attested. This is sometimes taken merely as an indication that the social sciences are still in their infancy; they are still at the stage of building up the data from which a stock of fruitful generalizations will later spring. But may not the explanation be quite different? May it not be that there is something about the material on which these sciences have to work, something about the nature of men, which makes it impossible to generalize about them in any way comparable to that which has made the success of the natural sciences? If this were so, the rather poor showing which men have so far made as anything but purely biological subjects for science would be logically accounted for.

The idea that man somehow stands outside the order of nature is one that many people find attractive on emotional grounds; so that it has to be received with some caution. It is, however, fairly widely accepted nowadays, even by philosophers who are supposed to be able to discount their emotional prejudices, and this for various reasons. One of them is of course the belief in the freedom of the will. It is argued that since men are free to behave as they choose, they are always capable of nullifying any generalization about their conduct to which they are alleged to be subject. If any such generalization is produced, it is only to be expected that someone will proudly or perversely exercise his option of rendering it false.

The trouble with this argument is that it simply assumes the falsehood of the position which it is intended to demolish. If the attribution of free will is construed in such a way that a man can be said to have acted freely only if his action is not susceptible of any causal explanation, then there will indeed be no question but that if men ever act freely, their behaviour is not totally subject to causal laws. This still allows for its being subject to statistical laws, but on the assumption, which the proponents of this view tacitly make, that a man is free on any given occasion to try to do anything whatsoever that he believes to be feasible, the possibility of there being even statistical laws about human behaviour which would be of any scientific value is effectively excluded. But now it is surely fair to ask for some justification of these very strong assumptions. What reason have we for believing that men ever do act freely, in this sense? There may be a *prima facie* case for holding that men are capable of acting freely in some sense or other; but it is by no means clear that an action which passes this test of freedom, whatever it may be, cannot also be governed by some causal law. Many philosophers have in fact held that what we ordinarily mean by speaking of an action as freely done is not incompatible with its being causally determined; some have gone even further to the point of holding that when we say that an action is free we actually imply, or presuppose, that it is determined; others who take the view that determinism excludes free will, as this is ordinarily understood, have concluded just for this reason that our ordinary notion of free will has no application. I do not myself think that we stand to gain very much by making a conscientious effort to discover what people ordinarily mean when they talk about free will: it might very well turn out that some people mean one thing by it, and some another, and that many people's idea of it is very confused. The important question, so far as we are concerned, is whether human behaviour is or is not entirely subject to law. If we conclude that it is, or even just that there is no good reason to suppose that it is not, then we may find it expedient to introduce a sense of acting freely which squares with these conclusions. We shall presumably want it to apply, so far as possible, to the same actions as those that most people would now regard as being free, though not necessarily with the same implications, but we shall rather be correcting ordinary usage than merely following it. If, on the other hand, our conclusion is that human behaviour is not entirely subject to law, then again we shall have to decide what provision, if any, this enables us to make for freedom of action; for example, if we make the absence of causal determination a necessary condition of an action's being freely done, we shall have to consider whether we can still preserve the connection between freedom and responsibility. But the point is that before we can usefully embark upon such matters, we must first decide the issue of determinism. How far and in what sense is man's behaviour subject to law?

It may appear, indeed, that this is not an issue which one could hope to settle *a priori*. Surely, it may be said, we can never be in a position to show that any piece of human conduct is inexplicable: the most that we can claim is that we have not been able to find any explanation for it, but this does not imply that there is no explanation, or even that the explanation is one which it will always be beyond our power to discover. But while this remark is perfectly sound, it may also be thought to miss the point. For what is most commonly maintained by those who wish to set limits to the extent to which men's actions are governed by law is not that these actions are inexplicable, but rather that the kinds of explanation which they call for do not conform to the scientific model. That is to say, they do not account for an action as resulting from the operation of a natural law. It is allowed that explanations of the scientific type are sometimes appropriate, as when we account for some piece of deviant behaviour by relating it to a disorder in the agent's constitution, but cases of this kind are said to be the exception rather than the rule. In the normal way we explain a man's action in terms of his intentions, or his motives, or his beliefs, or the social context in which the action takes place. Consider, for example, the simple action of drinking a glass of wine. As performed by different people in different circumstances, this may be an act of self-indulgence, an expression of politeness, a proof of alcoholism, a manifestation of loyalty, a gesture of despair, an attempt at suicide, the performance of a social rite, a religious communication, an attempt to summon up one's courage, an attempt to seduce or corrupt another person, the sealing of a bargain, a display of professional expertise, a piece of inadvertence, an act of expiation, the response to a challenge and many other things besides. All these are accepted as good explanations: if the circumstances are right, they render the performance of the action intelligible; but only in the case of the alcoholic is it clear that the explanation is of a scientific character. In the other cases we find the action intelligible because we are given a reason for its performance; it is explained in terms of the agent's purpose, or by reference to a social norm, or through some combination of these two.

This is a fair enough statement of the facts, but it raises a number of quite difficult questions which we shall have to examine rather carefully before we can draw any conclusions about the extent to which human conduct eludes the grasp of science. Exactly how do explanations in terms of purpose operate and in what way are they explanatory? In particular, how do they significantly differ from explanations in terms of causal laws? What kind of understanding do we acquire of an action when we are able to fit it into a social context, or see it as fulfilling a social norm? In what sense, again, is this an explanation of the action? And finally, even if a reason can be found for saying that explanations of these types are not, or not wholly, scientific, does it follow that the actions which they explain cannot also be explained in a way which does conform to the scientific model? Assuming that we do have to deal here with two or more radically different sorts of explanations, are we bound to conclude that they are mutually exclusive?

Let us begin then with the type of explanation in which an action is accounted for in terms of the agent's purpose. In the standard instance of this type, the agent has some end in view which he wishes to attain and believes that there is a causal connection between the performance of the action and the attainment of this end; he need not believe that the performance of the action is a necessary condition for the attainment of the end, since he may suppose that the end could come about, or even that he could bring it about, in other ways, and he need not believe it to be a uniquely sufficient condition, but he must at least regard it as part of a sufficient condition. This is most commonly expressed by saying that the agent takes the action to be a means towards the end in question. And correspondingly the end, or rather, to speak more accurately, the agent's desire for the attainment of the end, is said to be the motive for his action. It is not indeed essential that the motive should be conscious: we do sometimes explain a man's behaviour in terms of an end which he is not himself aware that he is pursuing. Sometimes we even discount the motive which he thinks he has in favour of the unconscious motive by which we judge that he is really actuated. However, the cases in which we speak of unconscious motives are modelled on those in which the motive is conscious. The reason why we credit a man with pursuing an end of which he is unaware is that his behaviour, in the given circumstances, not only indicates that he finds the end desirable but also resembles the behaviour which might be expected of one who was consciously pursuing it.

It is not necessary either that the agent's belief in the efficacy of the means should be fully articulated. That is to say, he does not have to formulate the proposition that such and such a course of action will conduce to his end. It is enough that he acts as though he took this proposition to be true and in the case where his motive is conscious, that he assents to it if it is put to him. The proposition may on occasion be false, in the sense that the means which are supposed to be sufficient in the attendant circumstances for the production of the end do not in fact produce it; and it may also happen that the agent is mistaken about the circumstances. He may adopt a course of action which would have been sufficient for his purpose if the circumstances had been what he took them to be but which is not sufficient as things actually are. This is a more common cause of failure than the other, but failure of any kind is less common than success. We should not be satisfied with the assignment of men's purposes as explanations for their actions, if they did not in general attain their ends.

The case which I have been taking as standard is that in which a man's action is directed on a particular occasion towards some specific end. In a situation of this kind, the action which the agent takes may not be the only one which he regards as suitable for his purpose, but the range of actions of which this is true is likely to be fairly narrow. There are, however, cases in which the assignment of a motive covers a rather wide range of behaviour, and these are usually also cases in which the end towards which the behaviour is directed is not very specific. I am thinking of the sort of actions which are done from what one might call a standing motive, a motive like that of ambition or avarice, or a love of learning. The end of being powerful or famous or rich or learned, or whatever it may be, is unspecific in the sense that it may take many different concrete forms and the means to it may be correspondingly various. The agent himself may not envisage at all clearly what form the achievement of his end will take, and he may even have no considered idea of the way in which he will set about pursuing it. His having the motive is rather a matter of his being disposed to accept whatever opportunity arises of achieving his end in one form or another. In cases where the motive is something like the love of learning, it may amount to little more than his seeking opportunities to engage in a certain sort of activity. It is, however, to be remembered that where an activity is mainly undertaken for its own sake, the description of it in terms of purposes or motives seems a little out of place. It is perhaps not incorrect to say that my motive for reading novels or playing bridge or going to the cinema is that I enjoy these pursuits, but if asked what my motive was for engaging in them I should be more inclined to answer that I had no motive at all.

In his book on *The Concept of Motivation* Professor Peters goes much further than this. He not only allows that there can be voluntary behaviour which is not motivated, but he does not think it correct to talk of there being a motive even in all cases in which an agent takes means towards a further end. The cases which he wishes to exclude are those in which our actions are habitual or fit into some conventional pattern. He thinks that the word 'motive' is commonly 'used in contexts where conduct is being assessed and not simply explained, where there is a breakdown in conventional expectations', and therefore wishes to restrict its application to purposeful actions which are somehow out of the ordinary and in particular to those in which we are inclined to pass an adverse moral judgement. There is indeed some warrant for this restriction in ordinary usage, in the sense that we do not normally inquire into people's motives unless we are surprised by their conduct or think that they are called upon to justify it. I should think it strange if someone asked me what my motive was in putting on my overcoat to go out on a winter's day, and I might be inclined to take offence if someone asked me what my motive was in asking a friend to dinner. But the reason why such questions appear strange or offensive is not that conventional actions are not motivated, or that motives tend to be discreditable, but simply that we do not bother to ask questions to which we already know the answers. The desire to keep warm, or the desire to give pleasure to a friend or to enjoy his company, are just as much motives for action as the more unusual desire to catch cold, say with a view to avoiding some disagreeable duty, or the desire to worm information out of a friend or to borrow money from him. There seems to be no good reason to exclude them merely because they are innocent and commonplace. It is not as if they functioned any differently, as springs of action, from motives which are ulterior in the pejorative sense.

I do, however, agree with Professor Peters, as against, for example, Professor Ryle,[1] that for an action to be motivated it is at least necessary that it be directed to an end. Professor Ryle has gone astray, in my opinion, through concentrating, almost exclusively, on actions which are done from standing motives, where, as we have seen, the ends are relatively unspecific; so unspecific, in fact, that Ryle effectively ignores them. In this way he comes to assimilate actions which are done from standing motives, like ambition, to actions like habitual chess playing which are not done in the pursuit of any further end at all, and so he finds himself able to conclude that motives can be wholly analysed in terms of dispositions, that to act from such and such a motive amounts to no more than being disposed to engage in behaviour of such and such a type. Accordingly he interprets explanation in terms of motives as if it were simply a matter of subsuming the particular under the general case, as when we say that a piece of glass has broken because it was brittle, or that a man is late on a particular

[1] In his *The Concept of Mind* (1949)

occasion because he is habitually unpunctual. This is not even a very plausible account of explanation in terms of a standing motive, and quite obviously wrong when it is applied to actions which are explained in terms of the agent's aiming on a given occasion at some specific end. Indeed one of my reasons for giving central importance to actions which are done from occasional motives is that the element of directedness there stands out more clearly.

Of course Professor Ryle himself has a motive for dissolving motives into dispositions. It is an important part of his campaign against the idea of the ghost in the machine to dismember the mechanical model, in which motives are conceived as 'ghostly thrusts'. And whatever the deficiency of his tactics his strategy has been successful. Thanks to him and also to Wittgenstein it is now almost a commonplace among philosophers that motives are not causes. But this is not to say that it is true.

Why is it thought to be true? There are various reasons, not all of them of equal weight. The most simple of them is that motives operate *a fronte* whereas causes operate *a tergo*: to put it crudely, that causes push while motives pull. A more sophisticated argument is that cause and effect are distinct events: so, if the motive for an action caused it, it would have to be a separate occurrence which preceded the action or at any rate accompanied it; but in many, perhaps in most cases of motivated actions, such separate occurrences are simply not discoverable; the specification of the motive is part of the description of the action, not a reference to anything outside it, and certainly not a reference to any distinct event. Thirdly, it is argued that in the scientific sense of 'cause', which is what is here in question, even singular causal statements are implicitly universal; to say that one particular event is the cause of another is to imply that events of these types are invariably connected by a causal law: this is not true, however, of statements in which a motive is assigned for some particular action; such a statement does not imply that whenever people have motives of the kind in question they act in a similar manner, or that whenever actions of that type are performed they are done from the same sort of motive. Finally, a point is made of the fact that motivated action often consists in following or attempting to follow a rule; that is to say, the action may be one to which normative criteria are applicable; the question arises whether it has been performed correctly; but this means, so it is argued, that we somehow impoverish the motive if we regard it merely as a cause.

Let us now examine these arguments in turn. The first of them need not detain us long. If the contention is that purposive behaviour is to be accounted for, not as the response to any past or present stimulus, but rather in terms of the future state of affairs towards the realization of which the behaviour is directed, the argument fails for the simple reason that there may not in fact be any such future state of affairs. Even if men generally succeed in fulfilling their purposes, they do sometimes fail, and the explanation of their embarking on the action must be the same whether the purpose is fulfilled or not. But this is enough to rule the end out of court as a determinant of the action. I do not share the qualms that some people feel about the idea of an event's being pulled into existence by one that does not yet exist, for these metaphors of pushing and pulling must not be taken too seriously; there is no great difficulty in regarding an earlier event as a function of a later one. But however little we are influenced by the metaphor, we cannot think it possible that an event may be pulled into existence by one that never exists at all.

But this, it may be said, is to take an unfairly naïve view of the argument. Its point is not that purposive behaviour is to be explained in terms of its actual achievement but rather that it has to be understood as tending towards a certain end, whether or not this end is actually attained. A general may not succeed in winning his battle, a chess player may not succeed in mating his opponent, but in order to make sense of their manœuvres, we have to know that these are their aims. If we want to explain behaviour of this kind, the question which we have to ask is not what impels it but where it is directed; and the same applies at all levels down to the rat, or even the mechanical rat, in the maze.

This is all very well but does it not concede the point at issue? For what is now singled out as the explanatory fact is not the end towards which the behaviour is directed, considered as a future event, but rather the agent's having this as his aim. The suggestion is that the agent behaves as he does because he has a conscious or unconscious need or desire for such and such a state of affairs to be realized. And why should not this be said to impel him?

At this point the first argument dissolves into the second. For the answer which will be given to our last question is that very often these desires and needs do not exist independently of the behaviour which they are supposed to impel. No doubt there are cases in which a man is impelled to action by a felt desire for the end which he believes that the action will secure him, but even in many cases in which an agent would be said to be conscious of his purpose, his action is not preceded by any psychological occurrence which could figure as his desire for the end in question. His consciousness of his purpose, in so far as it is anything apart from his behaviour, may just consist in his ability to say what it is if the occasion for this arises; it is not required that he should actually have formulated it even to himself. If the agent is not conscious of his purpose, it is still less likely that he will have had any distinctive experience which can be identified as the felt desire or need for the end towards which his action is directed. In such cases we may indeed conceive of the agent's desire as an unconscious mental state which drives him to act as he does; if we have a materialistic outlook, we may identify his desire or his need with some physical state of his organism; but to have recourse in this way to the unconscious or to physiology is to put up a theory which may account for the agent's having the motive that he has rather than to offer an analysis of what the motive is. What it provides at best is a problematic explanation of the existence of the motive; but what is wanted here, and what it does not provide, is an account of the motive as being itself an explanation of the action which it governs.

Again this is all quite true, but it proves very little. If one starts with the assumption that motives can cause the actions which they motivate only if they are 'ghostly thrusts', that is only if they take the form of distinctive experiences which precede or accompany the action, then indeed this argument will show that motives need not be causes. But this assumption is unjustified. It is true that a cause must be distinguishable from its effect, but there are other ways in which a motive can be independent of the action which it motivates than by figuring as a distinct experience, or even as an element in a psycho-analytical or physiological theory. The reason why we say that an action is done for such and such a motive may be no more than that the agent behaves or is disposed to behave in a certain fashion; but the point is that the description of the behaviour which constitutes his having the motive need not be identical with, or even include, a description of the action to which his having the motive leads him. On the contrary, if the assignment of the motive did not refer to something other than the action, if it did not associate the action with anything else at all, it is hard to see how it could have any explanatory force: merely to redescribe a phenomenon is not in any way to account for it. Yes it is, someone may say, if the redescription tells us more about the phenomenon; the assignment of a motive is explanatory in the sense that it enlarges our description of the action; it fills in an important gap in the story. But at this stage the dispute becomes merely verbal. If anyone wishes to give such a wide interpretation to the concept of an action that the motive for which the action is done is counted as a part of it, well and good: this is not perhaps a very felicitous usage, but it is manageable. The point still remains that if the initial description of the action does not include a reference to the motive, then the provision of this reference does link the behaviour which has been described to something beyond it, whether it be a distinctive experience or, as is more commonly the case, a further item or pattern of actual or potential behaviour; and it is only because it does this that the reference to the motive is explanatory. Indeed, this would seem to be the main characteristic of explanations in terms of motive, or more generally in terms of purpose. They serve to establish a lawlike connection between different pieces of behaviour.

This may operate in various ways. The simplest level of purposive behaviour is that which is ascribed to a homoeostatic system. The behaviour of the system on any given occasion is seen as exemplifying a uniform tendency to maintain equilibrium; it is purposive just in the sense that under varying conditions it operates so as to attain the same end-state. Much the same applies to the case of the animal, or the machine in the maze; what makes its behaviour purposive is that its agitation habitually continues until it emerges from the maze; in this instance the directional aspect of the behaviour is underlined by the fact that the individual trials may be stages in a process of learning, in which case they are related in a lawlike fashion to one another. If the animal is given a reward for its success, its appetite for the reward may be a measurable causal factor in the process of its training. The sense in which the animal looks for the reward, and so may be said to have this as its motive, is just that its behaviour would not be quite what it is if the reward had not been given to it on previous occasions. When it comes to simple human actions like putting on an overcoat to go out on a winter's day, our explanation derives its force from some such presupposition as that people in general under conditions of this kind do what they can to protect themselves against the cold. That this is the agent's motive on this particular occasion, rather than, say, a desire to appear well dressed, may indeed be discoverable only through his own avowal of it. But then his disposition to make this avowal, at any rate to himself, is a causal condition of his action. If he were not disposed to make it, then he would not in these circumstances be acting as he does. Otherwise there is no ground for concluding that this is his motive. In a more complicated case, like that of the general planning his battle, the general's desire for victory, if that is in fact his motive, may be exhibited in a fairly wide range of behaviour, apart from his conduct of this particular engagement. And here again, if the assignment of the motive is to have any explanatory force, we must be in a position to say that unless he behaved, or was disposed to behave, in these other ways he would not in the circumstances be planning the battle in the way that he does.

In all this there is little that is controversial. No one would deny that purposive behaviour fitted into some sort of pattern, and it seems pretty obvious that the assignment of motives could not be explanatory unless some lawlike connections were indicated by it. What may, however, still be disputed is that these connections are causal. It may be contended that the rough regularities in behaviour, which are all that we have seen to be required for the applicability of a purposive explanation, do not fit the standard model of the relation of cause and effect.

Once more this is partly a question of terminology. If we construe the causal relation in a strictly Humean fashion so that its terms can only be distinct events, then the objection holds. For we have seen that in many quite typical cases the motive may be present in the form of a disposition which, though distinct from the behaviour which it motivates, is still not exactly a distinct event. It seems to me, however, that even from the point of view of doing justice to the ordinary, let alone the scientific, use of causal language, this conception of the causal relation may be too restrictive. For one thing, we often want to be able to regard the absence of some circumstance as a causal factor, that is, to admit negative as well as positive conditions, and even this does not fit tidily into the Humean scheme. I have of course no quarrel with Hume's fundamental idea that causation must be in the end a matter of regular concomitance, but I suggest that causal relations should be regarded as holding between facts rather than events, where 'fact' is understood in the wide sense in which true propositions of any form can be taken as expressing facts. This involves no sacrifice since in any cases where it is appropriate, these causal statements about facts can be translated into statements about events; it merely extends the field of causal relations a little more widely. Then the sense in which an agent's motive may be said to be the cause of the action which it motivates is that, given certain conditions, an inference from the fact that he has the motive to the fact that he performs the action holds good in virtue of a causal law.

But just as the first of the arguments which we listed dissolved into the second, so, if I am right in what I have just been saying, the second dissolves into the third; for now the question arises whether there really are such causal laws. On the face of it, it seems at least very doubtful. As I said when I first referred to this argument, it is surely possible for someone to act from a given motive on a particular occasion without its being the case either that whenever anyone has a motive of this kind he acts in this way, or that whenever anyone acts in this way he does so from this kind of motive. No doubt there must be some degree of regularity in the way in which motives lead to actions, for us to find the connection intelligible. If people hold very queer beliefs, they may indeed take means to a given end that others would not take; in this sense the connection between motive and action may even be quite idiosyncratic. It remains true, however, that people in general do what they believe will enable them to achieve their ends, and that these beliefs though they may be false are usually backed by a fair amount of evidence. The result is that there is at least a tendency for similar motives to be correlated with similar actions. This tendency is especially marked in the case of standing motives. The range of behaviour which we are prepared to ascribe to jealousy, or greed, or ambition is fairly narrow. Even so, it will be objected, such tendencies, at their very strongest, fall a long way short of being causal laws.

All this is true, but possibly not decisive; for it may be that we are looking for our causal laws in the wrong place. The point from which I think that we should start is that when a man is said to have acted in consequence of having such and such a motive, it is implied at least that if he had not had this motive he would not in the particular circumstances have acted as he did. But this is to say that the existence of the motive is taken to be a necessary condition of the action; not indeed a necessary condition of anyone's performing the action at any time, or even of the agent's performing it at any time, but a necessary condition of his performing it at just this juncture. The question then arises whether it is also taken to be part of a sufficient condition, and this is not easy to answer. The ground for arguing that it must be is that otherwise the ascription of the motive would not properly account for the action; we should have to allow that even granting the agent's motive and the rest of the attendant circumstances, including all the other aspects of the agent's mental and physical condition at that time, we could not entirely rely on the action's taking place; and to this extent its occurrence will still be unexplained and indeed inexplicable. There may, however, be those who are prepared to accept this consequence, so long as they can hold that there is a high probability in this situation of the action's taking place: that is, they may be satisfied with the hypothesis that if the situation were repeated a great number of times the action would take place very much more often than not. But since this leaves an element of arbitrariness, in that we have no answer to the question why it should ever not take place, it seems preferable to make the stronger claim, unless it can be shown to be untenable. The suggestion then would be that whenever an agent can properly be said to have acted exclusively from a given motive, the circumstances must be such that in any situation of this kind, indispensably including the presence of such a motive, an action of this kind invariably follows.

It is clear that if so strong a claim as this is to be made to appear even plausible, a great deal will have to be included in the situation, both in the way of positive and negative conditions. We must, however, avoid including so much detail in the description either of the situation or the action that our claim becomes trivial; our ground for saying that there is an invariable connection between situations and actions of the sorts in question must not be that either the situation or the action is unique. In other words, the types of fact which our laws connect must be envisaged as repeatable.

But where are these connections to be found? Surely it is idle to maintain that these laws exist if we are unable to produce any examples. Well, perhaps we can produce examples of a rather humble kind. Let us begin with the hypothesis that whenever a person has a desire for the existence of a state of affairs S and believes that it is immediately in his power to bring about S by performing the action A, but not by any other means, and there is no state of affairs S′ such that he both prefers the existence of S′ to that of S and believes it to be immediately in his power to bring about S′, but not conjointly with S, then unless he is prevented he will perform the action A. This is not quite a tautology, since the existence of the agent's desire is supposed to be established independently of his taking any steps to satisfy it. On this account, indeed, it may even not be unconditionally true; there may be cases of inhibition which would have to be specially provided for. But even if this difficulty can be overcome, the hypothesis still falls short of what we want because its consequent is subject to a general proviso: the person who satisfies the antecedent will perform the action A unless he is prevented. The question is whether this proviso can be dispensed with.

The way to dispense with it would be to list all the things that might prevent the action from being done, and insert them in the antecedent in the form of negative conditions. This would seem, indeed, to be an impossible undertaking at this level of generality: we could hardly hope to draw up an exhaustive list of negative conditions which would at this point apply to any action whatsoever. But in its application to particular instances, our general hypothesis will in any case dissolve into a number of more specific ones, according to the nature of the case: and once the relevant type of action and perhaps also certain features in the situation of the agent have been specified, it does not seem to me obvious that the list of negative conditions cannot be completed. Thus, if the action is one which involves making a certain sort of hand movement, there may be a finite number of types of bodily disorder which would prevent it from being carried out; if it involves handling certain physical objects, there may be a finite number of ways in which they could become intractable: if the condition of the agent is specified, the types of psychological impediment to which he is then subject may again be finite in number: and if the number of these various factors is so limited, there seems to be no compelling reason to hold that they cannot be discovered and listed.

Of course we shall have no guarantee that the list is complete; but then we do not have such a guarantee in the case of laws of any other type. However carefully a generalization is formulated it must at least remain conceivable that it holds only under certain further conditions which we have failed to specify. Technically, if there are found to be such conditions, the generalization is falsified, though sometimes we prefer to regard it as having been incompletely stated. I do not, however, agree with those who would read into every generalization of law a *ceteris paribus* clause which tacitly protects it from being falsified through the operation of factors which the proponent of the generalization did not foresee. No doubt it is too much to require, as John Stuart Mill did, that causal laws should hold unconditionally, if this is understood to imply that they would still be true no matter what else were true; for one law often depends upon others, so that its truth would not be preserved if these other laws were false. It is, however, not too much to require that the law should hold under any circumstances whatever that actually arise. If the field which it is designed to cover is restricted, this limitation can and should be made explicit.

If *ceteris paribus* clauses were allowable, the task of finding laws in the sphere of human action would be very much easier, but, as our example has shown, these provisos would only increase the law's security at the expense of their scientific interest. Even as it is, our hypothesis contained a stipulation which would often not be satisfied. It is by no means invariably true that when someone is aiming at a given end he believes that there is only one means of attaining it which it is immediately in his power to realize. Very often he will be presented with a choice of such means, so that it needs to be explained why he selects one of them rather than the others. I have no doubt that a number of examples could be found in which I should not know how this was to be done, but I suggest that quite a lot of cases would be covered by the following hypothesis: Whenever the antecedent of our first hypothesis is satisfied, with the difference that the agent believes that it is immediately in his power to bring about S not only by performing the action A but also by performing the action A′, but that he cannot perform both, then, if he believes that A and A′ are equally efficacious in bringing about S, but prefers what he expects to be the other consequences of A to those which he expects of A′, he will unless he is prevented perform the action A. Again, if this is not to be tautologous, there must be evidence for his preferring the other expected consequences of A to those of A′, independently of the fact that he does perform A, but I think it fair to assume that this will usually be available. Our hypothesis does not of course commit us to holding that whenever an agent has a choice between actions of the kind A and A′ as means to a given type of end S, he will choose A. A man may well decide to walk to work on one occasion and take a taxi on another. But then the assumption is that there is a change in the circumstances, in the state of his health or his finances or the weather or some other combination of factors, which will sufficiently account for the variations in his preference. I admit, however, that until a set of such hypotheses has been formulated and tested, the degree of strength that we can attribute to generalizations about human conduct remains an open question.

The most that I would claim at this stage is that the difference between these generalizations and those that can be found to govern other natural phenomena is nowhere more than a difference of degree. What I have tried to show, in arguing that motives may be causes, is that there is no warrant for regarding explanation in terms of motives as something of a different order from the explanations that occur in the physical sciences. There is nothing about human conduct that would entitle us to conclude *a priori* that it was in any way less lawlike than any other sort of natural process.

But what of the argument that human actions conform to rules, that we are often more interested in judging whether and how far they are up to standard than in discovering how they came about? I cannot see that it is relevant. From the fact that we can estimate an action in terms of its conforming to a rule, it no more follows that the performance of the action is not causally explicable than it follows that the appearance of a rainbow is not causally explicable from the fact that it can be made the subject of an aesthetic judgement. To explain something causally does not preclude assessing it in other ways. But perhaps the suggestion is merely that to relate an action to a rule is one way of accounting for it, and, in the present state of our knowledge, a better way of accounting for it than trying to subsume it under dubious causal laws. I cannot even agree with this because I think that it presents us with a false antithesis. The only reason why it is possible to account for the performance of an action by relating it to a rule is that the recognition of the requirements of the rule is a factor in the agent's motivation. He may attach a value in itself to performing a certain sort of action correctly; he may see its correct performance as a means towards some further end; or it may be a combination of the two. In any event this is as much a causal explanation as any other explanation in terms of motives. The invocation of rules adds nothing to the general argument.

The same applies, in my view, to the argument that actions most often need to be understood in terms of their social contexts. A great deal is made by some philosophers of the fact that an action is not a mere physical movement. It has a significance which depends not only on the agent's intention and motive, but very frequently also on a complex of social factors. Think of the social norms and institutions that are involved in such commonplace actions as signing a cheque, signalling that one is going to turn when one is driving a car, saluting a superior officer, playing a card, shaking hands with someone to whom one has just been introduced, waving good-bye to a friend. To represent these merely as different sorts of hand movements, which of course they also are, is to miss their significance; it is indeed to fail to represent them in their character as actions.

All this is true, except that it seems to be an arbitrary question what we are to regard as constituting an action: whether, for example, we choose to say that the motorist's action is one of putting out his hand or one of signalling that he is going to turn. Earlier on, I referred to the action of drinking a glass of wine as an instance of the way in which the same action can have a different significance in different social contexts: it would have been no less, but also no more correct if I had described this as an instance of the way in which the same physical process can in such different contexts become a different action. Wherever we decide to draw the line between the characterization of an action and the assessment of its significance, the point remains that the physical movement has to be interpreted, and that in order to interpret it correctly it will often be necessary to understand its social as well as its personal implications.

But if we grant this point what follows? Certainly not, as the philosophers who lay stress upon it seem to think, that these actions cannot be explained in causal terms. For when it comes to accounting for the action, the only way in which the social context enters the reckoning is through its influence upon the agent. The significance of the action is the significance that it has for him. That is to say, his idea that this is the correct, or expedient, or desirable thing to do in these circumstances is part of his motivation; his awareness of the social context and the effects which this has on him are therefore to be included in the list of initial conditions from which we seek to derive his performance of the action by means of a causal law. Whether such laws are discoverable or not may be an open question; but the fact that these items figure among the data has no important bearing on it.

That human behaviour has a point or meaning, in this sense, is not even an argument against the materialist thesis that it is all physiologically determined. This thesis is indeed highly speculative; we are very far from having a physiological theory which would account for people's actions in specific detail, let alone from being in a position to apply one. But if the motives which impel men to act are, let us say, projections of the state of their brains, there is no reason why this should not apply to their social responses as much as to anything else. But surely no purely physiological account could be an adequate description of an action! Obviously it could not; even if the study of the agent's brain could give us all the information that we needed, beyond the observation of his physical movements, we should still have to decode it. But this is not an objection to holding that actions can be explained in these terms, any more than the fact that to talk about wave-lengths is not to describe colours is an objection to the science of optics. This also shows that even if I am wrong in assimilating motives to causes it will not follow from this alone that human behaviour is not entirely subject to causal explanation. For the fact that we can explain an action in one manner by referring to the agent's motive leaves it a fully open question whether it cannot also be explained more scientifically in terms, say, of a physiological theory.

None of this settles the issue of determinism. I do not indeed think that it can be settled at this level, since I agree with those who hold that it should not be interpreted as an *a priori* question. It is of course true that not every event in human history could in fact be predicted. Not only would the making of each prediction itself then have to be predicted, and so *ad infinitum*, but as Professor Popper and others have rightly pointed out, it would follow that no one could ever have a new idea. But however comforting this may be to those who dislike conceiving of themselves as subjects for science, it does not go any way to prove that not all events in human history are susceptible of lawlike explanations. The strength of the determinists lies in the fact that there seems to be no reason why the reign of law should break down at this point, though this is an argument which seemed more convincing in the age of classical physics than it does today. The strength of the indeterminists lies in the fact that the specific theories which alone could vindicate or indeed give any substance to their opponents' case have not yet been more than sketched, though this is not to say that they never will be. Until such theories are properly elaborated and tested, I think that there is little more about this topic that can usefully be said.

A philosophical question which I have not here discussed, partly because I do not think that I have anything new to say about it, is whether the denial of determinism is implied in our usual ascriptions of moral and legal responsibility. In common with many other philosophers I used to hold that it was not, that in this respect the antithesis between the claims of free will and determinism was illusory, but in so far as this is a question of what people actually believe, I now think it more likely that I was wrong. This is indeed a matter for a social survey which, as I said before, would probably not yield a very clear result. I should however expect it to indicate that if it were shown to them that a man's action could be explained in causal terms, most people would take the view that he was not responsible for it. Since it is not at all clear why one's responsibility for an action should depend on its being causally inexplicable, this may only prove that most people are irrational, but there it is. I am, indeed, strongly inclined to think that our ordinary ideas of freedom and responsibility are very muddle-headed: but for what they are worth, they are also very firmly held. It would not be at all easy to estimate the social consequences of discarding them.

15

PHILOSOPHY AND POLITICS

WHENEVER I have occasion to study the work of contemporary French philosophers, like Sartre or Merleau-Ponty, I am struck by the very great difference which there is between their conception of the scope and purpose of philosophy and the conception which has come to prevail in England in the course of the last thirty years. In many ways, I think that the difference is to our advantage, but there is at least one important issue on which it well may not be. They are very much less inclined than we are to regard philosophy as a special subject, with its own problems, its own technical terms, its own standard of proof and no very obvious bearing upon anything else. It is true that in France the connection of philosophy with science is even more tenuous than it is with us. This is due to the Cartesian divisions of the French academic system: philosophy belongs to the Faculté des Lettres and therefore not to the Faculté des Sciences. But, partly in consequence of this, the French do connect their philosophy more closely with literature, and they also connect it more closely with politics. Sartre's demand that philosophers should be committed (*engagés*) does not mean only that they are expected to have views on political and social issues, but that they should give their views a philosophical backing. One of the main questions which I want to discuss is that of the ways in which this might be possible.

To say that contemporary English philosophers are not concerned with political and social issues would be unjust. Many of them hold strong views on these subjects: and some at least are ready to engage in political and social controversy. The difference is that they tend to look upon these activities as extra-curricular. What we conspicuously lack is any serious contribution, on the philosophical side, to political theory. Who has done anything in this way since John Stuart Mill? There have been T. H. Green with his lectures on the *Principles of Political Obligation*, a respectable but hardly an inspiring work, and B. H. Bosanquet who defended a Hegelian theory of the state, and Bertrand Russell's *Principles of Social Reconstruction*, a brilliant attempt to domesticate a form of anarchism: but none of these books has had a lasting influence, and the most recent of them was written nearly fifty years ago. We have had very good historians of political ideas, but that is another matter.

This is not an entirely fair test, as I do not know that French philosophers either have made any very important contribution to political theory in recent times, but it is still broadly true that they are oriented towards politics in a way that ours are not. There are various reasons for this. Perhaps the most important is the difference in the strength and appeal of our respective Communist parties. Only a small minority of French philosophers are Marxists, but the others tend to find it necessary not only to take a view about Marxism, but also to show that they have a better line of goods to offer in the same market. The latest of Sartre's philosophical works is the seven-hundred-page *Critique de la raison dialectique*. In it he tries to show that most of current Marxist thinking is mistaken, but he also maintains that Marxism is the only serious philosophy for our time. Now Marxists subordinate philosophy to politics; they are inclined to judge philosophical theories by their tendency to promote political ends. The philosophers who have to compete with Marxism may not see any need to go so far as this, but they must be concerned with the political effects and implications of their views.

In this country, for better or for worse, Marxism is not a serious competitor. There are very few Marxist intellectuals, let alone Marxist philosophers, and their case very largely goes by default. Few of us feel the need, like Sartre or Camus or Merleau-Ponty, to measure and justify the extent of our disaccord with Communism. There was, indeed, a period in the thirties when this was not so. A characteristic line in one of Day Lewis's poems runs: 'Why do we all, seeing a Communist, feel small?' Because, at that time, the Communists looked to be the only people who were prepared to dedicate their lives to doing something about the social consequences of the depression, the rise of Hitler, the cause of Republican Spain. But the war and a greater knowledge of what was actually going on in Russia combined to blot that feeling out and there has not been a strong enough motive for reviving it since. Things have been different in France because of the different form of their class consciousness. With us, class divisions are mainly social; with them, political. To a much greater extent than ours, the French working class votes as a class and by tradition it votes communist. The result is that French intellectuals have been faced with a dilemma from which we escape. To go along with the Communists is to condone a great deal which is repugnant to the liberal conscience; to oppose them is, in local terms, to ally oneself with the forces of reaction. The attempts which have been made to organize an effective left-wing movement without the Communists, have failed through lack of working-class support. So the problem for these intellectuals, which was only put in abeyance by the paternalism of de Gaulle, is that the social conscience which drives them into politics also prevents them from taking any political standpoint which would make their intervention effective.

Here, since the war at least, the issues have not seemed so sharp. It is, indeed, easy to overemphasize the extent to which the two main parties agree in their political policies. Since they are competing for the vote of the emergent class of technicians, who are thought to be equally hostile to socialism and to hereditary privilege, both parties have an interest in fostering this belief, but the interest of the Conservatives is the greater. If people can be persuaded that the difference between the two parties is the difference between men rather than between measures, they are likely to vote for those who can claim not only a longer tradition of social respectability but also a greater experience of government. But whatever we may think of the conclusion of this argument, its presupposition is unsound. No doubt the two parties are drawing together in their policies, partly because no responsible English government nowadays has very much freedom of manœuvre, but, apart from anything else, there is still a difference in emphasis that practically amounts to a difference in aim. It matters a great deal whether or not one is prepared to say 'the devil take the hindmost', even if there is a diminished number of the hindmost for him to take.

What there is not, in spite of superficial appearances to the contrary, is any great difference in political theory. For a long time now, it seems to me, theoretical principles have played a very small part in English politics. There have been conflicts of interest, at different times setting country against town, land-owners against manufacturers, protectionists against free-traders, employers against labour, Anglicans against Roman Catholics and Dissenters, the Irish, the Scots and the Welsh against the English, even men against women, and of course always the rich against the poor, but in the main these battles have not been waged in ideological terms. There is often a coating of theory but the arguments in which it is deployed have been mostly *ad hoc*:

they have not stemmed from different theoretical systems. Conservatives, on solemn occasions, will still appeal to Burke, but Burke's is a second order theory; its moral is that one should not have any theory of the first order. 'Politics is the art of the possible; to find out what is possible you have to feel your way; if you tamper with ancient institutions, you will open the flood-gates to a tide which you may not be able to control; no human institution is perfect, but if one has stood the test of time it is better to leave it alone; what is entrenched is likely for that very reason to be good.'

Conservatism of this sort has gone out of fashion since the war, though it still has its advocates among the holders of academic posts in political theory. It is no longer thought to be practical politics. But this is not to say that any new theory has replaced it. The Conservatives have after their fashion taken over the Welfare State: but only on their old principle of catching the Whigs bathing and running away with their clothes.

The Whigs did have a theory, not so much the old aristocratic Whigs, whose theory mainly consisted in the belief that they ought to be in power, but the businessmen who took over the Whig party in the nineteenth century. They transformed it into the Liberal party which itself died in giving birth to the modern Conservative and Labour parties, its right wing forming the Conservative party, which has in this century been a party dominated not by landowners but by merchants and manufacturers, and its left wing developing into the Labour party which, as we shall see in a moment, is not so much Socialist as Radical. This very fact that it is the common ancestor of the other two main parties, that we are all Liberals nowadays, makes it difficult for the Liberal party to revive. Like the persons eaten by cannibals, who troubled Aquinas when he thought about the Resurrection, they have a problem in recovering their self-identity.

The theory which the old Liberals had was the theory of Malthus. If it is a law of nature that population always rises to the limit of food supply, then clearly any schemes of social welfare are going to be a waste of time and money. For it follows that if you raise the general standard of living, people will breed that much more, the number of extra mouths to feed will again bring the bulk of the population down to the subsistence level, and you are back where you started. So, the argument went, since government interference with the iron laws of supply and demand can anyhow do no good, the Government had better keep out of it. The Liberal party in the nineteenth century was the party of reform, but not of social reform, or rather not of the economic reform on which social reform mainly depends. The reform for which it fought was the reform of political institutions, precisely with the object of giving the manufacturers more power and the laws of the market more free play; to do it justice, it also cared about legal reform; outside the sphere of economic interests, it attempted to do away with traditional anomalies and barbarities in the domain of the law. These Liberals were not bad men; believing that most people were necessarily made miserable by nature, they did what they could to ensure that they were not made still more miserable by man, at least if it were not for any rational purpose. Their utilitarianism was quite genuine; they were not hypocritical, though their views did coincide rather closely with their interests: it was just that, thanks to Malthus, they had convinced themselves that welfare legislation could not achieve its end. In this context it is worth remembering that the factory acts in the eighteen forties, which put an end to the grosser evils of the system of child labour, were put through by Conservatives, like Lord Shaftesbury, against the opposition not only of the manufacturers but also of many of the workers who did not see how they could manage without the wages which their small children earned. That the reform would eventually lead to a rise in their own wages was not clear to them.

Facts of this kind create an awkward problem for utilitarians. The principle of utility is that we are to endeavour to give as many people as possible as much as possible of what they want; but at once the question arises whether this is to be what people say they want, or what they *really* want, that is, what we think they ought to want, or would want if they were enlightened. Most modern utilitarians are inclined to take the second view, but clearly it can lead to dangerous consequences, especially as with modern techniques of persuasion it is tempting to try to make people want what you desire them to want, whether in their interest or your own. Plebiscites in favour of dictators are not always faked; more often they do not have to be.

If one considers the world as a whole, it is not at all clear that Malthus's theory has been proved false: the pressure of world population upon world food supplies is going to be one of the most serious problems of the last quarter of this century. It can, however, be said that Malthus's theory has broken down in the more advanced countries of the West. The prosperity of the United States is the most convincing counter-example to it.

In my view, the local failure of Malthus's theory was one of the main factors in generating the outlook of the Labour party. It has made it possible for the party to be reformist rather than revolutionary and so in a large measure to dispense with any theory of its own. The radical sentiments by which the organized labour movement has always been characterized are based less on political than on moral and religious principles, the most important of them being a principle of egalitarianism, 'When Adam delved and Eve span, who was then the gentleman?' which goes far back in English history without, however, finding any very practical expression until quite recent times. What has been lacking for the most part is any very clear idea of the way in which these principles were to be satisfied. In the main the Labour movement has been content to fight for relatively short-term objectives, improving the conditions of employment of specific categories of workers, winning certain legal rights for the Trade Unions, carrying through schemes of social welfare, increasing the general opportunities for education. I am not at all saying that it was wrong to proceed in this piecemeal way. On the contrary, a systematic attempt to refashion the whole structure of society might well have achieved much less.

These campaigns have indeed been fought under the standard of Socialism, but the Socialism has consisted in a set of maxims taken over from Marx and cut loose from the main body of the Marxist system. 'Nationalization of the means of production, distribution and exchange.' Admittedly this was not just a battle cry. The manifest moral and social evils of the industrialism of the nineteenth century, extending indeed over most of the first half of the twentieth, were ascribable to capitalism; therefore, something quite different from capitalism, the very opposite of capitalism, was needed, if social justice and the general happiness were to be achieved. Not private but public ownership, production not for profit but for use. But this principle remained at a very high level of generality. Public ownership can mean many different things, and the way one effects the transition from private to public ownership makes a difference too; whether and to what extent one compensates the previous owners, whether or not one leaves the old managers in charge. It is a matter for debate whether the type of nationalization on which the Labour party embarked after the war was best suited to the industries concerned. It may also be questioned whether either the enthusiasm or the odium which is attached to the idea of nationalization derives from a dispassionate examination of the way in which it has been found to work. I shall not attempt to answer these questions here. The only point that I now wish to make is that it is only for a minority of its advocates that nationalization has been a political end in itself. By the majority it has been seen as a means to the achievement of greater prosperity and greater economic and therefore social equality: if these ends can be attained more easily by other means, well and good. There would be no sacrifice of principle, because the operative principles have been moral principles and these would not be sacrificed. No doubt harsh things have been said about private property, but the English Labour party has never gone so far as to maintain that all forms of private ownership are wrong in themselves. It has never taken Proudhon's position that property is theft—a contradictory statement as it stands since theft is an offence against property, but one sees what is meant. If you merely hold that certain forms of private ownership are not conducive to the general good, you need not be ashamed to change your mind if experience shows you to have been in some degree mistaken. You can call this yielding to expediency, but if expediency means a willingness to be flexible in the choice of means, it is a standard feature of modern English politics. Again I am far from saying that this is a defect.

The result of this prevalent empiricism—and here I am using the word 'empiricism' not in the philosophical but in the political sense, in which an empirical is contrasted with a theoretical approach—is that political science is reduced to a combination of economics and psephology. Can we and how can we afford to pursue various schemes of social betterment? Why do people vote as they do? How can they be induced to vote otherwise? About the social needs there is little open dispute, 'To raise the general standard of living. To give more protection to the old and sick.' No one is prepared to say that these things are not desirable if they are feasible. The moral difference arises only when it comes to deciding what constitutes their being feasible. Perhaps the Conservative acceptance of the idea of the welfare state is not entirely whole-hearted, but the hostility which may be felt for it finds little open expression. It is concealed rather in the laudation of individual enterprise, which again may mean many different things, ranging upwards from the attitude of 'Damn you, Jack, I'm all right.' And this is as far as one can seriously go. 'Odi profanum vulgus et arceo' is no longer an avowable position.

Conversely, in some quarters on the left, there is a display of much dislike for the affluent society, which is itself a proof of affluence, since only a fairly affluent society can afford to worry about the encroachment of material upon spiritual values. On this point I sympathize with Brecht: 'Erst kommt das Fressen, dann kommt die Moral.' We hear a good deal also about alienation, another Marxist concept which has been detached from its base, but little about the way in which it is to be overcome. How good it would be if we were all animated by a spirit of co-operation and everyone enjoyed his work. Again a social idea, which has yet to be given a political content. Socially, we are nearly all of us meliorists. Politically, we are inclined to be not exactly sceptical, but distrustful of the grand solutions. As so often, Dr Johnson, admittingly a high Tory, speaks for the deflationary element in English commonsense. 'Boswell: So, Sir, you laugh at schemes of political improvement. Johnson: Why, Sir, most schemes of political improvement are very laughable things.'

I am of course exaggerating a little, but broadly speaking I think that I am right in saying that our political life draws very little inspiration from political philosophy. Nevertheless the subject exists. Lectures are given on it, theses written, examinations taken. What does it consist in?

Mainly, it seems to me, in trying to answer a single question; one that would be likely to occur only to the members of a certain type of society; an individualistic society like that of Ancient Athens or seventeenth-century England. The question is: What is the ground of political obligation? Or, in more simple terms: Why should I do what the Government tells me to? This was the question which Plato raised in the *Republic* and from Hobbes through Locke and Rousseau to Bosanquet and T. H. Green it preoccupied the classical exponents of political theory. When I was an undergraduate the political theorists who did not much concern themselves with this question—Machiavelli, Marx, Lenin, Plekhanov, Pareto, Sorel—were comparatively neglected. Their work did not form part of the curriculum. I believe that this is still very largely true except that more official attention is now paid to Marx. And while Marx and his followers do not put the question in the foreground, they can also be represented as having their special way of answering it.

Their answer is only one of many. I distinguish thirteen, with brief attributions. The fact that four of these different answers were given by Hobbes, three by Rousseau and two by Locke does not necessarily entail that these writers were not thinking clearly. We cannot say *a priori* that there may not be several good reasons for political obedience.

The answers run as follows:

1. You ought to obey because you are forced to. Hobbes.
2. You ought to obey because you have promised to. Hobbes, Locke, Rousseau and other believers in the Social Contract.
3. You ought to obey because it is in your interest. Plato, Hobbes, Bentham.
4. You ought to obey because it is in the general interest. Locke, Rousseau, Mill, Green.
5. You ought to obey because it is you who are giving the orders. Hobbes, Rousseau, Bosanquet and other believers in the General Will.
6. You ought to obey because God wants you to. Medieval writers.
7. You ought to obey because the Sovereign is God's anointed. Absolute Monarchists.
8. You ought to obey because the Sovereign is descended from someone who had the right to be obeyed. Legitimists.
9. You ought to obey because people always have. Traditionalists.
10. You ought to obey because your government exemplifies the highest point yet reached in the spiritual development of man. Hegel. This can hardly be true of all governments.
11. You ought to obey because your government has history on its side. Marx. Again, this may not be true of all governments.
12. You ought to obey because you ought to obey. Some English moralists.
13. You have no obligation to obey. Anarchists.

This is not, to my mind, a very impressive list of answers, though there are one or two that deserve to be seriously considered. To begin with, we can eliminate all those in which the ground for obedience is placed in authority, whether the authority be human or divine. Even if there were a God the fact that he wanted something to be done, and that you knew that he wanted it, would not in itself supply a logical ground for doing it. It could supply a motive for doing it, a prudential motive in the sense that you might believe that he would reward you if you did it or make things very unpleasant for you if you did not, but then we move on to another plane. Your reason becomes one of self-interest. It is not a justification because it can never be a justification for doing anything that someone commands you to do it. There has to be the further premiss that you are obliged to do what he commands, and in this particular instance why should you be obliged? If your answer is that the authority is all-powerful, then it follows that he has the power to compel you to obey him. So either he exercises it or he does not. If he does, *cadit quaestio*. You need not bother to find reasons for doing what you cannot help doing anyway. If he does not, then the fact that he could compel you if he wished is nothing to the purpose. You still have to decide. If you decide on prudential grounds, then, as I have said, you are adopting a different principle and one that is also open to question. If you decide to obey on the ground that God is entitled to your obedience, you are evading the issue: the question why he is entitled remains unanswered. The only remaining possibility is that you decide to obey because you think that what he ordains is right. This is a perfectly respectable reason, but it has to be made good independently. The proposition that what God wills is good, or right, must be a synthetic proposition; it cannot simply be a way of saying that he wills what he wills. When believers say that God is good and praise or love him for this reason, they are not merely expressing the tautology that he is what he is, for this would be equally true of the devil. Admittedly, when a diabolist or a Manichean decides to espouse the cause of the devil, the chances are that he is doing what Socrates wrongly thought to be impossible: pursuing an end which he believes to be evil and not one which he believes to be good: but the logical point remains that if he did believe that what the devil rather than what God commanded was right, he might be merely perverse but he would not be guilty of self-contradiction. The upshot of this is that any reliance on authority involves an *independent* moral judgement, the judgement that what your authority enjoins is right, and therefore an independent standard of values. So we can leave God out of the argument. Even if he were known to exist he could not supply a ground for any form of human action: it would be a logical fallacy to try to found either morals or politics upon his supposed desires. This is not necessarily inconsistent with Voltaire's dictum that if God did not exist, it would be necessary to create him, for Voltaire was thinking of the deity only as a sanction, as supplying a prudential motive for making people do what they ought. But while this position is logically tenable, it represents a low and perhaps rather superficial view of the springs of human morality.

What holds for God holds *a fortiori* for his anointed. The answer to the claim of a divine right for kings is that even if there were any reason to believe that they were divinely appointed, it would prove nothing to the purpose. Of course, if one pledges one's allegiance to a certain form of government, if one decides that only the descendants of a certain family—the direct descendants or the descendants in the male line—have a right to command one's loyalty and obedience, questions of legitimacy become important. Given the appropriate assumptions, they can become questions of fact. The Jacobite who maintains that some Bavarian Count is the rightful king of England may well, on his own presuppositions, be saying what is true. But clearly this is not a fundamental ground of political obedience. For no answer is given to the question why anyone should obey the members of the privileged family in the first place. The mere practice of obedience, however long continued, does not constitute a justification.

The same type of objection is fatal to some of the other theories. There is an affinity here between Hobbes and Marx. Both held that you ought to do what, if they were right, you could not help doing. For Hobbes, the sovereign is defined partly by his power. It is wrong to rebel against the sovereign only so long as you rebel unsuccessfully. If you rebel successfully then by the mere fact that your rebellion is successful, he ceases to be sovereign. 'Treason doth never prosper, what's the reason? For if it prosper none dare call it treason.' The absolute authority of the sovereign is sustained by its being made *logically* impossible that it should be violated.

Let me remark in passing that there is a great deal more than this to Hobbes's system. His picture of the state of nature and his idea that 'Covenants, without the sword, are but Words, and of no strength to secure a man at all' have been much derided, and no doubt he does underrate the extent to which man is a political animal, but if one transfers his set-up to the international level, it works very well. In Hobbes's view, the main object of any form of political association was to obtain security, and it is very plausible to suggest that we are not going to obtain international security unless nations can be induced to relinquish their sovereignty to a supra-national authority. Of course this is not automatically going to bring about the millenium. A world government could also be oppressive and all the more oppressive because it would have so much power. Locke's gibe against Hobbes's theory of sovereignty that 'it is to think that men are so foolish that they take care to avoid what mischief may be done to them by polecats and foxes, but are content, nay, think it safety, to be devoured by lions' still has its point. A lot would depend upon the way that the world government was formed and how it was perpetuated. Nevertheless, I think it is the best solution, though not one that any of us is likely to see realized.

A counterpart of Hobbes's doctrine of sovereignty is to be found in Hegel's 'the real is the rational', the theory being that the justification of government is simply that it *exists*. Since you accompany the march of the Absolute Idea and cannot march faster than it does—though it would seem that you can march more slowly, in which case you might have an obligation to catch up—it is your duty to accept the institutions in which the Absolute Idea exemplifies itself at the time at which you happen to be living. But the trouble here again is that it is made logically impossible to go against the Absolute Idea, since if you do not accept current institutions and succeed in transforming them, this will still be the work of the Absolute Idea operating through you. It is amusing to note, however, that on this point also some of Hegel's followers attempted to turn him upside down. Instead of arguing, as he did, that because the Prussian state was real it was rational, they argued that since it was manifestly irrational it could not be real. Bismarck knew better.

In this matter Marx just follows Hegel, with the substitution of History for the Absolute Idea. We ought to take the side of the working class in the class struggle because history has decreed it to be the winning side. This does not quite come down to saying that you have an obligation to bring about what is bound to happen anyway, because the theory is not one of complete historical determinism. The victory of the working class is inevitable, but how it comes about and how soon it comes about depend upon the decisions that different people take. But once it is allowed that one is not naturally bound to work for Communism, in which case any question of moral obligation would be otiose, once it is allowed that one has a choice, then it is not clear why one should be morally bound to support the winning side. To take Mr Pickwick's advice and shout with the loudest may be prudent but it is not self-evidently a duty. The only argument for it is that it is silly to oppose when opposition is known to be futile; but the concession, the break in historical determinism, which makes it possible to be in opposition at all, also ensures that the opposition need not be futile. If one thinks that the triumph of the working class would be a bad thing (I am not saying that I myself think it would be but only considering the case of one who does), then something would seem to be gained if one were able to delay it; by fighting against it one might hope to mitigate some of its worse features. Besides, even if opposition were futile and recognized to be so, this is not a conclusive reason for changing sides; some would say not a reason at all. There is such a thing as heroic resistance. 'Victrix causa deis placuit sed victa Catoni.' An absurd attitude, if you like, but not ignoble.

Perhaps the most subtle but also the most deceptive of our answers is that you are bound to obey the government because you are then obeying yourself. It finds its strongest expression in Rousseau's saying that the criminal who is taken off to prison is being forced to be free. The assumption behind this saying is that freedom consists in obeying a law which you impose on yourself, a Puritan doctrine which became one of the cornerstones of Kantian morality, and one which I see no good reason to accept. If there is any ground for supposing that our actions are determined it applies as much to actions which are done from a sense of duty as to any others. But let that pass. The important point, in the present context, is that the criminal is held to be responsible for his own punishment because, even though he may strongly disapprove of the law which he has broken, or indeed of all such laws, still as a member of the community he has his share in the general will which the law exemplifies. The general will is one's own real will, writ large. Rousseau did not go quite so far as the English Hegelians, like Bradley and Bosanquet, who thought that the state was a more real version of ourselves, a version of ourselves because we were constituents of it and more real because it was larger and therefore a state nearer the Absolute which alone was really real, but the fallacy is much the same.

I say 'fallacy' for various reasons. In the first place, even if the criminal did make the law, if he actually voted for it, or even proposed it, it does not follow that he has to recognize it as binding on him. I am willing to concede that he is not morally entitled to make an exception in his own favour, though even this will not follow merely from the fact that he helped to make the law. But why should he not have changed his mind about the merits of the law? Might he not have come to think that the law was so bad in itself or passed by such improper means that he ought not now to obey it? Indeed, on the view which we are considering, it would seem that he would in these circumstances no longer be free to obey it; for if you are free only when you are imposing a law upon yourself, it follows that you cannot freely do what you believe to be wrong: a consequence quite alien to the spirit of Kantian morality and one which its exponents therefore tend to overlook. On the other hand, this discussion has no point unless it be assumed that one has a choice whether or not to abide by the law: and if one does have the choice, then the question at issue is whether one should always continue one's allegiance to a law which one has imposed upon oneself in the past: and then all sorts of considerations may intervene. No doubt one ought, other things being equal, to respect the law as such, but apart from the fact that other things may not be equal, this is a different argument. What is now in question is whether the fact that one has participated in the making of the law necessarily entails that one is bound in all circumstances to respect it; and I am suggesting that it does not.

But further it is just not true of most of us who do not hold political office that in any literal sense we do make the laws by which our society is regulated. We assent to them no doubt, or to some of them: if we are law-abiding people, we shall honour even those that we strongly disapprove of, but it is absurd to say that we are responsible for them. Rousseau said that the English were free only at election times: but what is it that they are then free to do? To declare their preference for one or other of a set of persons whom they have most probably had no voice in selecting and for one or other of a set of policies which they have most probably had no hand in framing. Note that I am not decrying our form of democracy or even saying that it does not deserve the name. There are all sorts of ways other than by merely voting in which people can bring pressure on the government; for example, by writing to the newspapers, marching in processions, making public speeches, badgering their representatives, militating in political parties. All that I am saying is that this does not amount in any literal sense to our enacting the laws by which we are governed. Even in the case of legislation by plebiscite, which was taken by Rousseau as his model, it is not true that those who are outvoted are the authors of the laws which are passed. They have had the opportunity to make their view prevail but the fact is that it has not prevailed. And even if it had prevailed, it might have been a view which they were tricked or bullied into holding. Recourse to plebiscites became a favourite device of fascist governments, just because it was found that on certain issues the mass of the population was very easily swayed. I do not infer from this that these people did not genuinely identify themselves with their government and its cause, but only that their succumbing to this propaganda, however wholeheartedly, did not commit them to putting their wills indefinitely and unconditionally into the government's keeping.

Of course there is something in the notion of the general will. There are groups of men who have a common purpose and an accredited machinery for carrying it out in which they participate in different ways. These conditions are satisfied by football teams, debating societies, governing bodies of colleges, borough councils and so forth. Whether they are satisfied by the groups which constitute modern nation-states, except perhaps in time of war, is rather doubtful. The point is of interest but it is not material to the argument. The fact that you belong to a group, which has in this sense a general will, and that you participate in the making of its decisions, may be a good reason for your abiding by the decisions, even when you think them wrong or personally dislike their consequences. But this is still not to say that the general will is your will, even though the exercising of your will is part of the machinery in virtue of which the general will exists. It is not your will. You can choose to subordinate your will to it, but it is a choice and one that you may find reason to go back on.

A more obviously fictitious idea is that of the social contract. There are indeed cases in which a social contract is known to have been made, not indeed in primitive times when men were emerging from the state of nature, but in communities which were artificially set up, mainly in the nineteenth century. One of the best known examples is the Oneida Community in the United States. But if my grandfather chose to join such a community, why should that bind me? Even if I myself had freely joined it, why should that bind me if I do not like what is going on? Because I promised that I would stay? But though it is true in general that promises should be kept there may be circumstances in which to break a promise is the lesser evil. And in any case if we are going to found political obligation upon moral principles, it would be better to do so directly, rather than appeal to a social contract which only a handful of people in very exceptional circumstances ever in fact subscribe to.

It may be objected that this literal interpretation of the theory of the social contract fails to do it justice. No one who still defends the theory regards the making of the contract as a historical event. The argument is rather that by remaining a member of a society, by taking advantage of the protection which it affords you and of the social amenities which it provides, you tacitly undertake to fulfil the demands which it makes upon you. As Hume pointed out long ago, this argument presupposes that you have a genuine alternative; otherwise, as he said, it is like telling a man who complains of the conditions aboard a ship on to which he was shanghaied in the first place that he is free to jump into the sea. But even when this condition is satisfied, the argument has very little weight. It is a good debating point for the chairman of a conscientious objectors' tribunal to say to an objector: 'Your country has done a good deal for you of which you have not hesitated to take advantage. Don't you think that you ought to respond to its present need, to do your bit along with all or nearly all the rest?' It may make the man feel uncomfortable: but not so uncomfortable as to override a genuine scruple of conscience. If he thinks it absolutely wrong to take human life in any circumstances, he will not be moved. And if he is told that he has tacitly promised to do even this, his answer can only be that this is just not so. A revolutionary in active rebellion against a government which he thinks tyrannical is not going to be deterred from his activity by the argument that though the police may have tortured him for his political opinions, they have at least directed the traffic for him and protected his property from burglars, and that so long as he has paid the bills his supplies of gas and electricity and running water have not been cut off. Does anyone seriously think that these considerations should deter him?

The answer to the suggestion that I ought to obey the government because it is in my interest to do so is that it frequently may not be. One has only to think of successful tax dodgers. Moreover, the fact that something is in one's interest, or that one believes it to be so, is not necessarily a sufficient reason for doing it. Those who have put this theory forward have usually done so because they believed, mistakenly, that it was psychologically impossible to act otherwise than with a view to one's own interest. Had they been right, there would be no problem beyond that of convincing people that obedience to the government really was in their own interest. Here again, there would be no sense in telling them that they ought to do what they were determined to do anyway.

Apart from the anarchist answer, about which I shall say something later on, we are now left with only two of our original list; the suggestion that you ought to obey the government because you ought, and the suggestion that you ought to obey the government because it is in the general interest that you should. If the first of these means that you ought to obey the government unconditionally, all I can say is that I just do not believe it: if it means that you ought to obey the government *when* you ought, it is true but not very enlightening. The only merit of this type of answer is that it draws attention to the fact that in the cases where it really matters the decision whether to vouchsafe or withhold obedience is a moral decision.

The utilitarian position is the one to which I feel most sympathetic, with one or two reservations. If we are evaluating political institutions and political measures, then I do think that what should primarily be considered is their probable effect upon the happiness of those concerned. Admittedly, the concept of happiness is vague and the process of balancing the satisfaction of one set of persons against the dissatisfaction of another is very rough and ready: but while it is absurd to look for anything like mathematical precision, I do not agree with the view that the utilitarian calculus is totally inapplicable. On the contrary, I think that politicians very frequently apply it, with a fair measure of success. Where its application is dubious is in the case of the individual. If I ask myself what would be the right action for me to perform in some particular situation, the task of working out the felicific sum with respect to each of the possible alternatives might well defeat me. It is only if I go by rule, as indeed I normally should, that I can apply utilitarian considerations not to the particular actions which are open to me but to the rules under which they severally fall, and even so I shall have difficulty in deciding on utilitarian grounds between the competing rules as they operate in these particular circumstances. It must, however, be remembered that Bentham never intended that the principle of utility should apply to individual actions. He was not concerned with the morality of individuals since he thought that they were in any case bound to do what they believed to be in their own interest. The position that he took up was that of a legislator who was benevolent in the sense that he happened to find his greatest self-satisfaction in promoting the welfare of others, and he then raised the question: What laws should such a legislator devise for the community over which he is in charge? The answer that he should devise such laws and institutions as will ensure as many people as possible getting as much as possible of what they want seems to me in a large measure acceptable: I am sure that it is the best single answer at this level of generality. One serious objection to it is that it does not sufficiently allow for the extent to which people are irrational: there is the difficulty, which we noticed earlier on, that people often think they want things which they would not want if they were more clear-sighted and, what is more vexatious, that they can be induced by propaganda to want things which we believe that they should not be allowed to have. I am not now thinking of the duty of imposing cultural programmes on people who would prefer to look at 'Double Your Money': one can hardly avoid the attempt to proselytize, but it need not go further than that. I am thinking of the much more serious case in which the majority of people in a given society are induced to approve of a regime which indulges in persecution and war. It is just possible, however, that if one puts into the balance the intense sufferings of oppressed minorities in societies of this type, these cases can be excluded on utilitarian grounds.

A second, more radical, objection to a thoroughgoing utilitarianism is that there are certain things like justice and freedom to which one might want to attach a value independently of the value of happiness. I do not agree with Pope's 'For forms of government let fools contest; whate'er is but administered is best'. I think it might be reasonable to prefer a rather less well-run society in which the average individual had a larger say in the management of its affairs, to a better-run society in which he had less, even though it could be shown that people on the whole were more contented in the second. I should, however, have to mitigate this by adding that the disparity in happiness between the two must not be very great.

But while I support utilitarianism in this qualified way, I doubt if it furnishes the answer to the question: Why ought I to obey the government? I have very often thought that the government was not acting in the general interest but never felt that this justified me in evading currency restrictions or fiddling my income tax returns or disregarding the policeman on point duty. Of course a utilitarian might reply that the evils of civil disobedience are normally greater in utilitarian terms than the evils ensuing from the government's policy; so that unless the government does something very bad, something that one thinks will have a disastrous effect on the happiness of the society, one will not be justified in refusing to obey it. There is, however, something rather artificial about the idea of our severally measuring our obligations as citizens in terms of a utilitarian calculus. The calculus applies to the choice of policies within the framework of a certain form of society, but only in exceptional cases to the maintenance of the framework itself.

The fact is that there is something wrong with the form of our question. Men do not choose to live in society, they are born into a society and into one of a particular structure. In rare instances they are in a position to exchange one form of society for another, and in very rare instances they may choose to opt out of society altogether by living as hermits, though this is not easy to accomplish; for one thing it is increasingly difficult to find anywhere to go. Now if there is to be a society, there must be some form of social organization: some set of institutions, some recognized machinery for taking decisions which will count as the decisions of the group as a whole. The machinery need not be democratic, but it must exist. This is a logical necessity; not that there shall be societies, but that if there is a society, there must be some form of social organization. The only question which arises is what form of social organization to have. The anarchist who answers the question: Why ought I to obey the Government? by saying that you have no obligation to, is in fact advocating a form of organization in which all decisions are arrived at as the result of a discussion in which everyone has the right to participate, and are freely adhered to without the imposition of any sanctions. This works, more or less, in families and clubs and perhaps even in some progressive schools, but unfortunately seems not to be a feasible way of conducting the affairs of a nation-state.

This gives us the clue to what political philosophers are really doing. The text books were in error when they represented them as dealing with a single moral question to which there can be a valid answer independently of the historical context in which the question is posed. The grounds which they offer for political obligation are persuasive in Professor Stevenson's sense. They amount to the advocacy of a certain form of political organization. Thus, Hobbes is saying that all that really matters is that the government shall be strong: Locke is arguing in favour of the protection of private property, the separation of powers and the accountability of the executive: Rousseau is arguing in favour of city states with town meetings and plebiscites: the theocrats are in favour of theocracy, the divine right of king's men in favour of absolute monarchy: Bentham and Mill maintain that political institutions, together with the whole legal system, should be assessed only in terms of their utility: Marx was in favour of a classless society made possible by increased production: Lenin thought that the first step towards attaining this end was to have a dictatorship of a small body of intellectuals acting in the name of the proletariat. But by the time that we get to Marx and Lenin, we are at a more realistic level than that of any presumed universal ground for political obligation.

Someone may protest that this advocacy of different forms of organization does not exhaust political philosophy. There is the history of the subject to be studied; there is the task of analysing political concepts. What exactly do we mean by 'sovereignty', 'democracy', 'political liberties', 'national self-determination', 'civil rights' and so forth? True; there are these questions. No doubt a careful investigation of the ways in which these terms have been understood at different periods and in different societies would yield some interesting results. But their interest would mainly consist in the fact that these different usages reflected different recommendations with respect to organization or policy. It is not, for example, a point of merely linguistic import that the Russians use the word which we translate by our word 'democracy' in a rather different sense from ours. If that were all there were to it our misunderstandings could be removed by finding a more accurate translation. It is that their usage reflects a different set of values, a different idea of what is important for a society, or at any rate for their society, a different structural model. These disagreements are not verbal and they are not to be resolved by any form of linguistic analysis, though an intelligent analysis may help to make clear what they are. The fact is, however, that we know pretty well what they are; what we do not know is what to do about them.

One reason why political philosophy is hardly a live subject in this country, so that more than most others it has the air of living on its past, is that our society is—if I may be forgiven the barbarous phrase—ideologically homogeneous. There are disputes about policies but not about the framework in which they are to be carried out. Even widespread nationalization in the form in which it is a political issue would not invite a radical transformation of our political or social structure. But the most important reason is that on fundamental questions of organization nobody has any new ideas. Only the fascists in the twentieth century have transformed people's political outlooks in the way that the Utilitarians and the Marxists transformed them in the nineteenth; and mercifully not here. So far as political theory goes our twentieth century is only a prolongation of the nineteenth.

In this matter I am like the rest; I have nothing new to offer. Only the old familiar liberal principles; old, but not so firmly established that we can afford to take them for granted. Representative government, universal suffrage, freedom of speech, freedom of the press, the right of collective bargaining, equality before the law, and all that goes with the so-called welfare state. It is not a heady brew. Such principles nowadays are a ground for excitement, a source of enthusiasm, only when they appear to be violated. For most of us participation in politics takes the form of protest; protest against war, against the aggressive actions of the major powers, against the maltreatment of political prisoners, against censorship, against capital or corporal punishment, against the persecution of homosexuals, against racial discrimination; there is still quite a lot to be against. It would be more romantic to be marching forward shoulder to shoulder under some bright new banner towards a brave new world. But I don't know: perhaps it is the effect of age. I do not really feel the need for anything to replace this mainly utilitarian, mainly tolerant, undramatic type of radicalism. For me the problem is not to devise a new set of political principles but rather to find a more effective means of putting into operation the principles that most of us already profess to have.

INDEX